Angela

Childhood in War-Torn Germany
The History Omitted from "Official" Texts

A Memoir

Angela Mailänder, Ph.D.

1st WORLD PUBLISHING

Angela
Childhood in War-Torn Germany
The History Omitted from "Official" Texts – A Memoir
Angela Mailänder, Ph.D.

Copyright © 2015 Angela Mailänder, Ph.D.

Published by 1st World Publishing
P.O. Box 2211, Fairfield, Iowa 52556
tel: 641-209-5000 • fax: 866-440-5234
web: www.1stworldpublishing.com

First Edition
LCCN: 2015907881
Softcover ISBN: 978-1-4218-3734-5
Hardcover ISBN: 978-1-4218-3735-2
eBook ISBN: 978-1-4218-3736-9

All rights reserved. No part of this book may be reproduced or utilized in any form or by any means, electronic or mechanical, including photocopying or recording, or by any information storage and retrieval system, without permission in writing from the author.

This material has been written and published for educational purposes to enhance one's well-being. In regard to health issues, the information is not intended as a substitute for appropriate care and advice from health professionals, nor does it equate to the assumption of medical or any other form of liability on the part of the publisher or author. The publisher and author shall have neither liability nor responsibility to any person or entity with respect to loss, damages, or injury claimed to be caused directly or indirectly by any information in this book.

**To my maternal grandparents
Maria Abrahmovna and Maxim Pavlovich Zeitner**

who lived through two world wars, internment in Siberia,
and famine – losing four of their nine children to starvation
and one daughter to rape. And yet,
my grandparents gained wisdom instead of suffering defeat.

**And to Victor Gollancz
(9 April 1893 – 8 February 1967)**

Victor Gollancz, a British Jew, understood politically imposed systems and saw beyond them. He predicted the slaughter of Jews in Germany. Yet he also opposed Dwight D. Eisenhower and Henry Morgenthau's efforts to annihilate the German people *after* World War II. Victor Gollancz documented and published accounts of the suffering of German civilians and former soldiers; he drew attention to postwar Allied atrocities committed against the German people, especially against German children.

Table of Contents

1. A Bombastic Name..................7
2. That "Good Morning"................19
3. The Russians Are Coming..............29
4. Your World is Gone................39
5. Escargot in Ursendorf...............47
6. My Mother in Fuchsia...............57
7. The Hog-Dogs of Peenemünde…..........69
8. Members of the Family..............79
9. The Ménage and the Pantry Window..........97
10. Brother Bühler's Spit..............113
11. Klaus Bach..................117
12. The Geese and the Shepherd............129
13. The Man in the Sun...............143
14. The Ménage Schools Me.............155
15. The Lord Works in Weird Ways..........165
16. One Horrible Imagination............177
17. Grandpa's Excellent Sidekick...........187
18. Learning to Read Plants and a Greek Tragedy......195
19. Dynamite..................207
20. Albrecht Leo Merz...............213

21. My Inheritance 229
22. Joachim and Vimsie 235
23. Explosion 241
24. Prisoner of War Train to Arrive from the East 251
25. The Village School and the Music of the Spheres 257
26. A Lousy Story 265
Appendix I 279
Appendix II 287

CHAPTER ONE
A Bombastic Name

"UNN-zhé-lah!!" my father, Rudolf Mailänder, yelled at the official between two bombs. KABOOM!! KABOOM!!

"What??!" bellowed the official, but a bomb drowned out the sound of his voice: KABOOM!!

"UNN-zhé-lah!" hollered my father again. KABOOM!! KABOOM!! KABOOM!!

"How do you spell it?" roared the official, even though silence reigned for several seconds.

"A-N-G-E-L-A," my father said evenly and smiled politely at the official.

"UNG-guh-lah! I...I am dreadfully sorry, *Herr Feldwebel*...ah... that is not a name in our register." (*Feldwebel*, "sergeant major," was my father's military rank. "*Feld*" means "field," as in "battle field," but God only knows what a "*Webel*" is—maybe it's a weevil). An ambulance driver in Hitler's army, my father had been somewhere on the Russian front when I was born on March 29, 1940, in Berlin, Germany. Soon after, my birthplace was experiencing the phenomenon of carpet-bombing, although I think it was called saturation bombing back then. By the time he came home on furlough to register me with the authorities, the British were bombing all night, and the Americans were bombing all day.

But in spite of many difficulties, my daddy had come home to give me my name, which my mother had been unable to get the "authorities" to accept.

"I don't give a rat's petunia about your register," my father, the Field Weevil, said to the official with a pleasant smile, "Just write it on her birth record," and another bomb gave him emphasis: KABOOM!!

"I…I…I'm…I'm dreadfully sorry, *Herr Feldwebel*, but we are not authorized uh to uh record non-Germanic names; "UNG-guh-lah" is not an Aryan name. So uh uhmm, may I suggest ah… 'Agneta'? 'Agneta' has the ring of nobility." KABOOM!!!! KABOOM!!!! "A truly aristocratic name."

"Are you out of your mind?" KABOOM!! "She'll be an old maid with a name like that," KABOOM!! "Can you imagine marrying an Agneta?" KABOOM!! KABOOM!! "An ice princess would make a better wife. My girl's name is Italian: UNN-zhé-lah." KABOOM!! "My father has arranged for her to marry into an Italian family we've known for generations." KABOOM!! KABOOM!! "She shall be Angela degli Alberti….No," continued my poetic dad in a thoughtful tone, "it can't be Agneta. The alliteration is good, but the first syllable 'uhgh' sticks in the throat—'Unn' in 'Angela' hums forever."

"What?....ah….With apologies um ah I beg to differ, *Herr Feldwebel*, 'Agneta' is a passionate name. It is derived from the Aryan name of the fire god, Agni. However--ah, if you don't like Agneta, may suggest Antje? Antje dellie Alberti has a very nice ring to it," KABOOM "Ahh!!" KABOOM!! KABOOM!! "'Antje is a very nice name, uh, very sweet," KABOOM!! "I suggest Antje."

"UNN-zhé-lah! UNN-zhé-lah!" boomed my father the Fieldweevil, hitting the desk with his fist for every "UNN-zhé-lah" he uttered in unison with the exploding bombs: KABOOM!! KABOOM!! KABOOM!!

In the ensuing silence, the official said in very reasonable tones, "But *Herr Feldwebel*, imagine how your daughter will *feel* when she goes to school, and she is the only one with a foreign name." A cluster of bombs precluded conversation for several minutes: KABOOM!! KABOOM!! KABOOM!! KABOOM!! KABOOM!! KABOOM!! KABOOM!! KABOOM!! KABOOM!! KABOOM!! KABOOM!! KABOOM!! KABOOM!! KABOOM!! When silence once again reigned, my father said patiently, but with careful and smoldering emphasis, "My daughter shall be called UNN-zhé-lah. I am her father, I shall give her a name, and the name I have chosen is UNN-zhé-lah" KABOOM!! "Angela Mailänder, to be Angela degli Alberti when she comes of marriageable age." My father, though German, had been born in Italy, and pronounced my future Italian name perfectly with the correct "r" and the right melody and rhythm.

"I am dreadfully sorry, *Herr Feldwebel*…" KABOOM!!

"If I hear you say you are dreadfully sorry one more time, I shall jump across this desk and strangle you," roared my father in an inimitable crescendo and with all the might a fieldweevil could muster. KABOOM!!!! "Her name is UNN-zhé-lah" KABOOM!! KABOOM!! KABOOM!!

"I…I'm, I am dread…ah, *Herr Feldwebel*, I shall have to clear this with my superior."

KABOOM!!!! KABOOM!!!! KABOOM!!!! KABOOM!!!! KABOOM!!!!

KABOOM!!!! The explosions were coming closer. Out the window, my father could see the planes. In such beautiful precision they came, flying in formation, bomb bays opening in unison, the tiny black specks falling from the planes' bellies and growing larger and larger. For a moment he allowed himself to wonder why the bombs, released with such military precision, almost immediately assumed random patterns—or, maybe, they only looked random from a human point of view. Maybe from God's point of view they were precisely ordered. But before he could formulate a coherent hypothesis, the official's superior arrived with an anemic little smile under his precisely rectangular little mustache.

"*Heil Hitler, Herr Feldwebel*," said the superior, clicking his heels together and bowing a correct and angular little bow while also and incoherently attempting the *Heil Hitler* salute. "Allow me to express my gratitude for your service to our beloved Fatherland, ahh, our precious Homeland," said the superior. KABOOM! "Congratulations are in order as well on the birth of your lovely daughter." KABOOM!! "May she grow into virtuous motherhood, bearing strong Aryan sons for our New World Order,"[1] KABOOM!! KABOOM!! "Now, uhmm, as regards her name…."

"Her name," KABOOM!! "Is UNN-zhé-lah," KABOOM!!!!

The superior cleared his throat, "*Herr Feldwebel*" KABOOM!!!!

---

[1] That term, New World Order, was indeed bandied about in Nazi Germany, as it is in contemporary American politics; the phrase in Latin (Novus Ordo Seclorum) appears on every dollar printed since the establishment of the Federal Reserve System in 1913, and is, of course, taken from Virgil's Aeneid. In my opinion, not enough mainstream historians are asking themselves how those facts connect.

KABOOM!!!! "*Herr Feldwebel,* our *Führer*" KABOOM!!!! "Our *Führer* in his divine wisdom has cognized the importance, ahh, indeed the profound significance, of ah primordial sound," KABOOM!!!! KABOOM!!!! KABOOM!!!! KABOOM!!!! KABOOM!!!! "A name, Herr Feldwebel, is divine essence." KABOOM!!!! "And with our Aryan names we proclaim our national unity…" Meanwhile (KABOOM!! KABOOM!! KABOOM!! KABOOM!! KABOOM!! KABOOM!! KABOOM!! KABOOM!! KABOOM!! KABOOM!! KABOOM!! KABOOM!! KABOOM!! KABOOM!!), the national unity was being bombed to smithereens.

"*Herr Feldwebel, Herr Feldwebel,* could we please conclude this business since we really must repair to the bomb shelter?" KABOOM!!!! KABOOM!!!! To his subordinate he said, "Put her down as Anke Mailänder." KABOOM!!!! KABOOM!!!!

"You miserable little ersatz Hitler," shouted my father as the glass of the windows exploded with a demonic laugh, "Her name is **UNN-zhé-lah!**" KABOOM!! "**UNN-zhé-lah!**" KABOOM!! "**UNN-zhé-lah!**" KABOOM!! KABOOM!! KABOOM!! KABOOM!!

"For God's sake," shrieked the small and miserable ersatz Hitler, (KABOOM!!!! KABOOM!!!!), "Let the man have his stupid way, write her down as Angela Mailänder, and let's get the hell out of here."

KABOOM!! KABOOM!!

After that, my father went back to the Russian front to drive his ambulance for the wounded and dying, never to be heard from again.

What I Remember Of My Father

That last phrase is not exactly true, but you know, it was a tempting way to gain closure on an explosive narrative, which tells you what my priorities are. Succumbing to temptation, I did notice a slight distinction worming its way in between beauty and truth.

It is certainly a fact that I do not remember the exchange between my father and the Nazi weasels. So this is your official legal disclaimer. I'm writing something of a fictionalized memoir, not an autobiography, and, in a world in which our shrinks tell us that human memory is malleable, our conspiracy theorists tell us it can be implanted, and our physicists claim that retro-causation is a viable concept, you're forewarned herewith. You should also know that I do not remember my life in chronological order, never mind sequential flow, though I will do my best to create something like such an order, but the truth is I remember people, events, images, conversations, a certain look, an understanding beyond words—not a chronological sequence. And then, there is the fact that what I remember of my childhood went on in German, not English.[2] I am tempted to call my work a *Bildungsmemoir* after the literary term *Bildungsroman*. Here is what Wikipedia says about it in one truly horrible sentence:

> In literary criticism, a Bildungsroman (German: "novel of formation/education/culture"), novel of formation, novel of education, or coming-of-age story (though it may also be known as a subset of the coming-of-age story) is a literary genre that focuses on the psychological and moral growth of the protagonist from youth to adulthood (coming of age), and in which, therefore, character change is extremely important.

Of course, in a memoir, the narrative voice is not supposed to change. But the character, me, myself, and I, does change. For example, I found nothing much to love in America when I first came here, but now, though there are infinitely more excuses for such negative emotions than I knew about when I was twelve, I neither love nor hate America. In fact, I don't understand the concept of loving a country. I love the world, and, at the same time, am aghast at its cruelty.

This is the story of my life as I remember it right now, as I am writing it down, here in Fairfield, Iowa,[3] U.S.A., as if a life could be written

---

[2] I have an MFA degree in translation studies and decades of experience in literary translation from languages I know and, à la Ezra Pound, from those I don't know. What I am suggesting here about writing down childhood memories in a language other than the one in which these events occurred is deeper than any translation process I've experienced. To comment on this adequately, however, current fundamental assumptions about the nature of the translation process would have to be questioned—in short, this is essay material, and so the present venue is not the place for it.

[3] What could be written about this town wouldn't fit on a cow's hide, as my grandmother

down. Note, too, that my early life includes the stories as I heard them recounted again and again by family and friends—and as I reconstruct them now. The important thing about the people of my childhood is that, like me, all of them had just survived a brutal world war, even two, a revolution, a famine, as well as hard times in Siberia; and their stories are part of me, especially since I remember the daily face of war and the post-war famine[4] in Germany myself, which means that their stories were more than just words to me. And so I write from a point of view that would have seemed omniscient to my five-year old self.

As it happens, my father did come back on furlough, and I remember three occasions before I was five—and those three occasions are all I remember of him. My mother barely spoke of him. One of those three scenes involved a small herd of elephants, and another one entailed a dozen of lions. The third one was his good-bye to me before he vanished somewhere on the Russian front (allegedly) and really never was heard from again. He did not say it, and I would probably not have understood; yet in some way beyond words we both knew he would not be back. Even so, I waited.

The twelve lions were carved of shiny black wood and formed the armrests of all the chairs around our dining room table. So when you rested your arms, they lay on the backs of two lions, whose tails curved up onto the backrests, and whose mouths were open wide in a hungry, yet silent, roar. Food was scarce, dangerously scarce, but the need to share my oatmeal with those lions was overwhelming—besides, I did not know food was scarce. When my parents came into the room, my father sat in the chair whose pair of lions had not yet been fed, my mother got busy retrieving and saving the oatmeal from the rest of the lions' maws while trying explain the existential situation of these lions to me. My father, meanwhile, asked if I could please help him into his uniform jacket.

---

would say. Indeed, several books have been written about this small town hiding among corn and soybean fields in the southeast corner of the state. I'll give you a brief run-down of this amazing place at the end of this chapter.

[4] This famine was deliberately engineered by General Dwight D. Eisenhower and Treasury Secretary Henry Morgenthau. See *After the Reich: The Brutal History of the Allied Occupation*, by British historian Giles MacDonogh. He "details how the ruined and prostrate Reich (including Austria) was systematically raped and robbed, and how many Germans who survived the war were either killed in cold blood or deliberately left to die of disease, cold, malnutrition or starvation…. His best estimate is that some three million Germans, military and civilians, died unnecessarily after the official end of hostilities." http://www.ihr.org/other/afterthereich072007.html. See also the work of Victor Gollanzc to whom my story is dedicated.

This was a routine I knew well and loved. His arm was in a plaster cast that held it in a wildly ironic *Heil Hitler* position. The cast had seven holes in it to provide air circulation to seven wounds. The holes were covered with gauze to protect the wounds and the maggots in them. And just so you know, maggots are what you put into festering wounds when there are no antibiotics to be had. The maggots keep the wound clean since they eat only rotting flesh. So, you either welcome the maggots or prepare to die of gangrene.

The sleeve of my father's jacket had been cut out leaving a hole. You slid that over the cast so as not to disturb the maggots. Then you climbed on the chair, and, crawling behind him, loving the back of his neck and shoulders, you brought the jacket around him to where he could put his other arm into the sleeve. Then you would collect a one-armed hug.

Whereas the reality status of the lions was in question, the elephants were real and alive. My father took me to the Berlin zoo, and as he crouched behind me, I stood between his knees, and we looked at the elephants, and the elephants looked at us. "Elephants are faithful," he whispered in my ear. And only today, as I write this sentence some seventy years later, I understand for the first time the sadness in his voice and the subtext: "As your mother is not."

And whenever I think of those elephants, I wonder: were they torn to shreds among exploding bombs? Of course they were, and you can be sure someone was grateful to cook and eat those shreds.

Did my father really go back to the eastern front? Wounded as he was? Of what use could he have been? The Papacy had a service for finding missing people after WWII (and which also helped an amazing number of high level Nazi war criminals go missing in Argentina). And because there was a mysterious connection between my father's family and Pope Pius XII, "His Holiness" personally oversaw the effort to find my father, or so my mother told me, and, at least allegedly, Rudolf Mailänder could never be found. Maybe he starved to death in one of Dwight D. Eisenhower's death camps—that would account for his not being accounted for anywhere as a POW (Russians, unbelievably, are even better at record-keeping than Germans are). Eisenhower called his prisoners DEF's (Disarmed Enemy Forces) so he would not have to abide by the humanitarian laws established for POW's under the Geneva Convention. That they were not called P.O.W.' s also made it impossible to learn who they were.

I know my American friends will be surprised to learn that Eisenhower[5] was a war criminal. In the age of the Internet, however, I do not feel the need to write a footnote here; nor would a footnote do justice to the facts. Just Google it, if you don't believe me, but note that you will have to go deeper than snopes.com. The issue seems to revolve around whether or not James Bacque's work, *Other Losses* (1989), is credible, and a number of American academic historians argue that it is not. However, having lived through two Ph.D. programs and subsequently teaching in academe for a number of years, I know how cheaply their opinions can be bought. I find Bacque's work to be solid; nor is Bacque the only source of this information. What all the reports I have seen have in common is that their accounts fit with what I remember people around me talking about as I was growing up. But if you do not want to read three library shelves full of books, read Martin Brech's memories of what he saw in one of Eisenhower's camps as a young American soldier. Brech includes good references. You'll find his statement in the "Appendix."

Fairfield, Iowa

When I came to the University of Iowa in 1975 for my first Ph.D., I worked with the International Writing Program under the direction of Paul Engle (who is allegedly a famous American poet), and one of the writers, a great friend, poet, and translator, the late Daniel Weissbort (of whom you'll hear more) told me, "You should write a memoir, since you've lived all over and through a lot, but remember, in the first chapter you have to plant your left foot." And so, I am herewith planting my left foot in Fairfield, Iowa.

I have indeed lived "all over": in Germany, of course, but also in France, in Greece, in India, and in China. In the US, I have lived in Ohio, Pennsylvania, Kentucky, California, Colorado, and Minnesota—

---

[5] While I have nothing good to say about Eisenhower in this chapter, I want to note that humans are never one-dimensional beings. Eisenhower strongly opposed and even felt sickened at the crime of dropping atomic bombs on a defeated Japan. And, upon leaving office in 1961, Eisenhower warned: "In the councils of government, we must guard against the acquisition of unwarranted influence, whether sought or unsought, by the military–industrial complex." This statement, an echo of Jefferson's warning about the dangers of "standing armies," does much to redeem Eisenhower in my mind.

and, of course, Iowa. I should also say that I have lived in the "other America." For 28 years, I was married to a black man, so I have lived in black America—and yes, it is a different country from white America. Almost every day a black American is killed by police or security forces in an extrajudicial murder—and those are just the official numbers; no doubt, many go unreported, as the police are not required to keep records on these things. Any time a black man is killed, it could easily be one of my grandsons. Such killings have never yet happened in a white community.[6]

Since 1992, however, I have lived in Fairfield, Iowa (minus two years in China and one in Minnesota). And since 1974, Fairfield has been the home of Maharishi University of Management (formerly Maharishi International University); the town is therefore also one of the biggest international centers of TM or Transcendental Meditation as taught by Maharishi Mahesh Yogi (1918 -2008). As noted above, books have been written about this place. Our town has also been mentioned in various national publications as one of the best places in the U.S. to live or visit. One of these publications dubbed the place "Sillicorn Valley" with reference to Silicon Valley (there are an unusual number of international computer businesses in Fairfield) and also with reference to the actual corn and the silly corn that are both produced here.

We have a somewhat labile population of 8,000-10,000. About 90% of the student body consists of foreign nationals, and they come and go. But so do the meditating community and the New-Age aficionados of various stripes. The original farmers, who still tend to look askance at the "Rus,"[7] stay put.

---

[6] Cornel West and Kareem Abdul-Jabbar are two black leaders who feel that what is happening today in black communities in America will spread to white communities, as both men feel that the militarization of the police is not without purposes beyond black communities. Cornel West characterizes the current political climate as "the Niggerization of America." Seems right to me. West and Abdul-Jabbar remind me of Martin Niemöller's famous statement, "First they came for the Socialists and I did not speak out...." And Glen Ford, responding to the notion that the American criminal justice system was "broken," said aptly, "The system works just fine. It does what it was designed to do. It acts with uniformity all across the United States and delivers like clockwork millions of black bodies to be incarcerated in the biggest Gulag in the world...." (Black Agenda Report)

[7] The local farmers and their attendant community in town dubbed the meditating folks who bought the bankrupt Parson's College in 1974, "Them fuckin' gurus." That term eventually got shortened to "Rus" and is no longer carrying as big a load of hatred as it once did—I even know some "closet meditators" among the "Townies" and farmers. These days, town Rus (as opposed to university Rus) use the term to refer to themselves and each other. Most of them

Fairfield is a religious town. I once lived in a hut in the forest just outside Emlenton, Pennsylvania, which then had a population of 800 souls (and some nastier entities as well); Emlenton had ten churches representing ten variants of Christianity. Well, Fairfield is even more religious. In addition to about thirty different Christian denominations (including two varieties of "independent" Catholic churches and two official ones), we also have countless Hindu temples (each representing a different deity), three Buddhist temples, and two Sufi houses. A casual traveler would not see these, however. Most of these places look like typical Iowa farm or town houses, but open the front door, and Ganesha, the Elephant God of India will welcome you. There are also an untold number of groups meeting weekly in order to share their "subtle experiences," as members coach each other to become "enlightened" and then go on to higher and higher stages of enlightenment, while arguing as to who is the most enlightened among them. There are many Internet discussion forums devoted to this most urgent issue.

However, in spite of the fact that a variety of religions are more or less welcome, there are those in Fairfield who do not tolerate competing Eastern gurus. When Ammaji (Mata Amritanandamayi) scheduled a meeting in Fairfield, she received death threats—anonymous, of course, but I very much doubt the local farmers had any intentions on her life. In spite of such strong feelings amongst some against "other gurus," there are followers of at least eleven different ones in Fairfield, counting only those actually from India. There are many Western gurus as well, who have Fairfield followers—though they usually give themselves Indian names upon becoming gurus. Fairfield is seen as a veritable goldmine of the gullible by a circuit of every variety of New-Age spiritual healers, angel healers, soul surgeons, past-life readers, exorcists, wannabe gurus, and senders to the light of lost souls, as well as channelers of various energies, of long dead gurus and saints, and of various celestial, intergalactic, and other-dimensional beings. Two Fairfield publications regularly offer a whole page advertising such occult this-week-only visitors offering seminars and services. Once, when I was jobless and saw how much money you could make by being a guru or healer of some sort, I thought I should really channel something—but what? Dolphins had

---

probably know that Sanskrit "ru" means "dispeller"; a "guru" is a dispeller of darkness. When, during one of the darkest periods of my life, a feral doggie came out of the blue and insisted on living with me, I named her Ru Dog. That doggie definitely was a dispeller of darkness.

been done—so, maybe, I thought, possibly perhaps, I could channel Lao Tsu's ancient turtle who was his guru. Needless to say, the turtle didn't fly.

But all that silly corn notwithstanding, Fairfield is an artists' and a writers' colony. When I first came to the University of Iowa, an artist had to have an Iowa City address in order to be taken seriously by the Iowa Arts Council. Now it's indubitably Fairfield. A vast variety of the finest performers also include our town on their tours. What other little prairie town gets visits from the Vienna Boys' Choir, just for instance? The first Friday of every month here is dedicated to a community festival, an "Art Walk," featuring local artists (sometimes including me) in about twenty different galleries. A national film festival is based here, and there is no shortage of musicians, actors, dancers, con artists, and poets. No question about it: I live in a spectacular zoo.

And why am I here? Well, by 1970 it was clear to me that, come the new century, I did not want to live in an American big city; I understood Henry Wadsworth Longfellow perfectly when he said, "Whom the gods would destroy, they first make mad." But I also did not want to live in an American small town since there is nothing on earth more boring than that. And, of course, back then, you really couldn't even think about living in an American small town with a black husband—that year, in the spring of 1970, he and I narrowly escaped a lynch mob, and that was in small town in northern Ohio, not in Mississippi or Alabama. So when I discovered Fairfield in 1975 just an hour's drive south of Iowa City, Fairfield seemed perfect. He and I drove down here, found the center of town, and gave each other a close hug and a big wet kiss while watching the reaction of the passers-by. Fairfield passed the test. I did not imagine back then that the town would become well known as a tourist destination. Nor did I imagine that one of my grandsons could be "raped" by our literally criminal justice system. You'll hear about him in volume three of this memoir.

Of course, there were many complicated and compelling reasons (reasons? Is life really about reason?) in addition to my dim views regarding the 21st century for moving here in 1992—and worries: what can someone like me do for a living in such a place—other than channeling a swamp rat or something? I could just see it: the wisdom of the groundhogs as channeled by the gifted psychic, Angela Mailander. By

1992 I could see Fairfield would not remain a totally anonymous town. And that worried me a bit. I ask myself, for example, why President Obama has come to our neck of the woods for secret conversations with our mayor about three times? What in the world did those two fellahs talk about? While I cannot answer that, you will hear all about life in Fairfield in due time, but first we will go back to the beginning of my life on this planet, which I have never yet understood—either the life or the planet, if, in fact, there's a distinction.

CHAPTER TWO

That "Good Morning"

Life was uncertain and full of horrors by the time I was three years old in 1943. Nobody got enough food, water, painkillers, or sleep. The Americans still bombed the city all day, and the British bombed all night.

But you have to hand it to the Germans—they are nothing if not organized and disciplined. After every air raid, all more or less able-bodied persons would form teams: teams to collect the dead and dispose of them; teams to stop the flow of blood wherever it seemed possible; teams to deliver the *coup de grace* where it was not; teams to search through the rubble for survivors; teams to collect orphaned children and babies; teams to collect old people wandering about in a stunned daze; teams to collect those who had gone totally screaming and shaking bonkers; teams to search for and fix electric lines that were jumping around torn and spitting fire; teams to fix broken water mains; teams to find broken gas pipes and mend them before they could blow up and cause yet more harm; teams to serve coffee on street corners and whatever food could be scared up for as long as these things were available; teams to search buildings for fire bombs that had not yet gone off and throw them out in the street where they would do whatever damage they might.

"You learn to throw them without looking where they'll fall or you'll hesitate too long," my mother told me decades later here in Fairfield, in her last months of life. She was so completely paralyzed that she could not move her finger to use the call button I had taped under her right hand. But she could talk, and she told me the stories that connected the images of my earliest memories for me. She died in early September of 1998. "The screaming..." she continued, "...the screaming of the wounded was there all the time anyway. You never get used to that, but you learn to make a space for it in your mind and then you could maybe seal it off. After a while so much of you is sealed off, you become a zombie."

That explains a lot, doesn't it? I was nursed by a zombie—until lack of food dried up her milk. It was a zombie who came to check on me when I screamed because my bed was full of broken glass after an all-night bombing. And it was a zombie who then didn't have enough presence of mind to figure out why I was screaming. And when I refused to eat boiled, mashed carrots, it was a zombie who locked me in the closet for three days and four nights, taking me out to give me water and offer mashed, boiled, carrots on schedule. My grandmother, both my maternal aunts, and even my mother—they all told me the story many times of how heart-rending my screams were, and then my whimpers, as I got weaker from the lack of food. They said I was nine months old, and this is what it took for me to learn that when your mother orders you to eat, you had better not refuse or you "vill starff to dess." My mother never quite lost her "Cherman accent."

"Well, there was no food other than carrots—and even they were hard to find and they were sometimes pretty far gone." That was her excuse, decades later, as I cranked up the bed and adjusted her pillows. "I was desperate to keep you alive," she continued, "and the doctor said, 'Let her get a little hungry; she'll eat the carrots'."

Some things have remained constant. I still am not fond of boiled carrots. And still the bombs are dropping. I have been in many places on this planet since those days. Somewhere the bombs are dropping day and night; they keep dropping, and it looks like they will for some time yet to come. We no longer call it war. We call it "humanitarian intervention" or "regime change" or "police action," we send military advisors, not soldiers, and we win the Nobel Peace Prize for it all while sounding no different from little boys in the school yard: "He started it"; "No, he did."

But back in 1943 something small with big political consequences happened to give us all a reprieve from the bombing and a chance to gather strength for the horrors that followed. We were coming out of the basement one morning after all-night raids. My mother was carrying my two baby sisters, and I was hanging onto her skirt while going up the stairs when a neighbor tickled me under the chin and said in a very annoying, cutesy sort of voice, "*Heil Hitler*, little Angela."

"Good morning," I giggled back at her. Or so my mother told me.

"Good morning!!" the lady screeched in outrage, "Alice Mailänder, don't you teach your children to say, '*Heil Hitler*'?"

In a killing voice my mother shot back, "'Good morning' will always be good enough for us."

And that "Good morning" got us out of Berlin and away from the bombs. My mother's friends and neighbors, Janek and his wife Elke, were behind her on the stairs, and both of them realized immediately the danger of what my mother had just said to a small-time Nazi official. My mother should have known better than to say something so utterly careless, stupid, and useless. She could have ended up in a labor camp, and my sisters and I would have been put into a state nursery where we would get the "proper" education. Janek phoned my Aunt Editta, my father's sister, who was miraculously able to pull some strings to get my mother transferred that same day to a munitions factory manned by prisoners and hidden deep in the pine forests near Dreetz, a small town about 45 miles northwest of Berlin. The factory needed an interpreter. As it happened, my mother spoke both Russian and German as native languages because she had been born in Russia, coming to Germany with her German parents when she was seven years old; she also was fluent in English and in French.

A few of the prisoners did speak English and French, but most of the workers at the factory were Russian prisoners of war. They had come to Germany before the war as volunteers, but when the war broke out,[8] they were classified as enemy aliens and were imprisoned. It was from this pool, in addition to the concentration camps, that many German factories drew their slave labor.

The area surrounding the factory near Dreetz was beautiful, and I, by then four years old, do remember. Trees with tall, slender trunks whose new bark near the top shone pink, rose gold, orange, and golden at sunrise or sunset. If you went close to those trees, you could see transparent amber beads on them that reflected light like diamonds, yet were warm with life even when they had caught and killed some

---

[8] "The war broke out." Had it been caged, then? History books are full of such phrases. So-and-so "came to power" is another example of History-textbook speak.

small spider or fly. The dark-needled branches at the tops of the trees formed a lacy canopy that threw dancing patterns onto the white sand in which these trees grew. Pure white and shimmering sand. The local squirrel population was the same fiery orange-golden color as the tree trunks, and, in addition to their charming tails, they had tufts of spiked fur sticking straight up at the tip of each ear. The deer, too, were reddish gold and white. So were the foxes: red gold on top, but their delicate feet and intelligent faces were white.

We, that is, my baby sisters, my mother and I, moved into a forest ranger's house in the middle of all that beauty, and my maternal grandmother, Maria Zeitner (a.k.a. Maria Abramovna), came to care for us, my two sisters and me, while my mother went to work at the factory. My grandfather, Max Zeitner (a.k.a. Maxim Pavlovich), stayed in Berlin where God's work desperately needed to be done, and he felt chosen and called. My aunt Maria worked in a factory in Berlin and looked in on her father whenever she could get away from her work, which, in those war years was grueling, and the hours were long.

The old head ranger lived not far away from the house we had moved into, but still quite a distance for a four-year old to travel by herself. I had to go through dense woods, cross a huge clearing, and then more woodland to get to his house, but the trip was always well worth it because he welcomed me and because many of the forest animals in his care were tame and would take food from his hands—especially the squirrels. That year, the old ranger was nursing orphaned fox pups. I have never since seen anyone to whom animals came so freely, and to this day my idea of heaven is a place where the animals are not afraid of me.

My grandmother told me many times not to go to the ranger's house alone, but what child could have resisted fox puppies? And you would think there could be no harm in going. When I was not in evidence, she always knew where I was. Then one day, after she had come to retrieve me, we were crossing the clearing together when an American fighter plane, a B-17, appeared out of nowhere. He dived towards us, so low we could see the ball-turret gunner's crazy, distorted face as he sprayed us with bullets from the plexiglass bubble clinging to the underside of the plane. My grandmother ran towards the bushes at the edge of the forest dragging me by the arm, not even taking time to lift me up and carry me. We made it mostly unharmed, though I had sustained a few deep scratches from being dragged through the field, and she had a flesh wound in her left arm, but it was not deep, and the bullet had not lodged.

How can I be so sure it was a B-17? Well, I described that plane minutely to my second husband's wonderful Uncle Harold decades upon decades later while he and I were watching the BBC WW II documentary series together. He said I did a great job describing a B-17 and that he had built models of them when he was a boy. I said I longed for a world in which children did not play war, and he said he was sure it could never happen. According to whispered family stories, Uncle Harold was a CIA agent.

After the B-17 episode, my grandmother tied me to a tree with a very long sewing thread. My mother laughed when she came home and said, "The child can break that thread any time she wants—she might not even notice it when she runs off."

"She can, and she knows it, but she won't," said my grandmother. "She is not disobedient; she just forgets, and the thread reminds her of her promise. Look how careful she is not to break it."

So all was not rosy and gold, considering you could get yourself shot while innocently crossing a field, especially since the gunner could see clearly that he was shooting at a middle-aged woman and a child—and I know he could see us clearly: If we could see his face, he could see ours.

Here is another image in my memory—the stuff of nightmares—from that time: My grandmother earned money for us by taking in sewing. Because of this, a Russian girl, Olga, came from the factory every day to help my grandmother with the housework. Olga and I were out one day to cut and gather cattails, whose stalks—white near the roots—are almost as good as asparagus. And we saw men dredging the canal and bringing up the bodies of people who had been dead for a while—probably shot by B-17's. As the bodies of men, women, and children came up, just breaking the dark water's surface, fat black eels jumped out of the eye sockets and stomach cavities and mouths of these bodies and boiled under the surface of the black water.

Just the snake-like black creatures roiling under black water will give you nightmares. There is archetypal horror in a scene like this, as there is in maggots crawling in the wounds in your father's arm.

Of course, we had boiled eel for supper on the night the canal had been dredged. And of course, you could not refuse to eat when my mother ordered you to eat, or it might be your last supper.

My mother apologized about the eels on her deathbed, but I just laughed and told her I did not remember having eel for supper that night. "We did," she said, "And you got so sick, we thought you wouldn't make it."

"Don't worry," I told her, "That was long ago and in another country."

"Well," she said, "There's a lot of things I'm glad you don't remember."

"What? Are you holding out on me?"

But she would say nothing more, while I wondered how much more terrible things could get than the horrors I do remember.

Eels and B-17's notwithstanding, our lives were easy in that pine forest compared to what they had been in Berlin and especially compared to what they soon would be.

Although things were not as bad as they were at some German factories that used slave labor from concentration camps, life for the workers at this munitions factory was still unadulterated hell. The German administration was cruel, food was tightly rationed toward the end of the war for everyone, so naturally the prisoners got even less than was allocated to the staff. Medical attention and supplies were practically non-existent for the prisoners, though there was a doctor for staff. Working conditions were unsafe, in part because the prisoners never got enough sleep, and there were frequent explosions in which workers burned to death—or, worse, nearly to death. My mother never did learn to deal with the smell of backyard barbecues in Mayfield Heights, Ohio, decades later—barbecues that made everybody else's mouths water.

The Russian workers, in spite of being cruelly oppressed and starved, were nevertheless lively and resourceful. And my mother was their friend. They called her by her Russian name: Alexandra Maximovna—which was not the name of an enemy to them, as her German name, Alice Mailänder, would have been.

Armed men guarded the prisoners; there were watchtowers with searchlights, barbed wire, and vicious dogs on short leashes that could be loosed any time. Even so, the prisoners had dug a tunnel out of the enclosure and, at night, they came and went freely. My mother asked them why they did not escape. There was nowhere to escape to, they told her. Russia would shoot them for having come to Germany voluntarily—if they made it as far as Russia in the first place. Then why bother digging tunnels and going out?

They were preparing for the end of the war, they told her. Any time a plane crashed anywhere near the factory they found it, dismantled what was left of it, and smuggled what they wanted back into the camp, or hid it somewhere in the pine forest before German authorities even found the crash site.

"How could that be possible—how could starved and cruelly oppressed Russian prisoners be more organized and efficient than Prussian bureaucrats?" I asked my mother, as I was getting ready to feed her lunch.

"The Russians were just ordinary people who did what they needed to do to survive," she said. "The German authorities were a cumbersome bureaucracy that was badly staffed toward the end of the war and crazy from hunger and lack of sleep. They couldn't fart without written permission in triplicate from Berlin. So they first had to request permission in triplicate, then they had to fill out endless forms in triplicate, then they got permission, then they had to acknowledge that they got permission, and then they could go look for the crash site."

"Did you say, 'fart'?" (I had NEVER heard my mother use such a word).

"I figure I better get it out, before I die."

"Don't make me laugh, or I'll drop your food," I said, as I was balancing a fork full in front of her mouth."

"It's really good," she said, "I didn't know you were such a good cook. What is it?"

"Shark steak."

"Shark steak? I didn't know you could eat shark."

"This one's special; it has dined on two Christian missionaries of two deliciously different denominations."

She nearly choked, she laughed so hard. (Since her father was a devout Christian, my mother was an equally devout atheist.)

Somehow the Russian prisoners had managed to appropriate two busses. When the busses went missing in town, I suppose no one suspected the prisoners at the factory because no one knew they could get out so easily. Those busses were hiding in the forest with full tanks of gasoline and several canisters of it stashed inside each one. The prisoners had also stolen enough bicycles so that there was one for every worker in the factory and a few more for my mother and her family. They had guns, ammunition, and, in case all else failed, cyanide capsules to commit suicide—all salvaged from crashed or shot down American and British bombers or German fighter planes.

Most importantly, the prisoners had a radio, put together from salvaged parts. It was a radio that could receive foreign broadcasts. It was hidden in one of the tunnels under the camp's basement and manned at all times day and night—by somebody too sick to work, so that his or her absence from the factory was accepted. The German population could not own such radios; I think my mother said that violators were shot. Germans were only allowed to have "*Volksradios*" ("people's radios"), which could only get German broadcasts approved by Goebbels, the Minister of Propaganda. We are much more sophisticated now. If there is indeed a minister of propaganda now, he remains entirely invisible. My guess is that there are a number of committees.[9]

Because they could not get foreign broadcasts, the German authorities at the factory did not know Germany was losing the war and quickly—Hitler successfully managed to keep hope alive all the way to the bitter end, even in early 1945 when twelve and thirteen-year-old boys were being drafted into battle zones.

The Russians told my mother around Christmas in 1944 that the end was near and that the plan was to get to American occupied territory somehow before Russian troops actually showed up in the immediate neighborhood. "They will be Mongolian troops," said the Russian prisoners, "You can bet on that—because they will really know how to take revenge on the German people. In fact, our own women won't be safe." Russia had lost thirty-seven million people in WWI, and German soldiers had distinguished themselves for their cruelty in that slaughter

---

[9] Since the Internet, it is more than obvious that the mainstream media is a propaganda organ. But even in the sixties, that was the case. Here is an example: When nobody in the country believed the Warren Commission's conclusion that Kennedy had been assassinated by the "lone gunman" Lee Harvey Oswald, the CIA sent a secret memo to all the media (CIA document 1035-960; http://www.jfklancer.com/CIA.html), instructing them to use the term "conspiracy theorist" on anyone who doubted that conclusion. This has been one of the most successful social engineering campaigns ever, as "conspiracy theory" has become an international cultural meme and thought stopper.

before they lost at Stalingrad by making the same mistakes Napoleon had made and because they thought killing people was more important than holding territory.

My mother and the Russian prisoners had learned from the hidden radio that the Russian army would advance to the Elbe River, which was to be the demarcation line between the Russian and the American occupation. So the plan was to get to the Elbe River and cross it into American territory at all cost and as soon as possible.

CHAPTER THREE

The Russians Are Coming

One fine Sunday towards the end of March, right around my fifth birthday, my two maternal aunts, Maria and Ruth, were visiting from Berlin. My mother had to work anyway—no time off for a German munitions factory in those days, obviously. She came home for lunch, bleeding from a gash across her forehead that barely missed her eye. Her clothes were bloody and torn. Everyone spoke at once. What's going on? What happened? Why are you bleeding? Are you OK?

She threw some backpacks on the kitchen table, laid a gun down carefully, and said to my grandmother, "Pack; the Russians are coming."

"How much time?"

"Plenty. We leave at nightfall. I have to go back to the factory—things aren't quite secure there yet."

"What are you talking about?" asked my aunt Ruth in alarm.

"You don't think the factory is just going to let us all walk out if the workers say that Russian troops are near, do you?" said my mother while re-loading her gun.

After grabbing some lunch, she went back to the factory, back into battle, while my grandmother started to pack. Because she had plenty of experience in these matters (in World War I), she knew the difference between what you need and what you might want. She knew, too, that everyone else would be on the road also, and that therefore you better pack what you need and what you might want separately, so you could prioritize guarding things from others in desperate need. Because starvation will make thieves and murderers of us all.

When my mother came home later that afternoon, she fell down into the big armchair and said to the ceiling, "We killed everybody except the doctor." Then she leaned forward with her head hanging, her elbows on her widespread knees and her hands shielding her eyes. She sighed, and added, "He's a bastard, but he might come in handy down the road."

"Did you kill Martin?" asked my grandmother softly.

I never learned who Martin was, and decades later my mother, dying, said, "It's not important; it was a battle, and in this one, everybody could choose what side they were on. Almost everybody on our side lived. No one was left on theirs except the doctor. They were outnumbered and they didn't expect an armed attack from the prisoners."

And then, maybe even on my fifth birthday on March 29th in 1945, the war came to our house. Of course, I had heard people talking with great fear about the war and I had formed the idea that it was a big black bird that would come and cover the sky—and when the war did come to my house, it seemed I had not been that far wrong. My aunt Maria said she was going to try to get through the Russian lines back to Berlin because "Somebody has to take care of Father; he can't even boil water, the poor dear."

"Bullshit," said my mother. "He walked through the Ural Mountains alone in winter—if he puts out that he can't boil water, then that's because he wants women to wait on him hand and foot. Anyway, YOU are going nowhere; YOU are coming with US," she said in a tone I've known too well, "Mother's got a heart condition; Ruth is always fainting at the drop of a hat; and I've got three babies to deal with. I need your help. And anyway, you'll never make it through the Russian lines."

Maria remained adamant: "Dad needs help too."

"You are running after some man," screamed my mother, "This is...."

And she used a term that's not really translatable into English: "*Sexuelle Hörigkeit.*" It literally means sexual obedience," but that doesn't get at the ugliness of the word "*hörig.*" "Bondage" is another possible translation, but that sounds as though you like getting tied to the bedposts in spare neckties, and that is not what it means at all. My mother said those words in such a way that, although I had no clue what they meant, I knew it was the most demeaning and sick thing in the world you could ever accuse anybody of, and Maria's reaction to my mother's accusation was entirely commensurate.

I do not remember what got said and by whom that day in our house in the pine forest—I do remember it turned into a screaming match among the three weird sisters. My two baby sisters, who were always crying or screaming anyway, were trying to outdo them. My grandmother said nothing and had been trying to hush the babies until my mother threatened to kill Maria.

At that point, my grandmother did get into it and said, "If you do, Ali, you might as well shoot me first."

The important thing for me about that screaming match was that it was different from three Italian or Greek women getting into a fight—that would be a completely different ball game—they could well be friends minutes later. But this scene was different. What I remember most of all about it was the black atmosphere of impotent hatred unfathomably deep. And though I could not name it or understand it, I knew that sex was very much part of this dark and evil picture. I hid in a corner, hardly able to breathe, and looked at my family and my home and knew the war was here, saw nothing but senseless darkness and evil, and was afraid the sun would never shine again.

Everyone has heard that animals can feel your fear. This sounds as if animals are somehow psychic, but I do not think that this is how it works. If a bee shows up in your environment, and you are afraid of her, that bee is completely over-flooded by your more powerful awareness. She does not read your fear like a clever spy, while remaining cool herself; instead, she feels it as her own mortal terror because your little bit of fear is huge to her. In that same way, I became that dark and deep and impotent hatred that had some vague connection with sex and that possessed my family, as I sat in a corner unable to breathe. Maybe my family and I were all over-flooded with the darkness that was Germany in those days.

My aunt Maria, as my mother had predicted, never made it through the Russian lines. She ended up in Waldheim and then Buchenwald for nine years. Buchenwald, as everyone knows, was a German concentration camp. But after whatever Jews had survived there had been liberated, the Russians filled it right back up again, mostly with Germans this time.

My grandmother packed while the three sisters were fighting and she dressed my baby sisters and me in so many layers of clothing that

I could hardly walk or breathe. After dark, two busses showed up in front of the house. I actually remember that they were blue. Bluebird blue. The seats had been torn out so more people could fit in, standing cheek to cheek. The one we boarded was already crowded. Some bikes and canisters of gasoline were stashed in the back, with more bikes and two bike trailers tied to the top carrier.

I refused to get in unless I could take my pillow, and my mother and grandmother almost got into another fight about that. This time my grandmother won. She said, "This child will have to walk through God knows what—at least let her walk hugging her pillow." My mother tried to make Maria come with us one last time, promising she would never forgive her if she did not come. And in fact, my mother never did forgive her, not even when Maria was dying, though later, when my mother was the one dying, she forgave all of life.

My sisters and I lay on nets stretched over bent metal tubes near the ceiling along with the baggage—mostly homemade backpacks. I do not remember much about that bus ride except getting sick and vomiting on whoever was standing beneath me and feeling really bad about it. We rode all night, stopping only to refill the tank from the canisters and for pit stops on some small path where the bus could hide behind trees and bushes, men on one side of the bus, women on the other.

There were no gas stations where we could have bought or stolen more fuel. To the extent fuel was available at all, it was allocated to the military. Nor would we have wanted to risk stopping and interacting with Germans. Then, when the blue bus ran out of gas, we filled the tank from the canisters, knowing that there would be a last time. That is why we had the bikes.

I do not remember how long we rode that bus. But when it was running out of gas for the last time, the driver took it down a footpath, leading deep into the pine forest whose floor was no longer white sand but sweet smelling dark forest soil, and I slept well that night between two tree roots, cushioned by my own pillow on deep moss with scent of pines all around me and the stars above.

At first light we were off on the bikes, my sisters and I riding in a two-wheeled trailer. We had orders to stay hidden under a tarp, but I had to breathe the air and see the landscape slide by. Our adults rode those bikes all through that day—a group of about forty of us. But the bikes only lasted one day before others equally eager to flee from the invading Russians stole them, and we were on foot. But for one day we had them and rode them for all they were worth.

And on that day we came to a place where the road divided around a huge circular field, and Russian tanks were moving into it at about the two o'clock position of the circle. I had never seen tanks before, but with tanks you do not need prior experience to know that they are evil. They were heading diagonally across the field towards the eight o'clock position, driving German soldiers and their equipment before them in a pitched battle.

The scene was utter chaos: mortar fire, machine guns, hand grenades and something called *Panzer Faust*—all exploding every moment. Men screaming, running, crawling, writhing, shaking uncontrollably, body parts flying around; blood, entrails, brains everywhere. Our group had tried to escape the battle by turning to our right, but we arrived at the eight o'clock position just as that mass of battling humanity was crossing the road there, and we had to ride right through that…whatever it was…a hell in which men were bayoneting each other.

We should have been killed. At least some of our group should have run into fallen soldiers or their equipment or slid on somebody's brains and wrecked their bikes. Some stray gunfire or shrapnel should have hit some of us. Nothing happened. Our group of riders leaned into the curve of the road as one and rode that curve as smooth and silent as the Tour de France on TV—and then, in perfect unison, we headed south at the six o'clock position of the field. Our group of riders and the men in the battle passed through one another like one wave passes through another without any effect one on the other. And even in the breath of the wind, I remember a self-contained silence and singularity that I still cannot quite name. Strange, such moments: I am not confined to a body or a time and space, nor am I any age; yet every detail is very specific, local, clear and saturated with light, with meaning-fullness, and things flow in slow motion and absolute silence even though there was obviously much noise.

Tired and hungry as our group of riders no doubt was, they rode those bikes all day until dark. The ex-prisoners wanted to continue through the night to put as much distance between themselves and the advancing Russian army as possible and get to the other side of the

Elbe River. But my grandmother could not do it. So we separated. They went on, taking the doctor who was a bastard with them; and we slept by the side of the road. In the morning, our bikes were gone, and so were two of the backpacks, but the pack with the two cooking pots and other cooking utensils, the gun, and some food was still there because my mother had slept with it in her arms.

Now we were on foot along with thousands of others. Everyone has seen them on TV or in the movies—refugees everywhere in the world look about the same. But nothing in those images of people walking, carrying babies and some odd and few belongings, tells the story of how much agony the human heart can bear.

I do not remember any of those thousands, except two. One was an old woman walking alone. She was carrying a grey parrot in a cage, talking to it and telling it not to worry, that everything would be OK. I felt so sorry for that bird. I was sure the old lady was talking through her hat—there was no way that bird would be OK. I dreamed about it for decades in terrible nightmares, trying to protect it and failing. After a while that bird became many birds in my closet or many beautiful fish, and I would be somewhere desperately trying to get home so I could feed them and getting there too late, much too late.

And then there was a soldier who had lost a hand, and the wound was healing badly. With his other hand, he pulled an egg out of his pocket, and I was instantly enchanted: I had never seen an egg. What an absolutely miraculous shape an egg has when you see it for the first time. You cannot bear not getting to hold it in your hands. His left wrist vanished, and all I saw was that egg.

"I'm your daddy," said the soldier, "Will you believe me? I'll give you this egg." I was not sure. Same uniform, same light brown hair, blue eyes. He made the egg stand on the tips of five fingers as he squatted before me: "It's good to eat—gold inside." Much later my mother told me that in those days, he could have bought a woman with that egg.

But I said, "No, you're not my daddy; my daddy has seven holes in his arm," and the soldier started to cry and said something tragic about a world in which children remember their fathers by their wounds. I was really sorry. Had I known how important this was to him, I would have lied and said that he was my daddy. And that is one of the many reasons right there why I had two marriages so disastrous that it borders on slapstick comedy.

It was shortly after that, when it happened—the thing nobody in the family ever talked about until my mother and I spoke, for the first time really, woman to woman, during the last three weeks of her life. She and my aunt Ruth had gone off to reconnoiter for food. In fact, they had been successful and were on their way back. Ruth had found a bag of rice so big that she could hardly carry it. She later said she had taken it from under a dead Russian soldier. And that rice lasted pretty much for the rest of our journey—part of it was soaked with blood. We cooked that part first. Later, tiny worms were crawling throughout the rice. We cooked and ate them too. After that, those worms turned into small, pale gold, winged things, and they, too, were cooked and eaten.

And my mother had found an enormous hunk of unrefined cacao, the raw material for chocolate. It looked like lavender-colored rocks and was chalky tasting and bitter as hell, but it was food, so we ate it, and it took decades before I grew to like chocolate. My grandmother said the stuff would be good for her heart, and it would give us energy. But that rice and that cacao had come at an incalculable price.

While Ruth and my mother were gone, my grandmother was minding my sisters and me in a lovely little clearing in a wood. The sun was out and the first spring flowers had begun to bloom, so the place was carpeted with flowers—in fact, my grandmother was digging up violet roots to give to the baby to chew on for her teething pain.

He appeared suddenly—a Russian soldier—I still remember his face, an Asian face with the same crazy distorted look I had seen in the American ball-turret gunner's face. First he raped my grandmother who screamed and then fainted, and then he raped my baby sister on a bed of spring beauties and anemones. My mother and Ruth must have heard our screams and came running—but too late. My mother shot the soldier through the back of the head, and his dead weight fell on my sister. But too late. She bled to death.

My mother revived my grandmother. Ruth began to get hysterical, but my mother told her roughly to shut the fuck up. Then Ruth started to dig a grave for my baby sister, but my mother stopped her again, not so roughly this time: "We have to decide if we want to live or die right now. If there was one, there are others. Maybe they heard the shot."

But before anyone could make a decision about whether to live or to die, we heard Russian troops marching. We heard their officers yell and the soldiers respond, yelling in unison. Even now, I find the memory of that sound disturbing. When I was in China, I was often awakened in the predawn darkness by troops of soldiers yelling like that: as one beast screaming out its mindless and deadly intention.

So we left them there among the flowers, the dead baby and the dead soldier, and slid more than scrambled down an embankment almost as fast as the huge bag of rice. Then we crawled into a big culvert under the road we had traveled. As we huddled together there in silence, my mother took out her cyanide capsules. We heard soldiers' boots echo loudly in the culvert where we sat in a small, slow trickle of water and waited. Ruth hugged her knees; my grandmother held my sister, and my mother held me between her knees. My mother and grandmother each had two capsules—one to give to the child she was holding and the other for herself in case the soldiers discovered us. My grandmother covered my sister's mouth, and my mother covered mine. I remember hating it not only because of the invasiveness of the gesture but because I understood there was grave danger and a need for silence—as young as I was; I resented the lack of trust and the imputation of stupidity.

Even after the soldiers were long gone, and all that was left was the sound of evening birds, we sat there in silence and in the presence of death, palpable in the form of cyanide capsules—a presence I somehow understood, though, again, could not have named. Finally my grandmother said, "We better choose life." My mother put her head on her knees. "I know what it is," said my grandmother gently, "To lose a child in such a way, but we have two more children to look after and they deserve life."

"DESERVE LIFE!!" said my mother, violently pushing out all the air in her lungs with those two words.

Then, after a long silence, she sighed and said, "OK. OK, let's find a place for the night." They divided the rice into three portions so it could be carried more easily, and we were on our way.

"*Sind wir bald da?*" I asked, possibly for the hundredth time. It means approximately, "Are we there yet?"

"Yes," said my grandmother, as she had every other time and would say a hundred more times as "*da*," the German word for both "here" and "there" took on the meaning of heaven for me.

Soon we found the warmth and safety of haystacks. Haystacks in April? But there they were, maybe from the year before, left there because there were not enough men left alive to bring in the harvest. There were also cows to milk safely out of sight. Some farmers were ready to shoot milk thieves.

You may wonder why I never mentioned my dead sister's name. As I said, I had heard no one in the family ever mention her and her horrendous death. I had only vague, fleeting and incomplete images of that scene and could not have written about it had not my mother in the weeks before her death told me what had happened in response to my questions. And in the silence after she finished her story, I asked as gently as I could:

"What was her name?"

She closed her eyes and remained still. And because she was dying, I let it be.

CHAPTER FOUR

Your World Is Gone

The going next morning was slow. Ruth fainted several times, my grandmother was bleeding down her legs and into her shoes, and her heart threatened to give out, but my mother drove us on. We walked from first light to nightfall for week after week and through town after town that lay in ruins. Not just a building or two, as in the World Trade Center incident, but the whole town—every building as far as the eye could see. Sometimes we saw cows in the fields, and my mother or Ruth would belly-crawl to try to get some milk. Sometimes they succeeded. More often the local farmers, who, for their own families' sake had to guard their possessions from refugees, drove them off.

Once we came down a road lined with fruit trees in full bloom—German highways are often lined with fruit trees. In each tree for what seemed miles a man hung by his neck, his dead weight and dark contour framed by pale pink and white blossoms, and big black birds were there to pick out his eyes and eat his rotting flesh. And everywhere the sick, sweet smell of carrion.

Then it began to rain every day for a week until, finally, after more than a month on the run, we arrived at the Elbe River, and the rain continued. The field by the river's edge as far as you could see up and down river was crowded with refugees and retreating German soldiers who were no longer organized into companies—just beaten soldiers with wounds, and no doctors, no pain killers, no medical supplies, no food. It was a cold and rainy spring, and whatever grass and plants had grown by the river's edge had all been eaten away—by humans.

There were no bridges. Any that had been left after Allied bombing, the retreating German army had destroyed long since in a scorched earth policy. River barges were going back and forth carrying refugees, and the Americans had built a pontoon bridge: you could walk across in single file and waist deep in water. We got in line, waiting our turn. The line was days and days long. When it was almost our turn, a woman in front of us with three children started across. She was carrying two of her babies, and a third child, chest deep in water, was hanging onto her skirt. When that one slipped, she went to grab it, and, in that move, she lost one of the babies she was carrying to the swift current. She did not even think, but jumped with her two remaining children, and the current swept them away.

Because of that, my mother decided to wait for a place on the river barges. It meant more waiting. More sleeping in the mud and the rain. And the scene was not just dismal and miserable and wet—it was a full-blown battlefield. For some reason, the Russian soldiers did not want the refugees to cross the river, and so they shelled the pontoon bridge and the river barges. The Americans on the other side of the river returned fire—I do not know why; Russians and Americans were supposed to be allies at the time, but they were in a battle against each other, and we were caught in the middle, mortar fire lighting up the horizon all around us.

There was no time or energy to bury the dead—nor any tools to do it. They just got stacked in a designated area; lime was thrown on them, and then they were covered with a tarp. And I just had to go see. Although the stench was unbearable, I lifted a corner of the tarp and saw a man's face almost eaten away by the white powder.

I ran back to my grandmother, "Grandma, Grandma, what's wrong with those people under the blanket, will they be all right?"

"Nothing is wrong with them," she said, "They *are* all right."

"They don't look all right, Grandma."

"Remember what happened when your feet got too big for your shoes just a couple of weeks ago?"

"Yes, Grandma, we threw them away."

"Well, in that same way, those people threw away their bodies—come, let's look at them again."

"But Grandma, the smell was really really bad."

"Yes, I know, but I want you to see that they are really not there inside their bodies."

And I saw that she was right: nobody was looking out of their eyes.

"Where did they go, Grandma?"

"I don't know; there are millions of places to go, here and there. When people throw away their bodies, that's called dying and then their spirits are free."

"Will I die too?"

"Yes, you will—we all do because we get tired of bodies."

"Will my body look like those people?"

"It won't matter to you what your body looks like. It will be like that pair of shoes. You'll just leave the worn out body behind and forget it, and then it rots and turns to dirt."

"Does it hurt when you die?"

"Sometimes it does; sometimes it doesn't. In any case, once you leave the body, the pain will be gone."

"Will it feel like electricity?"

"Electricity? What gives you that idea?"

"Well, remember the light bulb?"

"Oh," she said, "Yes, of course I remember."

Back in the forest ranger's house I had observed how people change light bulbs. After making my hypothesis about the nature of light bulbs and their sockets, I determined to put it to an empirical test, not that I put it to myself that way, of course. Still, there was a plan. I practiced making my hand into the shape of a light bulb, my fingertips coming to one point, and waited for my chance. One day when my grandmother was in the kitchen and my mother had gone to the factory, the floor lamp next to the armchair in the living room was waiting for a new bulb. They were very hard to find in those last war years. It was right around Christmas.

I climbed on the armchair and then onto its soft and rounded arm. When I gathered my fingers to a point, put them into the socket, and the electricity coursed through my body, I must have fallen off the armchair, and this broke the connection, though I really don't remember anything after the first shock. My grandmother had to resuscitate me.

The result of my first experiment was null-hypothesis: My hand and I did not light up like a light bulb, but it was an enlightenment of sorts anyway, and somehow, I associated electricity with the death I saw all around me and the screams of the wounded splitting your soul in two.

My grandmother said, "And so you do remember how horrible

electricity feels?"

"Uh huh."

"It can also be beautiful."

"It can?"

"Yes, it can. Light is beautiful, isn't it? And you have seen lightening, haven't you?"

"Yes Grandma."

"Well, isn't it beautiful? But if it struck you, it would feel very horrible. The only reason it feels horrible is because there is too much for your body—if it's just the right amount and flowing properly, it feels good."

"It hurt a lot when I touched it."

Artillery fire was all around us and lit up the horizon—I've heard people compare it to summer lightening, and the sounds of explosions to thunder—but there is no comparison between the two.

My grandmother drew my sister Ina (EE-nah) and me closer to her, as we sat on the tarp with one end of it folded over us to give some protection from the constant rain.

"Yes you do know what electricity feels like when it feels good," she said, "When you're happy and not tired and not hungry—that's like electricity. It feels good when it's just the right amount and flows properly." My grandmother had practiced herbal medicine and acupuncture in Russia, having learned from her mother and grandmother and even her great-grandmother, who had learned from a Chinese traveler. So it was this family tradition that made my grandmother think of the human body as a system of flowing energies. She continued her story:

"And sometimes, very rarely, electricity takes the shape of an animal. Then he is the most beautiful creature you have ever seen. Siberian foxes are usually white in winter...but when electricity wants to be someone, he becomes the Blue Fox of Siberia." I remembered the red-gold fox puppies and was instantly enchanted by the vision of a blue fox, the tips of his fur sparkling and his eyes electric.

"Imagine electricity; imagine lightening, but now it's not deadly, it's the best thing in the world and the most beautiful. Can you see what it would be like as a friend? Imagine a cloudless winter day on a white prairie under bright prairie light, electric blue sky, and little whirlwinds picking up the snow and making diamond dust whirl all around you;

and you are the Blue Fox: a dazzling creature of pure intelligence, wearing blue and silver fur and dancing in diamond eddies made in air within the blue and white brightness.

"The Blue Fox has many jobs, but one of them is to find creatures who have been caught in traps and he frees them. One day he found a beautiful white rabbit with pink ears. But his ears were much too pale, and the rabbit was almost dead because he was so tired and sad from struggling in the trap. When the Blue Fox came to open the trap, the rabbit crawled out, and of course he knew right away that this was no ordinary fox. The rabbit said, 'Thank you, Blue Fox, for saving my life, thank you for freeing me from this horrible and ugly trap.'

"The Blue Fox said, 'Rabbit, listen, a trap is only horrible and ugly when you are in it or imagining you are in it. Look at it now. Look how cleverly it is made. Look how it made you enter without suspicion or fear.'

"'Why yes,' said the rabbit, 'You are right Blue Fox. Now that I look at it from the outside, that trap is a fascinating piece of work. It is really very amazing—look, it was made exactly for me. Whoever made it understood me even better than I understood myself.'

"'Yes, Rabbit, that is the point of all good traps.'

"'Well, Blue Fox,' said the rabbit, 'That trap has made me understand myself much better than I did before—I see why you call it a good trap. I must thank you again.'

"'You are welcome, Rabbit. Do you think this trap could ever catch you again?'

"'No, Blue Fox,' said the white rabbit whose ears were once again bright pink, 'For the third time I must thank you.'

"'Be careful, Rabbit,' said the Blue Fox, 'There may be other traps you don't understand yet. But if you remember that they are only ugly from the inside, you may be able to free yourself next time.'"

***

The story ended, and we were back on the cold and rainy battlefield by the Elbe River. But the Blue Fox of Siberia became the hero of many of the stories my grandmother told and my sister and I encouraged her: "Grandma, tell a story about the Blue Fox.

Not far from us on that field by the river, the wounded were laid side by side—with a separate area for little girls who had been raped. One soldier with multiple wounds including a head wound was screaming in agony. I could not bear it. "He has a headache," I told my grandmother, "because he doesn't have a pillow."

"A pillow wouldn't help him."

"I'm sure it would help, Grandma, please let me give him my pillow."

"OK" she said. "OK, we can try."

We walked over to him in the rain. My grandmother knelt in the mud and lifted his head gently as I pushed my pillow under him. He died in that moment, but no one told me so until years and years later. I remember only his look of infinite gratitude and love.

The rain kept streaming down, the screaming of the wounded and the moaning and hard, rough breathing of the dying continued, and I saw a man hugging a horse around the neck and weeping. "Frieda, Frieda" he cried over and over, "Frieda, Frieda, my Frieda," and then he shot her whose name means "peace." She was stripped to bare bones in no time, and I knew that, given the right circumstances, people are piranhas, even though I did not learn about those fish and their name until decades later.

And we waited and waited while the world exploded all around us, and the river barges were sunk one by one, either empty coming back, or going and full almost beyond capacity with refugees and their children. It was then, that during a quiet moment the rumor went round that the war was over, and a woman's beautiful contralto voice began to sing, "Stille Nacht, Heilige Nacht" (Silent Night, Holy Night)…soon the whole muddy field soaked with blood and vomit and excrement sang with her. There were so many of us singing that the Americans and the Russians must have heard, and the shelling stopped for a time as the singing spread all up and down the river bank. Even now, many decades later, I still can not hear that song without tears coming into my eyes, though I am getting better about it, and lousy singers no longer move me at all. I have heard that something like this stopped soldiers from killing each other back in WWI also. If they can do it for a song, why can't they do it for human welfare?

As it turned out, the war really was over, as it was May 8th, 1945, one of the coldest and rainiest Mays on record. Eventually though, we had to stop singing, and then the Americans and the Russians resumed shelling each other, the river barges, and the pontoon bridge, even though the war was officially declared over.

When our turn finally came to get on a barge, the last one left, after sitting around and starving for almost three weeks in the mud and the rain among exploding shells and the horrors in their wake, a German officer showed up out of nowhere with a small company of men and pushed ahead of us. "Whatever happened to 'women and children first'?" said my mother.

"Somebody hand me a gun so I can shoot this bitch," screamed the officer.

Silence.

"That's an order!!"

And suddenly, his men laughed, and one of them said, "Fuck you, Friedhelm—it's much too late for that. Your goddam world is gone."

Still, the man barred our way onto the river barge, and my mother quietly took out her gun and told him to stand aside. No one said a word. His men did not help him. He just stood and stared at her. Then she said almost gently, "Get out of my way, Friedhelm, you wouldn't be the first man I've shot." He saw, I guess, that my mother meant it.

And so we crossed the Elbe River into relative safety in American occupied territory. On the way back to get more refugees, that last remaining barge was hit and sunk by Russian mortar fire.

CHAPTER FIVE

Escargot in Ursendorf

On the American side of the Elbe River, the Red Cross had set up a receiving station, and refugees were separated into ambulatory and non-ambulatory. Most of us were ambulatory since those who were not were still lying in the sea of yellow mud on the Russian side of the river. We were loaded onto a truck and taken somewhere to eat a thin soup of oatmeal boiled forever in a lot of water and then strained. It is one of the things you can safely give to starving people—and we definitely were starving, as no plants at all had been left growing in that mud by the river. Some of the refugee children's hair had even turned orange from starvation, and most of us had the characteristic swollen bellies. When the soldier had shot his Frieda, my family had not been among the beneficiaries, as there were thousands of refugees. Another thing we all desperately needed was sleep. So, again, we were loaded onto the back of a U.S. Army truck.

Only a very few buildings were left standing in this town whose name I cannot remember, and a kindergarten was one of these buildings. When we arrived there, a big black M.P. held up his hands to lift me off the truck. I shrunk back from him in utter terror. To my mind, no man, especially a man in uniform, could be trusted, and this one was black. I'd never seen a black man. But in that same instant, I saw him understand: he pulled some white gloves from his belt, took his theatrical time putting them on, and then offered his help again with a big smile. I let myself fall into his hands.

Inside the kindergarten, the intricate woodwork was painted in saturated colors so deep and so beautiful as they glowed in the evening light that I thought I was in a great king's castle—never since have I understood the practice of surrounding children with pastel colors.

Clean straw had been laid out wall to wall on the floor with only narrow walkways between each "bed." My grandmother, my mother, and my aunt Ruth stayed asleep pretty much for three days and nights, although the nurses kept waking my grandmother to make sure she did not die in her sleep.

They were kind ladies in white aprons with red crosses on them, and they took care of my sister and me, along with other shell-shocked children, since we could not stay asleep as long as the adults. After three days, however, these lovely nurses woke my family and asked us to go on our way to make room for others who also needed to sleep for three days and nights. There seemed to be tens of thousands of those others.

And again we were living like stray dogs, but this time there was less violence, the rain had stopped, and May was warm and beautiful and fertile as never before. I should add, though, that it was my adults who must have felt like stray dogs. I did not know that human beings ordinarily did not live like this. To me, nature still feels more glorious than a roof over my head, and I have never lived anywhere without surrounding myself with as many green plants as space will permit.

But though I loved being surrounded by nature, I would have preferred to do a little less walking. We had to walk and keep walking from first light until last light each day because the American military government had decreed that anyone with no address (and that was most of the country) could get ration tickets for food in each county seat for one day and one day only (Eisenhower had decreed 400 calories per person per day). If you wanted what little food that was made available, you could not get it in the same county two days in a row, unless the military government saw fit to issue a residence permit. So we had to keep moving, though we were weak from shock and hunger and fatigue.

One time, though, through an unbelievable scene that brought me nightmares, we did have plenty of chicken to cook and eat. We stayed hidden in tall weeds and bushes as we watched two crazy soldiers rape, and in that way kill a yard full of chickens. My grandmother covered my eyes, but I'd seen enough, and there was no way to keep from hearing the screams of those chickens and the animal whoops and grunts of the men.

This is how absurd and insane war really is. When, years later, I heard about the My Lai Massacre, I was amazed to learn that people believed it was an isolated incident, as the media had claimed. It could not have been. You have to make men crazy to be able to kill, and then, once they have killed, they go on killing, and they do not distinguish between soldiers and babies and chickens or anything else that lives. The problem is that these men then have to go on and live with themselves. No wonder that, according to the VA, 22 American veterans commit suicide every day.

The soldiers eventually left the chicken yard of the abandoned farm, and my aunt Ruth and my grandmother thanked God for the chickens while my mother shook her head and mumbled something about how the God in whom she did not believe could allow such cruel insanity. Nevertheless, that farm gave us a place to rest for a few days.

Then one day after we had been walking just about from one end of Germany to the other for some seven or eight months, sleeping by the side of the road, not eating enough, never even seeing soap, using leaves for toilet paper (burdock leaves are best), getting separated, finding each other again, and not knowing if we would ever get anywhere to settle down and live normal lives, my grandmother, who was experiencing all these horrors for the second time in her life, said, "This is it. This is as far as I'm going. You and the kids go on, but I can't do it anymore. Leave me in this ditch…"

More than likely, there were many grandmothers all over Germany who said just this to anyone around who could hear. Nor had it been the first time my grandmother had said, "Leave me in this ditch," but both her girls knew she meant it this time. So this time they did not beg her, "We need you Mama, we need you, come on, we can't make it without you." This time, we all sat down by the side of the ditch my grandmother wanted to be left in and said nothing for a while. I crawled into her lap afraid my mother would give her a cyanide capsule and leave her. Instead, my mother began a hateful speech about how her older sister, my aunt Maria, had let them all down by deciding not to run with them. Then she and her younger sister, Ruth, went off for a walk. They were gone a long, long time.

When they came back, my mother said, "I've made a decision, Mama, we'll leave you here, but we'll also leave the children." I was five and half; my sister Ina was four and covered with boils—even the bottoms of her feet. Ina needed to be carried. I had to walk. She was a pain in the neck, complaining, protesting, crying all the time. In my five-and-a-half-year-old opinion, if anybody was going to be left in a ditch, it should have been my sister.

"I can't die if you leave the children," said my grandmother.

"That is the point," said my mother not unkindly. "You can rest all day, except for gathering plants for food. This is a perfect spot. In the middle of nowhere. Fields with lots of weeds and a bit of forest for mushrooms—on the other side of those trees, it drops down to a little brook—so there's water. There are some big overhanging rocks down there too—you can get shelter from the rain unless the wind is from the east. We'll leave you most of the rice. Ruth and I are going to go on into the mountains. I think I recognize the countryside around here; this is where Rudolf and I hiked on our honeymoon. Irredorf can't be that far from here. When we get there, we'll come back and get you and the kids with an ox cart."

"You *think* you recognize the countryside?"

"No, I guess I'm sure I do."

"And you think you can find this village—Irredorf? It doesn't even sound like a real village. You're not making this up, Ali, are you? Irredorf sounds like a crazy idea."

My grandmother was referring to the fact that "Irredorf" sounds like a Swabian dialect version of "Irrendorf" or "Village of the Insane." The name is a corruption of "Ursendorf" or "Bear village" (cf. Latin, *ursa*, or bear), most likely named after Ursus, Prince or King, depending on which historian you ask. Ursus died in 884 or 5 and he was of the Merovingian bloodline. The village still exists, and it does lie on the migration route of Merovingians. Apparently, it changed its name back to "Ursendorf" some time after the war—I just found the place on the Internet and learned that it is in the area of Hohentengen, south of Stuttgart. Why, if we wanted to get to Stuttgart from up north, did we end up so far south of the city? I don't know, and there is no one left I can ask. But I can guess that the priority in choosing our way was always to avoid soldiers of any kind—and cities, since we depended on wild plants for food.

"Irredorf is a real village," said my mother, "Rudolf and I stayed there. There's an inn, and the innkeeper is an old family friend of the Mailänders from centuries back. He is a very kind man. I'm sure he'll help us."

"Are you sure you can find the place? How long do you think it will be before you can come back with the cart?"

"Couple weeks, maybe less; don't worry Mama, I'm sure. With you and the kids staying here, we can cover a lot of ground in a short time."

"What makes you so sure the innkeeper will help us?" My grandmother had seen too many Germans unwilling to help even their own people who had become refugees.

"The village probably needs a good herbalist," said my mother, "I don't think there's a single doctor left alive in the whole damn country. They'll welcome you."

My grandmother sighed. After installing us under the overhanging rocks, eating a small lunch with us, and making many promises that they would be back, my mother and Ruth lined their shoes with plantain leaves (socks don't survive the sort of trek we were on, and, often, shoes don't either), and they hiked into the foothills of the Alps on a small dirt road wide enough for one set of wheel ruts; grass and weeds grew on the hump in the middle. They walked over the crest of the hill eastward, and then, as they went down on the other side, they got shorter and shorter quickly until all there was left was a few grasses against the empty sky. My grandmother and my sister took a nap. I investigated the neighborhood—first climbing the hill to see if I could see my mother and my aunt Ruth on the other side, but I could not.

After their nap, we all went to gather wild vegetables for supper—or rather—my grandmother found the plants, but because she was carrying Ina, my grandmother would point at the plants, say their names, and I would gather them into the skirt of my red dress. She had stitched that dress together for me by hand somewhere on the road out of a discarded Nazi flag in which there were two shades of red: the faded rosy red of the flag's ground and the true red where the patch with the swastika had prevented fading.

As we wandered through the field gathering edible weeds, my grandmother, who had a really good soprano voice, sang her favorite song that she often sang when gathering plants, "*Die Himmel rühmen des Ewigen Ehre—der Schall pflanzt Seinen Nahmen fort…*" It means, very roughly, "The heavens praise the honor of the Eternal; the sound echoes His Name…"

But the German word for "echo" here is "*fortpflanzen*," a very strange word, which can be taken literally to mean, "to continue to plant," i.e. "The sound continues to plant His Name." It would be a long time before I finally realized that plant names are not generally regarded as names of God.

Years and years later, my grandmother told me, "When life gets really bad, and you can't see how you can survive, sing. Sing all the songs you know and then start over and sing them again." Recent studies have proved her right: singing is better than Prozac, and who needed a study for that?

We climbed around a few rocks, and my grandmother stopped suddenly and said, "Well, I'll be…look at this: foxgloves." She maintained ever after that if it had not been for those foxgloves (digitalis), she could not have made for herself the medicine that kept her heart going long enough for her daughters to come back.

Back at our campsite and waiting for my mother and my aunt Ruth to return, we ran out of rice after about a week and a half, but hazel nuts grew wild in those parts and were ripening. There was also plenty of lamb's quarter. I have no idea why lamb's quarters is not bred into a proper domestic vegetable. It is delicious, it thrives in the poorest soil, it seeds itself, it withstands drought, and it is good throughout the growing season. The same is true of purslane, which is one of the best plant sources of omegas in the universe. I still gather both and cook them in a variety of ways. There were also mushrooms and sorrel for vitamin C, which helped my sister to heal from her boils, various cresses by the brook, and nettles. Of course, the ubiquitous dandelion was there—as it is everywhere. True, it was fall, and most of the plants are better in spring, but they were edible, and so we ate them. Even dandelions are not bad that late in the year if they are growing in the shade, and of course purslane tastes great any time of year.

We had to stay out of sight of the road we had come on as much as possible, because if any occupation soldiers had found us, we would have been in trouble with whatever military occupation government was in charge. And then, you really never know when meeting soldiers if they are halfway sane or not.

My grandmother and I camped out in relative comfort. My sister, of course, was never comfortable because of the painful boils all over her body. It is a wonder we did not all catch them from her—maybe we did not because we ate a lot of plantain leaves. Ina had those boils from before the time we left Dreetz—no doubt a staff infection she caught from the Russian girl, Olga, who helped my grandmother with the housework—I do recall that Olga, too, had boils everywhere. It is strange how the act of writing calls up things I have not thought of for decades.

Then one day, after about three weeks of saying "soon" to my constant question, "When are Mami and Aunt Ruth coming back," my grandmother said, "Shhh!!" Ina and I shut up instantly. We were nothing if not obedient. You cannot get past soldiers and other crazies, through battlefields, air raids, and mine fields, unless your children are more obedient than my computer. If anyone in my family told me jump into a ditch full of icy water and hide, I did not ask questions or hesitate. So when my grandmother grabbed my sister and told me, "hide," I jumped into the nearest patch of tall weeds, which, unfortunately, turned out to be stinging nettles. But I knew my life depended on hiding when I was told to hide—and, if anything, the nettles made me even more motionless than I might have been otherwise. No motion, no stinging after the first shock, and I knew that as well.

The noise my grandmother had heard turned into a rumble, and, to everyone's infinite joy, it was not a military vehicle, it was the promised ox-cart coming down the dirt road. My grandmother and my aunt Ruth wept in each other's arms; my mother scooped me out of the nettles, and the innkeeper kept repeating, "*Noo, noo, noo, noo, noo, noo, noo...*" in low soothing tones. It means approximately, "Easy does it, everything's gonna be OK."

They had brought some food, and we ate while bouncing around in the ox cart on the way to Ursendorf, a village ancient and beautiful, though not wealthy. There was barely enough soil to cover the limestone beneath, but some spirit was there—maybe the same one that drives the igneous penetration of limestone and leaves rubies in its wake—some spirit that nourished Ursendorf, otherwise how would it have survived there for more than a thousand years?

The innkeeper's name was "*Kreuzwirt*"—"*Kreuz*" means "cross," and "*Wirt*" means "host." He was the host of the Inn of the Cross, and in that part of the world, what you did for a living often became your name—especially since what you did for a living was probably the same thing your father did for a living and his father and so on for ten or more generations back. Judging by the cross on the intricate wrought-iron shingle hanging over the door of his inn, I would guess Kreuzwirt's great-great-great-etc. grandfather probably had retired from political life to build this inn, back when the Templars were warrior monks protecting the likes of King Ursus, inventing international banking, and demonizing Muslims.

Kreuzwirt was happy to help us, as my mother had predicted he would be. Three reasons. One: he was a kind man and my father's friend, as his father had been my father's father's friend, and so on back centuries—and I would give anything to learn how a friendship like that came to be, and what it was that sustained it for so long until World War II broke the continuity.

Two: my grandmother's knowledge of herbal medicine was indeed welcome in Kreuzwirt's household and in the small village. Three: the village was occupied by French soldiers, and their officers were quartered at the inn. Village life became much easier just about immediately when we arrived because my mother and my aunt Ruth both spoke French. As for the extra expense of more mouths to feed, Kreuzwirt said, "No problem, no problem at all. We'll just tell them Frogs you're my cousins from Berlin, and they'll pay for it all—in fact, they won't even notice they're paying for it."

My mother and Ruth stayed long enough to get a little strength back—they had arrived at the village half starved. The first thing they did when they got there, after eating like really hungry people eat—in this case escargot of all things—was to create peace between the French commanding officer and Kreuzwirt's wife, Kreuzwirtin, the hostess of the Inn of the Cross.

The ruckus was all because of the escargot. The upshot was that the French soldiers got their own cooking pot and would no longer use Kreuzwirtin's pans in the kitchen to cook their snails. Those soldiers could use her pans for anything they wanted, but, Jesus, Mary, and a tiny bit of Joseph, not snails!! Disgusting slimy creatures they are to be sure and by all that's holy. Others, like the Frenchmen and us, thanked God that this local countryside was experiencing a plague-like abundance of escargot in the vineyards all around the village.

The French soldiers paid me for collecting them, once we were settled in. At five and a half years old, it was my very first job, and I felt hugely important. I have not seen snails or the silvery trails they leave behind in almost twenty years[10], but I can still see the snails I gathered into my skirt. I see their black eyes at the top of two little horns and see how, when you pick them up, they retreat into the lovely houses they carry with them and then close a tiny door.

Years and years later, I learned that my mother and Ruth also made a little money. They were not collecting snails, but selling sex to the French soldiers who were pretty hard up for women in a tiny Catholic village in which such things were simply not done, especially because the village was pretty much self-contained. And it bears mentioning, to the credit of these men, that no occupation soldier would have had to pay for sex if he did not want to.

My aunt Ruth and my mother left my grandmother, my sister, and me in Kreuzwirt's and Kreutzwirtin's care and took off for Stuttgart, shoes lined once again with plantain leaves. But this time they had backpacks with a few necessities as well as food and money for the road. Stuttgart was where my mother had arranged to meet my father in case he came back from the war. It was the logical place because that is where his family was from when they were not from Milan, Italy. "Mailander" is a word like "New Yorker." "Mailander" means "person from Milan," the German name of that city means "land of May." My father was born in Milan, which is something of a mystery I will get to by and by.

Meanwhile, in Ursendorf, my grandmother, my sister and I slept out of the rain in real beds with blue and white-checkered sheets, feather pillows, and blue and white-checkered duvet covers, in whitewashed rooms with well-scrubbed, white pine floors. We washed with warm water and soap that my grandmother had made out of bones and dead leaves. We got de-wormed and de-loused with the help of plants growing everywhere for all our needs. Of course we had parasites. We had two different kinds of worms, in fact, and I still had nightmares decades later in which worms were coming out of every part of my body, worms like the maggots in my father's wounds, or like the eels jumping out of dead bodies dredged from the canal, or like plain old pinworms and round worms in the toilet—they all became a snake pit for me, except

---

[10] The snails in southeast Iowa have become extinct because morning dew no longer exists to bless them.

that it was my body that was the pit, both source and host, of all those squirming creatures hungry for my life.

We ate regular meals lovingly prepared by Kreuzwirtin. And for extra treats, the pears were ripe and so were the hazel nuts, incomparable with their green elf caps turning yellow. John Keats shares my opinion of freshly picked hazel nuts: food for angels. And the creeping charlie that grew in the pear orchard in late summer still smells to me like heaven. I remember sitting at the top of a hill that was a pear orchard with other small children. We waited for a gust of wind to bring down some ripe pears; we'd run to get them, eat them, and then return to the top of the hill to wait for another gust of wind.

And then one fine day, with the hint of an unusually early frost in the clean mountain air, my mother arrived with an American soldier in an army jeep, and we left Irredorf forever and drove to Stuttgart. As we came close to the city, I could smell it. An evil smell. I asked what it was: Cars. Why are they allowed to do that, I wanted to know. If they keep it up, there will be no air left to breathe. And everybody laughed because I was so cute. It could never happen, they assured me. But I knew they were wrong and, not only that, I knew for the first time that my mother could be wrong.

CHAPTER SIX

My Mother in Fuchsia

Ursendorf had been a taste of heaven, but Stuttgart, in spite of the evil smell of cars, turned out to be its full blossoming, though of course, any heaven is bound to have its demon seed. Still, the place where we settled was heaven for me, though I doubt it was heavenly for my mother or my aunt Ruth or my sister Ina. Our new home was not actually in Stuttgart; we lived in Sillenbuch, a village that was in process of turning into a suburb of Stuttgart.

When my aunt Ruth and my mother had arrived there, they at first made their living as they had in Ursendorf. My mother was sleeping with soldiers herself and also procuring customers for my aunt Ruth. They were American soldiers this time instead of French. It had been one of those American soldiers, in fact, who had driven my mother to Ursendorf in a topless army jeep to bring us all back to Stuttgart. How they had managed this when there was a non-fraternization order from General Eisenhower, I do not know. Other women showed up as well with the same work in mind, and so my mother became a madam—she loved being in charge. When she died, it was of Parkinson's disease, which is called the disease of dictators: Hitler, Mao Tze Tung, and Franco all had it—not the kind that makes you shake like a leaf, but the kind that is a progressive paralysis until you are as stiff as a board—as if rigor mortis is setting in even before you are dead.

The money my mother made as a madam was not great, barely enough to support us all since there was no shortage of beautiful German women making a living the only way they could to feed their fatherless-children in a country whose farming and industry were utterly destroyed—*after* the war was officially over—by orders of Eisenhower.

In addition to the money, there were other compensations for selling sex. Through these connections with soldiers, my mother and her sister were able to get residence permits for us, and a residence permit was needed to rent an apartment and obtain ration tickets for food. In fact, this was a catch-22 situation: you had to have ration tickets to get a residence permit and you had to have a residence permit to get ration tickets. Moreover, you had to have an address to get a residence permit, and you had to have a residence permit to get a place to live. Finding an apartment would ordinarily have been all but impossible, but it was no problem for us since my father's sister, my aunt Editta, had at sometime in the past, sold two antique dinner plates from the Mailänder family's collection of art and antiques, and with the proceeds, she had built an apartment building next to her house in Sillenbuch.

To get to the city of Stuttgart you took the yellow streetcar number ten and rode through a beautiful ancient forest of beech trees called Silver Wood, and from there the number ten crossed town, right through the middle of it past the train station, and then went all the way out to the west side to a little pleasure palace or hunting castle of some ex king, probably named Eberhardt, where it then would turn around and come back through the city, Silver Wood and, finally, back to Sillenbuch. (Google "beech trees" and you will see incomparable beauty).

The German names of Sillenbuch and Silver Wood (*Silberwald*) occupied my five-and-a-half-year-old mind, and I started to ask questions. Aunt Editta was the one who came closest to understanding them. And she also came closest with answers, as she taught me the etymology of those words. "Silver" was obvious in the name of the wood, and the word "book" was part of Sillen*buch*. The words "book" and "beech" are cognates or blood relatives, and beech staves were used to stamp or carve with runes. What's more, the words for "read," "letter" (as in a, b, c…), and "syllable" were also present in the name of the village. And how this could be so involved mysterious stories of magical and wise old women who picked up beech staves thrown on the ground to tell fortunes.

I spent time in that Silver Wood, convinced there was something there I was to read, and the black markings on the silver bark sometimes looked like writing and sometimes looked like eyes looking at me very seriously. My grandmother would take my sister and me there to collect mushrooms and beechnuts, and then she would grind them in a mill to make oil. When my grandmother and sister were with me, the woods were still truly beautiful, but they were woods. When I was there alone, the living presence of the trees seemed to whisper something just barely out of hearing.

And if that magic forest were not enough, within easy walking distance from where we lived, there was (and still is) a nature preserve called Eichenhain, or "Oak Grove." If you go to Google Earth, you can zero in on and actually see the individual ancient oaks of the Eichenhain. Both forests, that of old beech trees and that of even older oaks, were as important to me as the adults in my life.

I had permission to ride the yellow streetcar number ten any time I wanted as long as I did not transfer, and I rode to the end of the line and back often—I was too young to have to pay, and it was better than television, especially since there were no television sets in Germany at that time, even though television had originally been a German invention. The little castle on the west side of Stuttgart was built during a time when it was fashionable to call your summer residences something like "*Sans Souci*" ("No Worries") or "*Solitude*," and it was lovely, as were its gardens. I did have to time my rides properly since the streetcar would often be so crowded that people were hanging from the running boards or catching really dangerous rides by standing on the coupling between cars.

Times were different then; the concept of babysitting, for instance, did not exist in Germany when I was a child. And the apartment made me stir-crazy. I had been used to walking all day every day—after all, we had walked from one end of the country to the other in a circuitous route—and staying put just did not feel normal to me. My grandmother sometimes packed a boiled potato and some salt in a little rucksack for me and then showed me where the sun would be in the sky when it was time for me to turn around and come home. I would supplement the potato with wild greens, and all the springs and brooks still had clean water—in fact, there was a folksong, which suggested that the best water to drink was that which flowed over mossy rocks.

So I was often exploring the countryside all around Sillenbuch, ambling half a day out while also studying plants and rocks and foxholes and the structure of flowers. The comings and goings of an anthill could keep me silent and watching for an hour or more. Then, I would travel back home, all the while engaged in the same minute examination of my world, often collecting strange things to ask about when I got there.

Riding the streetcar itself was another one of my favorite pastimes, especially since one of the drivers spoke in nothing but rhymed iambic hexameters, even when calling out the names of the stops or just giving directions to a passenger like myself. My mother said they were just rhymes, not poetry, and that talking in rhymes like that was a form of insanity, but what did I care—I learned his schedule by heart so I could time my trips across the city to coincide with his and listen to him recite endless verses like this:

Mein lieb' Kind, Du willst heut Solitude besuchen?
O wie gern gewähr ich Dir Dein schön' Ersuchen.
Bis dann, schau nur, das Laub der Buchen ist licht grün.
Rosen glühn darunter, und die Zweige, hängend,
Verbergen Reh und Rehlein. Geschwinde rennend,
Sind sie rasch davon, wenn wir vorüberziehen.

My lovely child, you wish to visit Solitude?
It is my joy to grant your wish, and lift your mood.
'Til then, regard the silver trees in leafage green,
And roses, wild and sweet, just budding in between.
The overhanging branches hide a doe with twins;
When we pass, they'll bolt and flee, swifter than the winds.

And so they did—but that would be the following spring. For now, it was late fall. No fawns. In fact, it was a while before there were any animals, including cats and dogs, in the starving country. Still, anytime I wanted, I could get a rhymed guided tour like this all the way from the east to the west side of a historic city rich with stories.

I seriously wonder about the gods who arranged my childhood. What were they thinking?! First they throw me live into World War II in Berlin like a fish in China who is often skinned and thrown live into a painful marinade—and it is astounding how long a skinned fish can flop around in such a marinade made of salt, acid, and alcohol, before it dies. And then these same gods arrange for a pastoral streetcar driver to make it all OK again. And the magic is, he did much. With the virtually absolute power of language. And the nearly absolute innocence of childhood. Not only do I wonder about the gods who arranged this, I also wonder about your political forces that made it all so excruciatingly real. Who are these human beings that live on this planet and make it into a hell for so many?

Sillenbuch was so charming a place that single-family houses and villas had been built on its outskirts long before the war, when the Weimar Republic had promised peace and democracy. And as I said, one of these houses belonged to my aunt Editta and my uncle Walter, the man she had married to cover up an affair to be discussed later. My Uncle Walter was known to the entire village as the "Asshole of Sillenbuch," a title he enjoyed immensely, as his "arrangement" with my aunt Editta meant he did not have to work for a day in his life. I do know that my uncle Walter's title completely breaks the narrative tone of my story here, but there is nothing I can do about it. Everyone in the village called him that: "*Das Arschloch von Sillenbuch.*"

On the other side of our apartment building was the farm of an original Sillenbucher whose family had no doubt lived in the same place and farmed the same land in the same way, both organic and sustainable back when it was just called "growing food" for a thousand years. Right after 1945, for a few years farmers once again used horses and oxen to till the land and bring in the harvest with implements made by the local smith, since Eisenhower had destroyed whatever machines they had had before. Besides, there would have been no fuel to run these machines even if they had survived.

And so, for all practical purposes, I grew up in a 19th century village. Many of the one-family houses were occupied by American officers and their families. I do remember that one day a rumor went all over Sillenbuch about how the wife of an American officer occupying one of those houses had spray painted a crystal chandelier pink. "Americans have no taste," said my aunt Editta, and I wondered how that could possibly be. If they had no taste, would they know what to eat?

In my aunt Editta's apartment complex, we got a one-bedroom railroad flat plus living room, dining room, kitchen, bath, garage storage space, garret room, and a space in the coal cellar for coal and wood—palatial accommodations after the road trip we had just been on.

The wood stove in the kitchen also heated the adjacent bedroom a little bit. A tiled stove, accessible from the hall, heated the living room and the dining room—if we had wood or coal, which we often did not, but we were immensely grateful anyway because plenty of people were sleeping in the snow in the winter of '45 with predictable consequences.

We moved in, and almost right away an older refugee-couple my sister and I called Aunt and Uncle Kellermann joined us, taking the bedroom. Aunt Kellermann got busy telling stories about giants and dwarves working the silver mines in the mountains of Silesia—and who would know about those beings better than a refugee actually from that place? And her husband, Uncle Kellermann, immediately began teaching me to write my letters with infinite care and beauty in the modern Latin script as well as the traditional Gothic that had just been abolished and banned by the American occupation government, probably because they had a hard time reading it. Uncle Kellermann had been a government official of some sort, a scribe, really, and his handwriting was picture perfect. In order to write as he did, I worked on a little black slate in a wooden frame until time expanded me, making my letters virtually indistinguishable from his, and we both glowed with pride.

My mother was always gone all week, often longer. But we would hear from her regularly. She sent people bringing letters from her to my grandmother, and these people were the most fascinating characters in the entire galaxy. Sometimes they would need a place to stay for a few days, and my grandmother always found a way to accommodate them some place in our flat. Sometimes these stray folks stayed for quite a while. A young man named Michael Ende in his mid teens, who owned nothing but a lute, a guitar, and the clothes he wore, moved into the coal cellar after arriving with a letter from my mother. The coal cellar was a tiny, unheated room that had a shaft leading to the ground outside. It was designed so a man could shovel coal from a truck into a wheelbarrow to be dumped down that shaft. On the other side, the room was accessible through a locked door so the neighbors could not steal your coal. We are such a fascinating species.

The wall that held the door and the door itself were both made of slats, which meant that Michael Ende did not really have any privacy—although, of course, most other residents of the apartment building would not be coming down to get something in the middle of the night—there was nothing to get. Besides, he only slept there. During the day, he was in the apartment with us, filling it with music.

Michael Ende found a way to fix up his space. Miraculously, he was able to get newspapers somewhere in a land in which paper hardly existed, not even toilet paper. He put them on the floor, stacking them to use as a mattress, leaving some to be his blanket and some to be curtains over the slats. "Paper is excellent insulation," he told me, "Look at this: I'm the news, I am the new-hoo-hoos," he sang, as he held a piece of newsprint to his body as if trying on a shirt, and then he sang, "Oh no, no, no, look at this date, I'm not news, I'm history, oh my God I'm historee-hee-hee! Maybe I can crumple some of this stuff up and make a quilted jacket." Michael Ende was definitely glad to be alive.

Michael Ende played music anytime I wanted to hear it and he taught me dozens of songs ranging from scandalous Latin lyrics he did not translate for me, to medieval German songs, to Mozart opera tunes, to songs Beethoven wrote half in German, half in Italian, complaining about his physician who would not come when the great composer was sick, and so on to the Three-Penny Opera, and American Swing. Michael had been a "Swing Kid" in Hamburg, kids who had loved American music (Swing, obviously) and who had resisted Hitler, and suffered the consequences. The thing that is amazing to me still is that teens were politically engaged and active. No computer games back then.

***

My mother's career as a madam, meanwhile, was extremely short-lived. Not long after we were established in our little apartment, she got jailed for running a prostitution ring. She was turned in by one of the johns who had got a little rough with my aunt Ruth, and so my mother got a little rough with him, making the mistake of kicking him where it hurt most and in front of his buddies—all of which I learned only decades later from my aunts Maria and Ruth since one's mother obviously would not tell stories about her adventures as a madam—at least that is true of my mother. I can see the scene. She was only just over five feet tall, but no one to tangle with. Obviously, however, it was not all right for a woman in a defeated country to get rough with an occupation soldier.

The upshot was that the American military judge in the case noted that although the Nazis had thrown her out of high school for anti-Nazi activities, she had managed to get a really good education on her own (with the help of an old librarian in Berlin).

"And why is an educated lady in, ah, your line of work?" asked the judge.

"I've got two children and my mother to support, Your Honor—If I couldn't find any other job in Germany without a high school diploma, it wasn't for the lack of looking. Believe me—I don't really love my job all that much, but thanks to your political forces, I didn't have much choice."

"I believe those were *your* political forces," said the judge, "But I see your point."

"I was using the word 'your' in the impersonal sense, Your Honor, as Hamlet does when he talks about 'your philosophy' with Horatio."

"Uh-huh…I see, and what exactly did you do in that anti-Nazi organization you say you belonged to for which you got kicked out of school?"

"Nothing really. We smuggled Jewish friends into Holland, where it turned out they weren't safe either."

"I see your English is fluent. Do you speak any other languages?"

"French and Russian—and German, of course."

"Russian? Why do you speak Russian? Are you a Communist?"

"No," lied my mother, or maybe, by then, she was no longer interested in politics, just survival. "Your political forces" with an impersonal "you" sounds politically detached to me, rather than politically engaged.

"So why do you speak Russian?" asked the judge.

"I was born in Russia. And my parents were born there too, but they had retained German citizenship.[11] After World War I started, we were interned in Siberia in 1915 as enemy aliens, but we managed to get to Germany in 1922."

And how many people, I wonder, hearing or reading a sentence like that, know how much human agony is contained in it?

"So your Russian is kind of native?" asked the Judge.

"Yes, it is, your Honor, it was my first language—speaking German was dangerous when I was born, so my parents couldn't risk teaching me. And then, even after we lived in Berlin, we spoke Russian at home."

---

[11] Amish people and Mennonites had fled from Germany to Russia, just as they had fled to the U.S., to avoid serving in the military. There were several waves of such immigration to Russia, and most such people retained German citizenship.

"But by this time your German sounds native too? Can you speak the Berlin dialect?"

"Yes, your Honor; I was only seven in 1922—children learn fast."

All this was useful, most useful.

And that is how my mother became a secret agent. She started going into East Berlin and other points east behind the Iron Curtain on secret missions she never really explained to anyone, not even as she lay dying here in Fairfield, Iowa, but I am pretty sure I figured it out after her death. I was helped along by some pretty amazing coincidences.

Maybe being a gun carrying secret agent was not really her idea of a career path—maybe the Americans had offered her that fascinating exemplar of American justice, the plea-bargain: jail for prostitution, or run a few nasty and dangerous little errands for us, and we wipe the record clean. This they must have done, or we would never have been able to come to America in 1952 during the McCarthy era: she had been a Communist, and she had also been a prostitute.

We saw her less often after that—not only because she traveled, but also because the headquarters of the American Military Government was in Frankfurt. She was often there during the week, preparing for a mission when not actually on one—so we saw her only on weekends when she was not traveling behind the Iron Curtain. The money got better, and life must have been pretty exciting for her. She had high-ranking American officers fly her to Paris in military planes to shop for evening gowns in which she looked smolderingly stunning—and, maybe, she had not given up on all of her customers after becoming a secret agent. I swear her life would make a great movie.

I loved my mother, of course, but I also lived in abject terror of her. There was something unspeakably evil and dark about her that I could not name or fathom. In retrospect, it is not hard to understand at all: not everybody's mother shoots men or threatens to shoot them while you get to watch at the tender age of five, all thanks to "your political forces."

As soon as I was old enough to read, I read horror stories because I thought—not very consciously of course—but still, I thought I would get to the bottom of what was so scary about my mother. My favorite one was about a beautiful girl with a scary mother. (The gods must think we're beyond dense, considering the way they make some things extra obvious). A young man falls in love with this girl, and then the two of them learn by slow and increasingly terrifying degrees who or what Mom really is. The terror builds and then culminates in absolute horror as the young lovers creep through the bushes at midnight in the cemetery and see that Mom belongs to a group of people with a secret passion for feeding on dead bodies. When the man leaves the girl because he does not really want to marry into a family like that, she gets drawn into the group and starts eating dead bodies also.

I read that story about a thousand times, determined that I would not be drawn in like the girl in the story who ended up doing what her mother did. But when mine got dressed in a dark fuchsia silk taffeta evening gown from Paris that whispered evil thoughts when she walked, while the moiré pattern shifted shape, when she added lipstick and nail polish darker even than the dress, and then, in total morbid excess, put on a black hat that looked approximately like spider webs and long, black gloves that reached above her elbows, I knew deep fear, while she, casually, flicked the ash off her cigarette in a long, silver holder.

Though I did read that horror story over and over, what I remembered of it turns out not to be accurate. Just today I found an old book in an old box, and in it was my anthology of horror stories, *The Salamander Must Glow*. And in it is the story, "Hyenas" by E.T.A. Hoffmann. I recognized it right away, and dead human bodies do get devoured with wolfish greed, but the plot line is a bit different from what I remembered. Makes one wonder about the rest of one's memories, does it not?

One fine day, my mother arrived out of the clear blue in an American military ambulance transporting my grandfather who was only half conscious. That event would have been much less surprising if my mother had called first, but of course, we did not have a telephone. It was good news and bad news. My grandfather was alive, though just barely, but it also meant that my aunt Maria evidently had not made it through the Russian lines to find him. So where was she? Was she alive?

But my grandfather was home with us, half conscious, and dying of a kind of typhus fever that attacks people who are already dying of starvation anyway. And my mother said, "Well, here he is, and there's no doctor left alive in the whole damn country, so see what you can do with your weeds and your Chinese needles—if, in fact, you want him to live. I have to get back to work."

My grandmother told the military men who were carrying the

stretcher where to put my grandfather, after which they left with my mother. My grandmother took my grandfather's pulse and then issued orders: Michael Ende and I went on an herb-gathering mission even though an early winter had almost begun. We were to gather sloe berries and *uva ursi*, which remains green under the snow, and I knew just where to find all that, since our nine-month trek had been an excellent herbal education for me. Sloes are best after a light frost. Aunt Ruth, meanwhile, went to the kitchen to boil water, make dough of water and flour that my grandmother would use to enclose any lice she found on my grandfather. She would then make him swallow those dough pills with living lice inside.

That is a really interesting way to deal with typhus fever, and we shall hear more about it in due time. The sloe berries and the *uva ursi* turned out to be for all of us, not for my grandfather. Drinking medicines made with them would keep us from catching what he had, according to my grandmother. According to my mother, it was just hocus pocus, though she allowed that a beyond mysterious placebo effect might keep us all safe. According to research done after my mother retired, the stuff does do something: the effect of its astringency is that bacteria cannot lodge in tissue long enough to multiply and thus cause trouble. Instead, they're flushed out of the system. And pulse diagnosis, which my grandmother practiced, is practiced today, as it was in ancient times in India, in China and in parts of Russia—and for a few years now, it has been taught at the Harvard Medical School from where it has spread to other places such as the University of Iowa Hospital and Clinics. It is amazing to me to ride in the elevator there and hear young interns and residents talk about how the newest research indicates that pulse diagnosis can often catch things better and sooner than a lab test.

CHAPTER SEVEN

The Hog-Dogs of Peenemünde

So my mother had somehow figured out a way to smuggle my grandfather out of East Berlin. How exactly? We heard on the radio every day that people were shot and killed by the dozen trying to get across the border from East to West or trying to help others get across, and here was my mother with my grandfather who was too sick to walk. Not only had she gotten him out, she had somehow commandeered an American military ambulance to assist her. When I was a child, everything was most ordinary and highly miraculous at the same time. What kinds of questions could you ask about such a world at age five? But later, and it is astonishing how much later, I did wonder.

She never said much to me about her trips to East Berlin and other mysterious places behind the Iron Curtain—a name that I took quite literally as child, picturing miles and miles of corrugated metal hanging from the sky. But now, looking back, I can piece one or two things together thanks to two meetings—one of them was probably not merely by chance, and I'll get to that in due time. The other one was certainly pure chance, just a few of years ago.

I had an appointment in Iowa City at the University of Iowa Hospital, and after the vampires there had drawn my blood, I went to the New Pioneer Food Co-Op, a glorious place, in whose establishment I had had a small hand back in the seventies when I was getting doctorate degree #1. So I was fond of the place. I got a salad, and went to sit on a bench outside. A handsome young couple with a charming little boy were already sitting there, and they moved over to make space for me. They looked like congenial types to me: the man wore sandals and blatantly miss-matched socks. "I love your socks," I told him, and from there it was not more than two minutes before he and I realized we both shared an interest in the history of the 20th century, particularly Nazi Germany, and its secret connections to the current political scene here in the U.S. The young man ran to his rust bucket truck and brought back a book: *Secret Agenda: The United States Government, Nazi Scientists, and Project Paperclip, 1945-1990* by Linda Hunt (New York: St. Martin's Press, 1991).[12] "You have to read this," he said, handing me the book. "Paperclip" sounded deeply familiar, but I could not quite drag it out of the depths of my consciousness. The young family was in a rush to get somewhere, so we exchanged phone numbers and went our separate ways.

This is one of the things I really love about America. In Germany or France or Greece or China or India—all places where I have lived—no stranger would ever lend you a book, so this detail about the guy in the miss-matched socks would most likely not be believable to a reader from those countries. As a rule, if you smile at a stranger in France or Germany, he thinks you are an escapee from a loony bin—though I hear that this has changed in recent years. If so, I would love to see it. The only exception to this rule when I was young was if you are on a walk in the Alps—there, strangers have always been expected to say hello to each other.

Once home from Iowa City, I looked at the table of contents of *Secret Agenda*, and the title of Chapter Three, "Peenemünde on the Rio Grande," knocked the lid off worlds of forgotten memories, beginning with a childhood scene, as the words "*Peenemünder Schweinehunde*" jumped up in my awareness like a jack-in-the-box. I do not think I have ever devoured a text more quickly or more ravenously.

And here is a long ago scene from my childhood in Stuttgart-Sillenbuch: my aunt Ruth and my mother had come home for a weekend and were spending long hours together at the dining table pouring over maps and floor plans, my mother interrogating my aunt Ruth. And I do mean interrogating, not questioning—obviously, Alice Mailänder had learned something from her experience with the Gestapo about effective interrogation techniques. My aunt Ruth, close to tears, did not want to talk,

---

[12] Since then, other researchers have confirmed Linda Hunt's work. Two recent works are: Ratline: Soviet Spies, Nazi Priests, and the Disappearance of Adolf Hitler by Peter Levenda (2012) and America's Nazi Secret: An Insider's History by John Loftus (2010). Blowback: America's Recruitment of Nazis and its Destructive Impact on Our Domestic and Foreign Policy (2014) by Christopher Simpson should also be mentioned.

but my mother relentlessly pumped her for any and all details my aunt Ruth could remember about Peenemünde.

My aunt Ruth had worked there in some capacity even before she was out of her teens, as a telephone operator, according to her. But why would a telephone operator's memories of a work place be so painful? According to my mother and my aunt Maria, my aunt Ruth's life in and out of mental hospitals dated back to her time in Peenemünde, but that is all anybody ever told me, and so Peenemünde sat around dormant in the basement of my mind. Now, thanks to the man in the miss-matched socks, I know that even if a telephone operator was all she was, to get to her workstation, she would have had to walk past mounds of stacked up, tortured, and skeletal dead bodies of Jews, Gypsies, Jehovah's Witnesses, homosexuals, protesters, journalists, the retarded, handicapped, and others not deemed fit to live—horrendous reminders of what would happen to you if you did not shout, *"Heil Hitler"* enthusiastically enough.

That day of the maps and the floor plans, my mother was determined to get information out of my aunt Ruth. And when my mother was determined to do something, she got it done—none of us would have lived through the war, or our flight from the Russian army, without her iron will, her courage, and her resourcefulness. And, just as clear as my aunt Ruth's reluctance to talk about Peenemünde was the fact that my mother was livid with rage concerning the folks in that town *and* with her American employers. In fact, the only reason I remember this small scene was because of her rage, which always scared me to death.

Peenemünde had been a harmless fishing village on the white sands of the Baltic Sea until the Nazis put their Army Research Center there. It included, among other important and sensitive organizations, their Guided Missile Development, their Aerodynamics Institute, their Homeland (!) Artillery Park, and their V-2 Production Plant—all in that hapless village. And Wernher von Braun, technical director of that research center, was chief among the *Peenemünder Schweinehunde* in my mother's mind.

"*Schweinehund*" is one of the worst and most colorful terms of disapprobation you can use in German—it literally means "hog-dog." I have not done definitive research on the history of the term, but it is pretty obvious that a hog-dog is not an animal used for herding swine—for that would be an honorable profession for a dog. Instead, a hog-dog is a human being with a dog for a father and a hog for a mother or, even worse, a swine for a father and a bitch for a mother. The plural is "*Schweinehunde,*" and in my memory, the two words go together: *Peenemünder Schweinehunde.* They form a slant rhyme, and so the phrase is memorable for that reason alone.

As my aunt and my mother worked together over the maps and the floor plans, with my mother taking notes, the words "*Peenemünder Schweinehunde*" would explode from her at regular intervals. Although I could form no clear idea of what the two women were talking about, it was abundantly clear that a *Peenemünder Schweinehund* was even lower than a regular *Schweinehund,* and that my mother was in some way, and most unwillingly, involved with them. She traveled to Peenemünde many times, and I would hear snippets of conversation—meaningless to me—between her and my grandmother about her trips to Peenemünde—and other places behind the Iron Curtain—*Mittelwerk* and *Dora*[13] were other place names I heard often in conversations.

Linda Hunt's book gave me a context for those snippets of childhood memories. What was happening in Germany in 1945 was that, even before the Allies had laid down their guns, they started fighting over the more or less dead and cut-up body of the Fatherland. The spoils of war, glorious always, if not exactly clean, in this case included thousands of scientists, who were, in many fields, a decade, sometimes two, ahead of the rest of the world. Now, why that was the case is a really interesting story that has never yet been told, but one thing is certain: Germans are not smarter than any other humans on the planet, or more evil—what Germany proved capable of, all nations are capable of. It is a simple matter of social engineering, and we disbelieve it at our peril.

Space exploration was an aim as far back as Nazi Germany, so rocketry and related war machinery, including chemical and biological warfare, were areas in which Germany excelled, as was medicine, and why not? They had human guinea pigs readily available in the interment camps.

Naturally, everyone wanted a piece of that brain trust after the war.

---

[13] "Mittelwerk (German for "Central Works") was a German World War II factory built underground in the Kohnstein to avoid allied bombing. It used forced labor from the Mittelbaur-Dora concentration camp to produce V-2 ballistic missiles, V-1 flying bombs, and other weapons. (Wikipedia). Most of the operations in Peenemünde moved to Mittelwerk after Allied bombing began.

And, for the most obvious of reasons, America very much did not want Russia to get her hands on all that sensitive expertise in the arts of death and destruction, as well as in the conquest of space. If you do a little research, you would find that flying saucers are not UFO's. German engineers were designing them. Of course, you could always insist that they were "back-engineering" them.

So Nazi scientists and their expertise were wanted, but on the other hand, one could not really justify importing a bunch of ardent Nazis who should have been brought to trial for war crimes. "Ardent" was the legal term for "rabid" with a precise definition which included a whole slew of criteria, among them how much power and rank a person had held, what kinds of crimes he had committed or ordered, what organizations he was a member of, how early in the game he had joined, and how publicly he had spouted off.

My mother had been a sometime interpreter at the Nuremberg war crimes trials, and the one thing I can conclude from what I have read and from what she told me is that those trials were a brilliant PR move, and that is about all they were, even though some of the worst offenders were imprisoned. Or executed—which, to my mind, does not improve the world at all. However, these trials also set international legal precedents—according to which it is your duty to disobey immoral orders and to publicize anything you know of that you deem a war crime or even just harmful to people. I do wish that these laws really were binding. According to this precedent, Chelsea Manning was doing her duty in exposing war crimes—her lawyers didn't bring up the Nuremberg war crimes trials and the legal precedents they set because in an American courtroom, it is the judge who decides what can and cannot be said. Add the notion of plea-bargaining, and you have a broken system.

So here was a dilemma for the U.S. According to Linda Hunt, the United States, while officially condemning the Nazis, helped thousands of them to escape to the Middle East and South America, especially to Argentina, with the assistance of the Vatican over the so-called "Ratlines."[14] These Nazis went from monastery to monastery using false papers and wearing monks' robes. But if those war criminals were scientists, they

---

[14] Some of the people who escaped Germany via these ratlines included Franz Stangl, commandant of Treblinka, Gustav Wagner, commandant of Sobibor, and their boss, Adolf Eichmann, who had organized the transport of millions of people, first to all the ghettos and then to the concentration camps. Adolf Eichmann was later captured and tried in Jerusalem.

were imported to the U.S. as secretly as possible, and their Nazi past was obliterated as much as possible, to be replaced in some cases with pure fiction—well, not pure, but fiction. In many cases these scientists also had to be shielded from the public eye because they kept right on doing what they had been doing in Germany.

Another imperative was created by the fact that many of these scientists found themselves in East Germany in 1945, i.e. in Russian occupied territory, such as Peenemünde, for example, and so as far as the Americans, the British, and the French were concerned, scientists and their papers had to be gotten out of East Germany at all cost and as quickly and as furtively as possible before Moscow snapped them up. Linda Hunt says they were kidnapped, but you cannot really call it kidnapping when the victim is co-operating, and is indeed grateful for the chance to get away with murder yet one more time.

The biggest prize of them all was Wernher von Braun, as mentioned, the technical director of the Nazi "research" center, the man who went on to become the father of the American space program. According to what I can gather, he had turned himself in to the Americans on his own, but the various stories about him do not tally. My mother had met him—I do not know under what circumstances—and she had a seemingly most unreasonable hatred for that man. I later learned things about him that made me sure he never stopped being an ardent Nazi.

Given Linda Hunt's research on "Operation Paperclip" and given also what I remember from my childhood, I am virtually certain that my mother went to Peenemünde, and other places in East Germany, as part of a team that was getting scientists out for processing and shipping to the U.S. I do remember hearing the term *Paperclip*, and *Peenemünde*, *Dora*, *Mittelwerk*, and *Kohnstein* were definitely household words—made the more interesting and memorable because violent emotion were connected with them and because all questions I asked about them were answered with, "This is nothing for children."

Since my mother had joined a Communist organization to fight the Nazis, and since they had caught her, tortured her, and denied her the education she needed to become the medical researcher she dreamed of being, it must have struck her as bitter irony that the closest she got to science was to "kidnap" *Peenemünder Schweinehunde* so they could go on being what they were and continue doing in America what they had been doing in Germany. Even in later years, when Braun was in the news for his title role in the glorious American space race, my mother would spit out the words *Peenemünder Schweinehund* with all the contempt she could pull up through her feet from the very center of the earth on which she stood. "History will never know the truth about this man," she would say, and if she had been a snake, she would have struck him right between the eyes, right through the television set. As it was, she had to content herself to merely hiss, "*Dieser ekelhafte Peenemünder Schweinehund hat so 'n richtiges Ohrfeigen Gesicht,*"[15] as she stood, impotent, in her second husband's suburban ranch house in Mayfield Heights, Ohio.

So that is a hint of how she got my grandfather out of East Berlin, commandeering an American military ambulance in the process. Ambulances would have been one of her preferred means of travel, taking Russian military ambulances and East German ambulances to the border between East and West, and then an American military ambulance for the rest of the way to Frankfurt, the headquarters of the American Military Government, where she was stationed, coming home to Stuttgart only on those weekends when she was not on some secret mission.

Later, when she sent my sister and me to a German boarding school, the *Hermann Lietz Schule*, for my last year of high school, I met a teacher, Dr. Droste, who would tell me more to confirm my guesses as to what my mother was up to that made it possible for her to bring my grandfather home in an American military ambulance. But I will get to Dr. Droste in more or less chronological order. For now, I will say that Dr. Droste—not his real name, and I doubt the name he went by was real—Dr. Droste and von Braun had been classmates at the *Hermann Lietz Schule* and then colleagues in Peenemünde.

My mother's story on getting my grandfather out of East Berlin mentioned nothing about *how* she got him out. Here is the story she told my grandmother.

"Finding Papa was easy and difficult at the same time. I went to his apartment on *Blücherstraße*, and there he was. He was so sick that he didn't recognize me right away. But finding the place and getting there was almost impossible. So many buildings are bombed to the ground. Streets are impassable because of the rubble, and they're really

---

[15] "That disgusting bastard (hog-dog) has the kind of mug you just want to keep on punching."

dangerous: you can crash through something, and be buried forever.

"I didn't recognize anything—none of the familiar landmarks are there. The buildings that are left standing look really unfamiliar without their neighbors, they look…well, they look…bereft. There's no public transportation because the streets are impassable. There's no way to get anywhere except by military vehicle."

(And I see the vehicle. I saw such military vehicles on our flight from the pinewood near Dreetz. They can drive over any ground and they can even drive into a river, swim across, and drive out on the other side. I saw them drive through the muddy field and cross the Elbe River. They look like unstoppable black and evil armored insects).

"Papa's apartment building was the only structure still standing in the neighborhood," continued my mother, and my grandmother interrupted at that point: "Well, don't you remember Ali, he predicted it would be. Nobody believed him, but he did say many times, 'God will spare this building.'"

"Yes, I remember," said my mother, "It certainly was a strange coincidence, but I don't see anything divine about it. Those few people left alive in those few buildings are starving to death and dying of thirst. They live in a rubble desert. And rescuing survivors wasn't exactly the first thing on Russia's mind after they took over what was left of the city. Fortunately, I was able to bring out everyone that was left alive in Papa's building."

I, too, have difficulty believing such things as, "God will spare this building," even though I have had the experience of clearly knowing a future event ahead of time myself. It took time for me to give up belief after belief, but it took even longer to give up disbelief. And yet, that does not mean I understand the mechanism that makes such vision possible, never mind fathoming the deep and far-ranging implications. Neither can I control it: it comes or it does not. Nor can I say how such a thought differs from any other—yet it does.

My mother also told us the story she had heard from my grandfather's neighbors about his doings in Berlin:

"While I was getting Papa ready to travel, the neighbors came over and told me this typical Papa story. When Russian soldiers arrived in Berlin, Papa stood in front of the apartment building and welcomed them into the city—in God's name, if you please. Sounds exactly like the kind of crazy thing Papa would do. And I can just hear him say it: *Radi Boga—dobro pozhalovat v Berlin*. Who would say a thing like that? To invading soldiers! 'In the name of God, welcome to Berlin'. I mean, really! He also mentioned to these soldiers, by the way, that they'd have to kill him first if they wanted to come into the building to rape any of the women. Then, after three days and nights of welcoming the Russians, when he was about to collapse from fatigue and hunger, a troop of them came and arrested him as a spy. Why he didn't know that this would happen is beyond me: he was speaking Russian like a native to Russian soldiers in Berlin! Of course, he'd be suspected. The neighbors thought that would be the last they'd ever see of him.

"But a few weeks later, a Russian captain who spoke German brought Papa back to the apartment in a Russian military ambulance and left him in the neighbors' care—Papa was pretty sick with hunger typhus already. The captain brought them food and clean water. He told them that a Russian military court had found Papa guilty of espionage. The captain said he didn't believe Papa was a spy, but there was nothing he himself could do about it. There was no evidence, he said, and Papa's insane faith seemed real and seemed to rule out nefarious activities such as espionage, especially since it seemed clear that he loved Russia and didn't have much good to say about Germany. The captain also said that the story Papa told the court about his life in Russia, starting out as an apprentice in a foundry to becoming a wealthy industrialist and then being sent to Siberia, as an enemy alien, had all sounded very genuine.

"Even so, they sentenced him to death. And Papa being Papa, refused the blindfold and told the soldiers on firing squad duty that he was innocent, but that if God wanted him home, they would obey the command to fire; but if God had further duties or adventures in mind for him, then they'd refuse the order to fire. Either way was just fine with him, and he would not hold it against them if they shot him. On the contrary, he was sure God would bless them because he, Maxim Pavlovich, would put in a good word for them with the Almighty—it all sounds pathetically just like Papa. And, unbelievable as it seems, the soldiers refused to obey the order to fire."

When my grandfather got well enough to talk, he told the same story beginning with, "In my fever, I didn't recognize Ali right away because she was wearing a Russian military police uniform—how in the world...."

"Shhhhh..." said my grandmother and then whispered, "She's working for the *Amis*." "*Ami*" is German slang for "American."

"No!" said my grandfather.

"Yes," said my grandmother, "How do you think she's supporting all of us and how do you think she got you out?"

"But they..."

"Max, leave it be; she didn't have a choice."

CHAPTER EIGHT
Members of the Family

Had my grandfather been allowed to finish his sentence about the *Amis*, it would have been: "But they are war criminals!" I know, of course, that this is not what the history books say. As has often been observed, however, it is not the losers of wars who write the history books.

As noted earlier, my maternal grandparents were declared "enemy aliens" while they lived in Russia and were sent to Siberia—my grandfather was taken first, and then my grandmother and her children made that journey about four or five months later when my mother was a new-born. Miraculously, they were re-united in Siberia. But for my grandfather's ingenuity[16], their lives would all have ended in one of the Siberian mines where life expectancy was about two miserable years. They all managed to escape from Siberia when she was four or five years old. She told me she remembers begging for bread in a Russian village: *Radi Boga, daietye minye kussok khleba* " ("In God's name, a piece of bread, please") She was seven by the time they got to Germany in 1922, where my aunt Ruth was born in a refugee camp. My aunt Maria was fourteen then, the age her older brother, my uncle Franz, had been when they had been sent to Siberia. My grandmother credits Franz for keeping her, Maria, and the newborn baby alive on that journey by horse-drawn sleigh through the Siberian winter prairies. My grandmother's other five children did not make it out of Russia. They starved to death, except one, who, like my baby sister, died as a result of rape.

Already a fine horseman, my uncle Franz had perfected his skill, first in Kirgizstan and then in Kazakhstan, which is famous for its riders. My grandmother claimed Franz could ride a horse bareback at a full gallop

---

[16] Think about what a 2.5 hour movie is hiding in that word.

and bend down to pick up his girl's silk handkerchief with his teeth. Of course, the Russian cavalry would want a rider like that and so they had inducted Franz—that is what they called it—it seems like kidnapping to me and my family, especially since, legally, he was a German citizen. We never saw him again, although the hope that he would somehow be able to come home to us was alive in both my grandparents. My uncle Franz was the hero of many of the stories I heard as a child. Here is my favorite one:

Just before they were sent to Siberia as enemy aliens, my grandparents were doing very well, and life seemed without a care. As the family story goes, thirteen-year old Franz had persuaded his mother to let him visit my great-uncle Alexander's twin boys of the same age in the neighboring village. My grandmother had had misgivings—it was winter—and she told the boy and the servant, as they were harnessing the three horses to a sleigh, a troika painted with fantastic flowers, to be back well before dark. They promised and took off: a bright thing flying over the sparkling snow, high-spirited, the man, the boy, the elegant Arabian horses, and the silvery sound of sleigh and harness bells.

Uncle Sasha's boys were raising an orphaned bear cub, and, in spite of the old servant's admonitions, the boys just could not stop rolling around in the snow with the young bear. So it was too close to dusk when Franz and the old servant set out for home.

With darkness came wolves, and the three horses ran for their lives. But more wolves came and gained on them. The boy and the man were weeping for what they had to do; nevertheless, they cut loose one of the horses to give themselves more time to reach the village gate—but not enough time, and with the screams of the first horse still in their ears, they cut loose the second horse to be torn apart by wolves.

The last horse, a strong, black mare, was white with foam and ran like the wind-drinker that she was, almost flying above the snow as only Arabians can, but the wolves closed in. "There is only one way," the old servant yelled over the howling wind, the harness bells, and the wild laughter of the wolves, "You must obey my words exactly now—always—your life depends on it." Franz nodded.

"Promise as you love God," insisted the man.

"I promise," shouted the boy almost in a rage. Handing him the reins, the old man yelled in his ear, "DON'T LOOK BACK!" and jumped into the moonlit snow.

My grandmother thanked God for those last words every time she told the story. Then she would conclude it for me by telling me that, later, Franz killed as many wolves as it took to make a great sleigh blanket of their fur; and all around its perimeter, he sewed on wolves' ears to make a scalloped edge.

When I first heard the story, it never occurred to me to wonder if it was true—since then, however, I have taught teenaged boys, never forgetting the while that Alexander the Great was only sixteen years old when he conquered the world. But when I was a child, my concern was for the wolves my uncle Franz had killed. I understood killing them to pay for the old servant's life, but the ears seemed excessive to me, and an unnecessary insult to all wolves. "Possibly you're right," said my grandmother, who had mixed feelings about wolves.

Just a few months after the old servant had been lost to the wolves, my grandfather's factory making farm machinery was confiscated, and he was sent to Siberia, leaving my pregnant grandmother and her children to starve. Then, a few days after my mother was born, my grandmother and her children were sent to Siberia also.

My grandmother and her children rode through endless snow for weeks in a caravan of horse-drawn sleighs. At night they would circle the sleighs, keeping the prisoners and the foals inside the circle. The mares stood outside its perimeter facing inward, so that they could kick any approaching wolves in the teeth with their hind legs. The stallions ran around the circle all night to protect the mares. And outside that circle, at some distance, you could see another circle: the eyes of the wolves glowing in the darkness. "Sometimes they sang," said my grandmother, "And in their singing you could hear that they, too, loved God."

The amazing story of how my grandparents were reunited in Siberia, how they survived there, and how they eventually fled to Germany is for another time.

***

On their flight from Russia, my grandparents had lost track of my grandfather's brothers Alexander ("Uncle Sasha") and Otto, and I heard constant stories about them as well as Franz. In that same way, I heard stories of my father, who would also come home some day—some day soon.

So there were four absent men in the family, men who were nevertheless a palpable presence, and the stories about them were alive with love and longing and loss. Perhaps it was because of them, that I somehow formed the notion that there was yet a fifth uncle who was missing. He, too, was present in important ways and often part of the conversation, and that was my unseen uncle Adolf Hitler, though it was abundantly clear that he was very different from our other missing men.

At the time when my uncle Hitler was thinking about his beer hall putsch, my mother was beginning to learn German. No more than seven years old in 1922, she told her parents and teachers, "I don't want to learn German; it's not even a language: it's a sore throat" (*eine Halskrankheit*).

My mother's family was eeking out a bare subsistence on a small farm near Berlin. I heard stories about bringing in the harvest by lantern light and about a pig named Steppke who loved everyone, and everyone loved him. Steppke was later slaughtered, and nobody felt like having dinner that night because Steppke had been a member of the family. Somehow, the farm did not make it; Steppke had been the last straw, and the family moved to Berlin where my grandmother supported them by sewing for one of the big fashion houses.

My grandfather and my mother both hated my uncle Hitler from the start, though their hatred of him was also the occasion of hatred and a personal warfare between the two of them. My grandmother stood aloof, and my aunt Maria worshiped Hitler, as did my aunt Ruth, the youngest of my grandparents' children. By the time I was five years old in 1945, it was no longer fashionable to adore Uncle Adolf. Yet he remained an immeasurably important part of the family's conversation, as they and all of Germany tried to awaken from the nightmare and come to terms with it.

My grandfather was not the sort of man who would go through two world wars, a revolution, and a famine without educating himself about "your political forces" that made it all happen, and he saw it as his duty to educate me. There were rules about teaching me religion (absolutely NO religious instruction), but politics was fair game. Simply put, his view was that Hitler was a puppet with a very big mouth, that the money to fabricate him had come mostly from Wall Street, and that the Vatican had pulled the strings and taken care of the on-the-ground political machinations, while Prescott Bush[17] (Grandpa Bush) paid the mercenaries that crushed opposition against Hitler.

And so my grandfather identified Hitler-worship with "Popery" and idolatry for good reason: The mayor of Bremen, for example, had said, "We don't need priests and clergymen! We are in direct contact with God through Hitler. He has many Christ-like characteristics." Nor was the mayor of Bremen voicing an unusual opinion. A group of Rhineland Christians of both denominations voted for a resolution worded as follows: "Hitler's word is God's law; his decrees and ordinances have Divine authority." And after it was all over, Germany's first post-war chancellor, Konrad Adenauer, wrote a letter to a Catholic clergyman, in which he says, "In my opinion, the German people and the bishops, as well as the entire clergy, carry great responsibility for the events in the concentration camps. It is true that afterwards there wasn't anything that could be done. The responsibility was incurred earlier. The German people, the bishops, and the clergy fell for the National Socialist propaganda to a great extent. They fell into line without resistance and even enthusiastically. In that lies their guilt."[18]

According to my grandfather, Adenauer told a half-truth, which is worse than a lie. The bishops did not fall for anything, he told me again and again; instead, they were some of the engineers. Consider some basic facts:

1. The editor or, more likely, the ghostwriter of Hitler's book, *Mein Kampf* (which lays out the plan for the Holocaust) was a Jesuit.[19]

---

[17] Senator Prescott Bush was deeply involved with the Nazis. In 1942 he was indicted for trading with the enemy. In 2001 two Holocaust survivors sued the U.S. government and the Bush family for a total of $40bn in compensation. The plaintive charged that both the U.S. Government and the Bush family materially benefitted from Auschwitz slave labor during WWII. The evidence seems conclusive to me. Among many other things, Prescott Bush commissioned his attorney, Allen Dulles, to hide his money and its trail.

[18] Here is the German text: Nach meiner Meinung trägt das deutsche Volk und tragen auch die Bischöfe und der Klerus eine große Schuld an den Vorgängen in den Konzentrationslagern. Richtig ist, daß nachher vielleicht nicht viel mehr zu machen war. Die Schuld liegt früher. Das deutsche Volk, auch Bischöfe und Klerus zum großen Teil, sind auf die nationalsozialistische eingegangen. Es hat sich fast widerstandslos, ja zum Teil mit Begeisterung gleichschalten lassen. Darin liegt seine Schuld.

[19] Bernhard Stempfle was either a Hieronymite or a Jesuit, depending on whom you ask. Given the history of the Jesuits, he was probably both and then some.

2. Monsignor Ludwig Kaas was the head of the Centrist Party that elected Hitler. The vote for Hitler was mandated from the pulpit of every Catholic and Protestant church in the country. The only reason Kaas was not promoted to Cardinal was that this would have made his political activities and his connection to the Vatican much too visible.
3. Once Hitler was elected, Monsignor Kaas was instrumental in passing the treasonous "Enabling Act" which gave Hitler absolute power.
4. Hitler's vice chancellor (for a time) was Franz von Papen, a "Papal Chamberlain." He wrote in the official Nazi Newspaper that Hitler had "reinstated (in Germany) the sacred principles of the Papacy," i.e. the divine right of rulership, which had been so badly damaged in the French Revolution. Von Papen was profoundly involved in the deep state and played a vital role in bringing Hitler to power as early as 1913 when he was a military attaché to the German ambassador in the United States. There is some evidence that he worked with Paul Warburg, one of the designers and first chief of the Federal Reserve Bank. Warburg, as is commonly known, was the model for the character "Daddy Warbucks" in the cartoon series "Orphan Annie." It bears mentioning also that Warburg's brother, Max Warburg, was head of the German financial system at that time and chief of the German secret service.
5. Eugenio Pacelli was the Vatican's ambassador in Germany for twenty years before he became Pope Pius XII and then signed the *Reichskonkordat*[20] with Hitler (whom he had known intimately while in Germany). The Reichskonkordat was an agreement according to which it was the duty of every Christian "to love, honor, obey, and protect" the Nazis.

Of course, I took my grandfather's word for everything as a child. Since then, I have done extensive research, and it does not seem to me that my grandfather's position was unreasonable. In 2001, for example, I was the research assistant to Marc Halberstadt, a brilliant independent

---

[20] The original text of this agreement, signed by Hitler (a practicing Catholic) and Pope Pius XII, is German. I am translating the words "to love, honor, obey, and protect " the Nazis from the original. It is noteworthy that some translations into English omit these words.

filmmaker and comedian. I researched (among other things) the history of the American Indians. In that capacity, I found that the so-called "residential schools" for Indian children were really concentration camps with an average death rate of 50%. In Canada, these camps were run by the Catholic, Anglican, and United Church of Canada (leading me to some suspicions as to whether major Protestant denominations are indeed still independent of the Papacy). In the U.S. these concentration camps for children were administered by the Federal Government through the Bureau of Indian Affairs—and there is reason to believe that the Catholic Church was, once again, behind it.[21]

In a personal interview here in Fairfield with Russell Means (1939-2012), the founder and leader of the American Indian Movement), he told me that most of these "schools" closed in the mid-to late seventies, but that he thought there were some still operating in secret locations. Others I interviewed agreed.

"Operating" in this context means that we are talking about nuns and priests torturing and killing children. "How can that be?" I asked myself a hundred times, and, while I do not have an answer I can document, I can imagine that the practice of confession allows the Church to identify families in which child abuse runs from generation to generation. It is a given in the field of psychology that many such children grow up incapable of resisting the urge to abuse others and, also, these children are easily controllable as adults. When I discussed this with Russell, he said, "Well, yes. Some of the abused Indian children in those concentration camps grew up to be useful guards in them. Remember Viktor Frankl: 'the abused take on the values of the abuser.'"

The information presented above is the tip of the iceberg of the available evidence that the Papacy was intimately and knowingly involved in Hitler's regime and the Holocaust. In the Croatian Holocaust the connection to the Vatican was even more evident on the very face of it. It is matter of official record that the plan for Croatia was to exterminate one third of the population, expel one third, and forcibly convert the remaining third to Catholicism.

As to the involvement of Wall Street in financing Hitler, that evidence is readily available online, and so I will only mention the basics. In 1947, when it was all over, Senator Homer T. Bone said to the U.S. Congress,

---

[21] See Rulers of Evil: Useful Knowledge about Governing Bodies by F. Tupper Saussy (1999)

"Farben was Hitler, and Hitler was Farben." He had reference to the German corporation, I. G. Farben (Paul Warburg, the first chief of the Federal Reserve, sat on its board of directors). Senator Bone's statement is another expression of what Mussolini had said about fascism: It should really be called "corporatism," he had maintained, as it is the union of big government and big business. So the question is, who financed I. G. Farben? The answer is that there were categorically *no* German financiers of either Farben or Hitler who were not entangled with American high finance. And, as America's ambassador to Germany reported to President Franklin D. Roosevelt, there were over a hundred U.S. corporations on an unregulated (precisely the point of fascism) feeding frenzy in Germany. So, what Senator Bone had said of Farben could be equally well said of General Electric, IBM (who located and kept track of the Jews to be interned), Standard Oil, Ford, General Motors J. P. Morgan, ITT, Texaco, Alcoa, Du Pont, Dow Chemical, and Bayer (aspirin), and a slew of others.

Now, here is my favorite part of the story, which would make a fabulous movie. Two guys blow into town—Munich, that is. One of these two guys just had cocktails with Paul Warburg in New York City on Wall Street. His name is Moses Pinkeles (a.k.a. Ignaz Trebitch-Lincoln; a.k.a. Abbot Chao Kung, a.k.a. Lama Djordi Den). The other one is Adam Alfred Rudolf Glauer (a.k.a. Erwin Torre; a.k.a. Baron Rudolf von Sebottendorff; a.k.a. Sefik Hüsnü). Adam had been adopted for his nefarious talents at age forty by the German expatriate international banker, Baron Heinrich von Sebottendorf. This noble banker was also a member of a slew of secret societies. Does it get better than this? Think of all the excellent stories behind the a.k.a.'s of our two guys. We suspect there is some intelligence behind them; there certainly is money, and, so far as I have been able to research it, no historian has been able or, possibly, willing, to reveal its source. Like Hamlet, we want to ask these two miscreants, "Were you not sent for?" It is an amazing story: these two fiends help to create a crucially important planetary situation of profoundly evil and mythic proportions and then, when they are ready for retirement from the world stage, after a few other notable adventures, they fake their own deaths (one in China, the other one back home in Turkey) and both vanish into thin air. These are not your average attendant lords to swell a progress, start a scene or two; no, these boys come straight out of the movie, The Usual Suspects.

When they first get into town, they start out small. They form a club, a kind of "New Age" society where you can meet like-minded seekers, learn meditation, and all kinds of other groovy and occult yogic stuff—of course, it wasn't called "New Age" back then, but there is indeed nothing new under the sun. The cultural climate was right for such little ashrams, and they'd been springing up like mushrooms all around the land as if someone had thoughtfully spread a rich manure.

Mose and Rudy are good at what they do. Like sweet and sticky fly paper, they attract people from all walks of life and all levels of society. They watch the membership grow, all the while looking for certain kinds of talent, capabilities, means, connections. And, somehow, it just happens that the folks with names that say "old nobility," and names with Ph.D.'s behind them, and names, small and ordinary, but with big money at their back, are initiated at a higher rate into the more advanced and secret teachings of the ashram. Yet there are some few lower class types as well, folks without means—of the monetary kind that is, who make it into those high ranks: butchers, bakers, fishermen, fakers, and ordinary foot soldiers with special talents. The society had put an ad in the papers. It said, "We are looking for a dictator." Really? Yes, really!

One of these soldiers who had joined the society, a somewhat artistic young loser, who had done nothing more interesting than feed the mice in his army barracks, looked to Mose and Rudy like he had the right kind of stuff they were particularly watching for. They had tested a number of likely candidates, and this young chap stood out. He was perfect. "He's got a big trap, he could be useful," one of their trusted initiates had said—Mose and Rudy were no longer working alone.

So they provide this young soldier with the best of mentors and teachers, giving him also amazing yogic techniques and initiating him into the secret teachings of the Sufis, the Tibetan Lamas, the Vedas, and, for good measure, the Japanese Society of the Green Dragon. They convince him he is Arjuna on the battlefield about to establish heaven on earth for a thousand years. His teachers buy this promising young chap new clothes, they correct his grammar and his pronunciation so he'd pass in high places, and then, through the membership they've built, they introduce him to "Society." And they've done their job programming this hapless young man very well: he is a hit among the glitterati.

They have fun. They have lots of weed and peyote and other psychotropic drugs. They know just how to make this young soldier feel special, perfect, chosen. They encourage him. They tell him stories that go to his head. He hardly knows what to make of them—or of his own good luck, but they tell him it is not luck, it is Providence, it is Divine Will. And, by gosh, they are serious. They start a political party, and they buy him a newspaper (with the help of Bush and Harriman).

Now I ask you, is this not a much more fascinating and engaging story than what you get in your average history book: Hitler came to power in 1933. What a boring sentence that is, given the realities behind it. By the time I was twelve in 1952, I knew this story inside and out (except for the part about weed and peyote) since my grandfather had told it to me many times.

Back in 1933 my grandfather joined the Jehovah's Witnesses, not because he believed in their version of Christianity, but "in order to do something about Hitler." Indeed, the Jehova's Witnesses were one of the major groups protesting and documenting Hitler's every move. For this, they were sent to the concentration camps by the thousands, and where the Jews wore the Star of David on their prison uniforms, the Jehovah's Witnesses wore a purple triangle. The real difference between them was that the Jews could never leave; the Jehovah's Witnesses, on the other hand, could leave any time they renounced their religion. None ever did, at least not enough for Hitler to parade, and they endured unbearable torture and death.

My grandfather became a missionary for them and distributed their weekly publication, *The Watchtower*, in the Russian émigré community in Berlin. That he did not end up in a concentration camp for that activity borders on the miraculous. It was not as if he tried to lay low either. He wrote exceedingly long letters to Hitler, Göring, Himmler, Goebbels, and a whole slew of other high and low party officials, telling them all in abundant detail where their Godless ways would lead them and the whole country, and why their ways were Godless in the first place—all on official Jehovah's Witnesses' stationary.

As my grandfather had joined the Jehovah's Witnesses to do something about Hitler, my mother joined the Communist party for that same reason when she was fifteen years old in 1930. My aunt Maria, who loved Hitler, was twenty-two and still living at home. My aunt

Ruth was only eight and she adored Maria and Hitler both together. The dynamics at the dinner table must have been interesting, with my grandfather proclaiming:

"You're a Godless creature, Alice,"

"So are you, Papa, since there is no God."

And then my aunt Maria put in: "There is a God, and Hitler is our direct link to Him, and that means he is God in his essence. Hitler is our Savior."

"That is sacrilege, Maria," answered my grandfather, "He is our direct link to Satan's dark power, and Germany will go straight to hell."

My grandmother said gently: "Can't we talk about something nice at dinner?"

Then my aunt Ruth silenced them all with: "Hitler *is* nice, Mama, all the teachers in school say he is."

I am making light of it, but the reality was soul and gut wrenching for everyone, and things became ugly just over three years later. While the family was still living on the farm, my mother took the train to Berlin every day to attend a school, one of the best in the country, where she had received a full scholarship through the efforts of her teachers in elementary school. She did her homework on the train, coming and going, because at home there was farm work to be done. Still, even though she put in her hours as a farm hand, my grandfather did not like her school since it was "very progressive" and he blamed it for his daughter's atheism. On the other hand, she was an exemplary student, especially in the sciences. She was planning to attend medical school to study research pathology ("So I wouldn't have to deal with stupid patients," as she told me later). A doctor in the family seemed to promise a comfortable retirement for the doctor's parents. Then, in 1933, after Hitler was in place, after the *Reichstag* had burned, and after Monsignor Ludwig Kaas had engineered the treasonous Enabling Act giving Hitler absolute power,[22] the Gestapo came to my mother's school, dragged her roughly out of her classroom and hauled her downtown.

She was in solitary confinement on rations of stale, moldy bread and water; she was interrogated under bright lights, deprived of sleep, and tortured. *Where did her Communist cell meet? Who were the other*

---

[22] Notice how eerily similar some things are: Bush is in place, 9/11 goes down, and the Patriot Act guts any semblance of "democracy."

members? Who had introduced her to the group? What were the activities of the group? Who were the group leaders? When and how often did they meet? What were their plans? Whom did the leaders report to? They almost broke her when they told her that her father had denounced her as "a Communist and a Godless creature." But in the end, my mother proved a tough nut to crack; through it all she denied belonging to a Communist cell, and, five weeks later, they let her go, but she was not allowed to graduate with her class, which meant no university in Germany would ever accept her. They also denied her the privilege of learning any kind of trade, effectively condemning her to the life of a laborer.

She came home wounded in body, mind, and spirit, but not broken, and, still in her mother's welcoming arms, she accosted her father with a voice that seemed to come from some other world: "Denouncing your daughter to the Gestapo—is that your Christian love that you've got plenty of for strangers but not for your own family except when you want to end up making another baby no one can feed?!"

"How dare you talk to me like that! And what makes you think I denounced you? I denounced no one!"

"You told them I was Godless."

"And so you are! That is no more than the truth—I'm sure they didn't arrest you for that—what did they arrest you for?"

"You don't know why they arrested me?"

"No I don't. They wouldn't tell us. They came here and asked about your character, but they wouldn't tell us why you were in jail or when you were coming home. What did you do?"

"I don't believe you."

"I was here, Ali, your father is telling the truth," said my grandmother."

"You didn't tell them I was a Communist?"

"I did not—are you?"

"I wouldn't tell you if I were. But I can tell you that they are more humane than the Nazis."

"That's only because they're not in power here," said my grandfather, "Hitler and Stalin are both subhuman monsters."

"Maxim, *pahzhalsta*, please be careful," said my grandmother in Russian with a nod towards Ruth, "Remember what happened to the Schreibers."

"What happened to the Schreibers?" asked my mother.

"Robert said something unflattering about Hitler, and Hans repeated it in school. The boy is in an orphanage now. Robert and Hanne were taken away. Nobody knows what's happened to them."

"Oh, my God!" said my mother, the atheist.

When my aunt Maria came home from her secretary job and her Nazi women's group meeting later that evening, the air was still dark in the house. Maria was in high spirits, though, and as everyone was silent around the supper table, she chattered away, "Remember I was telling you about Hilde—well, we finally caught her. She *was* dating a Jew. We really let her have it, we beat her so hard, she literally messed her pants."

"Maria!!" said my grandparents in unison.

"Don't look at me like I'm the criminal. Hilde is. It's racial desecration is what that is, and it's against the law and it's against science, too. We practice eugenics for racial purity and evolution."

"Did you denounce me to government?" asked my mother with carefully managed calm.

"Yes, I did, and it serves you right, too, always pretending that you're the only intelligent person in the whole world."

My mother stood up so violently, her chair fell to the floor with a crash that seemed to cut everyone to the heart. "I'm not living in this house anymore," she said, rushed to her room, and started to pack her clothes into her pillowcases. Her father was not far behind her.

"Where do you think you're going?" he demanded to know.

"None of your business."

"You're still under age and you don't have a job."

"I can always be a prostitute."

That was more than my grandfather could handle, and he left huffing and puffing.

"You have stolen my children from me," he told his wife. "Go and see if you can talk some sense into her."

But nothing doing, my mother left for Berlin on the last evening train.

She did not become a prostitute, at least not until much later. In fact, she got lucky. She stayed with a classmate in Berlin until she got a job: cleaning the library. The head librarian caught her reading Heidegger in the philosophy section instead of washing the floor. He took an interest in her and trained her in all she needed to know to run a library—soon, she was his assistant. "The Nazis won't be in power forever," he told her, "So you should keep up with your studies as much as you can."

And she did, with the discipline of a German farm hand. Soon, she could afford to share an apartment with a couple of friends, two young men, Potus and Ariel. I do not know how Potus got his name: POTUS? I never saw it written, and have only heard my mother's stories about the two young men.

Ariel was named after the role he had played brilliantly sometime before Hitler was installed—afterwards, Shakespeare did not play in German theaters, even though Hitler secretly admired the British; after all, they *had* kicked ass, empire-wise.

Soon my mother was part of a group of young Bohemians and felt completely at home, maybe for the first time in her life. While Hitler was burning books, my mother and her friends were trying to save as many as they could, hiding them in the basement and the attic of the library as well as the attic and the basement of the theater where Potus and Ariel worked. And they read all the forbidden foreign literature they could get their hands on, mostly the work of the American writers of the time, Sinclair Lewis, John Galsworthy, Erskine Caldwell, Henry Miller, Thomas Wolfe, Gertrude Stein, and especially Pearl Buck, who shares a Chinese home town with me.

I imagine my mother doing the Berlin cabaret scene with Potus and Ariel. She never talked to me about what that scene was like, except I heard from her much later, about how intelligent a thing a cabaret was in comparison to what was called a café in America in the fifties.

Potus and Ariel were lovers, and my guess is that the whole thing was a ménage à trois. My aunt Maria, with whom there was a sort of reconciliation about then, told me only one detail about my mother's living arrangements in Berlin: "The lamp that's supposed to hang over the dining room table was not hanging over the dining room table," she said and added, "That was so stupid. You need it over the table—that's why it's there. But your mother's lamp hung around somewhere useless, just to make the statement, 'I'm different. I am not a herd animal, and I am very far from bourgeois.'" My aunt Maria, on the other hand, was so petit bourgeois that I am amazed she even knew the word.

Whatever the relationship was between Potus, Ariel and my mother, it was cut short. Potus was a Jew, both men were gay, and too many people knew it. There had been too many warning incidents to show what the future might hold. And so the time came when Potus and Ariel needed help to smuggle themselves across the border and into Holland, where, as it turned out, they would not be safe either.

I do not know what happened to them, but I know I would have enjoyed meeting them: Potus and Ariel. It is easy to imagine Ariel—for no doubt whoever directed Shakespeare's Tempest at the Berlin State Theater in the late twenties/early thirties had imagination, intelligence, and a budget. No amount of money can make up for stupid casting or lousy acting, but the Berlin State Theater was famous for doing everything brilliantly. So of course I can imagine Ariel, and I am totally in love with him. I imagine that is just how Potus felt about it too. And Potus—what a guy! He is living with Ariel and my mother! Given that scenario, I am 100% certain that Ariel had blonde curly hair, laughing eyes, the face of an angel, and a physique like my mom's, petite, well-proportioned, lithe—except he had male accoutrements, where hers were female.

Ariel, the blithe spirit, so present in the moment that he seems fleeting, barely there, to ordinary mortals—to them, he looks flaky and irresponsible because he does not fear the future or drag the past with him like a ball and chain. And my black-haired, green-eyed mother had begged for bread in the streets of a Siberian village; she had survived a time in Russia when 28 million people were starving to death all around her as her family wandered homeless for years—she saw three of her siblings buried in shallow graves by the side of the road. Then she had to abandon her mother tongue and learn German—that is a trauma not well understood just because it is so deep.

By the time I knew him, my grandfather was kind to all living things, but that represented a sea change: he had been brutal with my aunt Maria and with his wife, my grandmother, while my mother watched from a corner, learning that life gives you a choice: tyrant or victim, and given that choice tyrant is better because anger, while it destroys the mind, is easier to bear than grief which can almost eat away your soul. And then there were those five weeks in Gestapo custody. No doubt about it, there was something dark and smoldering about Ali, something determined, almost manly, something dangerous. Potus had his hands full, all right—Potus who wanted to love both heaven and earth.

When time came for Potus and Ariel to leave Germany, the threesome engaged the aid of a friend who had joined them often at parties, at the cabarets, and at the theater: a young artistic type with connections in high places and with money to burn. His much older sister ran a travel agency, not because she needed to, but because she had been in love with some "very high level Vatican official," who had chosen his religious vocation all rolled up with political aspirations over her, according to family stories. On the rebound, she had then married a real jerk: my uncle Walter, the famous Asshole of Sillenbuch. Because of my uncle Walter, it was a lot more fun for my aunt Editta to take groups of expensive travelers to Italy than to stay home with him. It was she who had arranged to transfer my mother out of Berlin to the ammunitions factory near Dreetz, and it was she, who had arranged for Potus and Ariel to travel to Holland with false papers.

***

Now, here is another family story, which is so outrageous, I hesitate to even mention it, yet I did grow up with it, as it was part of the amazing tapestry of stories each of us is made of, learning only late Penelope's art of unraveling by night what the day has woven. So, here goes nothing:

My father was born when my grandmother's other three children, two sons and a daughter, Editta, were already grown. "Of course," said my mother, "Think. There's a grown up, unmarried, beautiful daughter spending too much time, including evenings, at the Vatican's German Embassy, and, all of a sudden, she and her mother go on vacation together in Milan, Italy, where they've had villas for centuries, and you already know there are strange, underground family connections to the Papacy, also through untold generations…so that your father being born in Italy was not unusual. Lots of German, Protestant Mailänders were born in Italy. So mother and daughter vacationing in Italy was nothing unusual either.

"But here's the thing: mother and daughter go to Italy together, visit some spas along the way, and then, nine months or so later, they come back, and everyone's amazed: your grandmother's had a baby so very very late in life. Whose baby do you think that really was?"

"But, Alice," I said to my mother as I am balancing a spoon full of dripping oatmeal in front of her mouth, "If that's the case, then I'm the granddaughter of some high level Vatican dude pretending to be celibate, and Aunt Editta is really my grandmother, not my aunt?!"

"What do I know?" she said. "All I really know is family rumor and innuendo. Pope Pius XII definitely remained a friend of the family, though distant after he became Pope." That conversation took place in the late nineties in Fairfield, Iowa, when my mother was completely paralyzed and dying.

Decades earlier, waving Potus and Ariel out of sight, my mother and the youngest son of the Mailander family were left alone on the station platform. Then, maybe right then, they fell in love, and by 1939, they were married, World War II had begun, he had been drafted to the Eastern front, and my mother was alone and pregnant with me.

CHAPTER NINE

The Ménage and the Pantry Window

My mother must have been great as an undercover agent—and in spite of her hatred for *Peenemünder Schweinehunde* (hog-dogs), I think she must have loved her job. She was intelligent, creative, and as cold-blooded in the face of danger as her father, though, unlike him, she did not attribute her fearlessness to any kind of divine being or the hope of a glorious afterlife. In addition to getting my grandfather out of East Berlin, I know of one other secret adventure of hers in East Germany, but that time, she was not successful.

On one of her missions, she had managed to track down my aunt Maria's whereabouts, learning that she was in Waldheim, a notorious prison. My mother was somehow able to get our Stuttgart address to Maria. We got a 5x7 page from her once a month after that, and although the prison authorities had often blackened out half the letter, we could read enough to know she was alive and as well as could be expected in an East German prison.

As my mother had predicted when my aunt Maria decided to make her way back to Berlin, when we were about to run from the invading Russian army, she never made it through the Russian lines. Russian soldiers took her, kept her for a week or so to gang rape her repeatedly, and then were getting ready to hang her when she, standing on the bed of a truck with a rope around her neck, begged for her life in Russian, revealing for the first time during her ordeal that she spoke their language like a native. They did not hang her, but instead, like my grandfather, she was tried for espionage and war crimes. She was found guilty and was sentenced to life imprisonment. How my mother found her, I do not know.

Somehow, my mother had also learned that my aunt Maria, along with many other female prisoners, would be transferred by train from Waldheim to Buchenwald. And along with some of her team, all of them dressed up as East German police this time, my mother had devised a plan to intercept this transport of prisoners and to "kidnap" Maria—in an ambulance. But for reasons my mother and her team could never discover, the date of the transport was changed, and they could not find another opportunity to get my aunt Maria out. She was released in 1954 as part of some prisoner exchange program, having served nine years of a life sentence by then.

I still have a hard time getting my mind around the idea that my mother had a career as a secret agent. I mean, spies and related creatures are characters in movies, not in your own family. She was a very scary mom, but also a wonderfully interesting woman. And like any secret agent, she had a cover. When she was not busy traveling behind the iron curtain with false papers, fake uniforms, very real guns, and God only knows what other disguises for what missions and at what cost to her peace of mind, she also had a job helping to set up and run the America House Libraries all over the American sector of Germany. And in that capacity, there were apparently legitimate reasons for traveling to West Berlin—from whence she would vanish into the mysterious East.

The America House Libraries were an important vehicle for the "re-education" and "de-nazification" of Germany. Well, it was probably the other way around: first you de-nazify, and then you re-educate. I have some clue about how you educate, but how you "denazify" is a mystery to me. A short while ago, I saw online that if you are unemployed in Germany, and unemployable due to carrying the burden of a Ph.D., which over-qualifies you to do most anything, you could take a course which would "un-phid" you, so to speak. I got in touch immediately. I asked if you had to take two of their courses if you had two phids, and they said one course would do the trick. However, they would not let me take the course online. Is something seriously physical involved in the process?

Back in the late forties/early fifties, the de-nazification and re-education programs offered plays, films, and discussions by panels of experts—all in the service of getting Germans fit for democracy and teaching them about America, the greatest country in the world, the land of endless opportunity, equality, classlessness, "racial tolerance" (think about the strangeness of that concept), and political as well as religious freedom—all things I admired fervently and believed with all my heart. How I managed this, while, at the same time, believing my grandfather's stories about America as a war criminal and profiteer is one of the mysteries of childhood.

When my mother came home on weekends, she would often bring with her an entourage consisting of various kinds of artists, painters, sculptors, musicians, writers, philosophers, scientists, journalists, actors (and gorgeous actresses), foreign dignitaries, famous folks from America, coffeehouse intellectuals, university professors, scoffers, bums, and poets. One particular group of artists impressed especially my grandfather: a troupe of performers from Karamu House in Cleveland, Ohio. They were touring all over Germany with "Porgy and Bess," and my grandfather loved one of the songs, so much that he learned the English words and could be heard singing, "It ain't necessarily zoh...the sings zat you're liable to read in ze Bible, it ain't necessarily zoh...." His religiosity was apparently a bit more complex than my mother thought.

And while my mother played the part of a French intellectual superstar holding *salons* in between spy missions, I would sit under the table or behind the couch and listen to people talk and talk and talk until late into the night. Sooner or later someone would discover me and I would be sent to my bed, which was the top shelf in a small pantry opposite the kitchen. And next to that shelf, was a small octagonal window, a window to a world beyond imagining, a window we shall return to.

Our railroad flat in the apartment building at number four *Zundel Straße* in between my aunt Editta's house and the ancient farm of an original Sillenbucher, as I have said had three rooms, a kitchen, and a bath. And there was, of course, the coal cellar, where Michael Ende slept. Every apartment in the building also had a small, unheated room in the attic, a room intended for storage, as built-in closets did not exist in Germany back then, so this space was needed for out of season clothes and bedding, suitcases and so on, of which we owned none, so that room stood empty for a short while. But before long, we were housing thirteen human bodies of various sizes in all the available spaces.

That might seem like an excessive number of people to stash into a one-bed-room apartment until you realize that not only was Germany bombed to the ground, it was also the case that:

> Between 1945 and 1950, Europe witnessed the largest episode of forced migration, and perhaps the single greatest movement of population, in human history. Between 12 million and 14 million German-speaking civilians—the overwhelming majority of whom were women, old people, and children under 16—were forcibly ejected from their places of birth....They were deposited among the ruins of Allied-occupied Germany to fend for themselves as best they could. The number who died as a result of starvation, disease, beatings, or outright execution is unknown, but conservative estimates suggest that at least 500,000 people lost their lives in the course of the operation.[23]

Two of these 14 or so million of "displaced persons," the couple from Silesia, the Kellermanns, had the back room, which was indeed intended as a bedroom. Aunt Ruth and my mother (when she was home) shared the living room, which was also the *salon*. My grandmother and grandfather slept in the dining room, which was also my grandmother's sewing room. My sister and I slept in that pantry across from the kitchen, as I said—she had a lower shelf because she tended to sleepwalk or fall out of bed. I slept on an upper shelf, right next to that magical and octagonal window which led out onto the garage roof.

Then, one fine day, a very young woman, Klara, and her baby showed up in amazingly theatrical fashion to be detailed below, and they slept in the attic room. Yes, it was unheated, but German feather duvets are designed for that. And you put a couple of hot water bottles into the bed about an hour before bedtime.

Not long after Klara had settled in, a boy about the same age as Michael Ende showed up out of the blue. The new boy's name was Klaus Bach and he came with a lady whom my sister and I were to call "Aunt Lilo." They had a letter from my mother telling my grandmother to make room for them. So Klaus Bach shared the coal cellar with Michael Ende, and Aunt Lilo slept in the living room with my aunt Ruth. Like Michael Ende, Klaus Bach was a major presence in my life and as different from Michael as night from day. I have no clue at all as to Lilo's background.

---

[23] http://chronicle.com/article/The-European-Atrocity-You/132123/\. This is but one of the many sources for this information.

However, I do suspect that she was one of my mother's lovers. The reason I suspect this is that, one day, when Aunt Lilo was helping me to get dressed, she touched my future breasts in a way I knew instantly to be invasive, and I firmly told her "No." She left me alone after that, and it meant, that somehow, she really no longer had any authority over me at all—though we both pretended.

So when my mother was home, twelve people sat around the table for meals. And then a stranger, beyond mysterious, appeared with a letter from my mother, and he had to remain hidden, so he did not sit at the table with us; instead, his meals were brought to him secretly in his hiding place under the eaves of the roof next to Klara's attic room—he deserves a chapter unto himself.

That was our *ménage*, a survival band, sharing skills, resources, ration tickets, and bright ideas about how more food could be scared up than the ration tickets allowed. And you had to do that: Eisenhower's 400 calories per person per day were half as many calories as the Germans allowed in Hitler's death camps. Some things could be bought and sold on the black market—which puzzled me for a while, since I could see no market that was black anywhere in Sillenbuch or in Stuttgart, but I would to get to know it soon enough.

And here, just off-hand, is a truly ravenous event. One day, when no one seemed around, I climbed on the counter in the kitchen and ate the monthly butter ration for twelve people. I got caught, too, but not before stuffing the last lump into my mouth. As I recall it, the monthly butter ration for twelve people was not more than a stick of butter as it is packaged in America now. Everyone expected me to get very sick. I disappointed them all and still think that butter, European unsalted butter, is the most heavenly food on earth.

Eleven people who were sharing that three-room flat with me, each one of them stuffed to the gills with endless stories, and all serving as a small child's family—all of them were not pleased with me for almost a whole week because butter was such a rare treat. I got lots of lessons regarding the rights of others from everyone except Klara's baby, who did not have an opinion.

Michael Ende and Klaus Bach, the two boys who shared the coal cellar, did not have jobs. They were both still in their teens and worked full-time preparing for high school equivalency exams on their own, which, in those days, were considered the equivalent of two, sometimes three years at Harvard University in any major. Even at that, a German high school graduate would not have had to struggle at Harvard. I am not exaggerating either—I do not think there is an American educator alive who can begin to imagine what what kind of standards are possible in a school system—but more of that another time[24]. But think about it: are there many American educators who are not themselves products of the system?

So, Michael Ende and Klaus Bach were busy, as busy as students are in China today, where no child over the age of twelve gets more than six hours of sleep each night, and you can forget time to play—it breaks the heart of many of their parents to see it, too.

But even though they were busy, both Michael Ende and Klaus Bach made time for me. Michael, as I have said, was made of music. Klaus Bach taught me to play chess and to have useless philosophical discussions, but which nevertheless lingered and lurked in my mind.

Klara stayed home with the baby. Aunt Lilo worked at the Stuttgart branch of the America House Library, and Aunt Ruth got a job as a secretary there also, after my mother became a secret agent—Aunt Ruth's job had been part of the deal when my mother accepted the plea bargain from the Americans. The Kellermanns and my grandparents were retired.

As near as I could figure, Aunt Lilo's function in the household was to make sure my sister and I learned table manners and related rules that seemed unimportant and extremely annoying. To learn the continental style of wielding a fork and a knife (or two forks in the case of fish) required the practice of doing so while a book is held tight to the body under each elbow, leaving only the lower arm free to move. Aunt Lilo was so strict about table manners that it would be a wonder if she had a normal relationship with food.

Aunt Lilo's most important job, however, as I figured out by myself without too much trouble, was as my mother's spy. She was supposed to make sure my grandfather followed the rules of the breadwinner, and the breadwinner, well, that was my mother. Actually, there was only one rule: my sister and I were to get no religious instructions whatsoever from my grandfather or from anyone else. My mother most vehemently did not approve of religion of any kind.

---

[24] See ....#17

Oddly though, Bible reading was OK because the Bible was literature—there was no harm in reading the Bible. I guess my mother did not know that Bible-reading was punishable by death throughout centuries of Church history, and that was because the Bible is, in fact, a dangerous book. In any case, Bible reading was not an issue for her, nor was memorizing Biblical verses or whole passages, as long as there was no religious indoctrination. She trusted Klaus Bach and Aunt Lilo to undermine all Bible readings.

Both Aunt Lilo and Klaus Bach had the German art of scoffing down to a T, and they practiced it avidly on the Bible and on my grandfather himself. They were like two black crows hacking at his religiosity, and, strangely, he really never seemed to mind it at all. He laughed with them and occasionally even added fuel to their fire by quoting Biblical verses that seemed to prove them right. I remember once Klaus Bach said, "It's all just words anyway." My grandfather smiled and said, "Yes, it's all vanity, as Solomon says, all silver threads and golden bowls and they will all be broken."

Now, the reason I know Lilo was a spy is because I overheard several conversations about religion between her and my grandfather since it cannot always be easy to distinguish between a discussion of what a Biblical passage means and religious indoctrination. I thought my grandfather would be upset that there was a spy in our family, but he was not. He just smiled and said, "I certainly know my daughter." If Bible reading was OK, then that was all that mattered to him. He read the Bible all the time—not really out loud, and not silently either, but in a sort of chanting half-voice, and I loved to sit under the table, lean against his knee, and let the cadences of Martin Luther's German or those of the synodal translation into Russian soak into my bones. Often he would read the same passage in both languages back to back several times, and then murmur something about the difficulties of the translation process.

So far as I could tell, we were all very comfortable—considering my age, this probably meant only that I was comfortable. Still there seemed peace in the household—I could tell my grandmother did not like Klaus Bach very much, yet she bore it silently.

But my sister was definitely never happy. Ina had cried all the time on our flight from the Russian army and then on our cross-country trek from the Elbe River to Ursendorf because she had those angry and painful boils all over her body. And then she just got used to crying until crying was her life. Everyone simply accepted it as a fact: "Ina has built her house too close to the water," is the way my grandmother put it. Ina later studied psychology in order to figure out whom to blame for this waterfront residence of hers, in which she had assumed squatters' rights. Last time I talked with her, she was still convinced that she was an unwanted child. It is true that my mother was partial to me until puberty, when she changed her mind, and Ina became the favorite. But before that, I was the golden child, probably because I did not cry all the time and because I made precocious comments at my mother's *salons*.

My mother, however, was rarely home. Even while we were still living in Berlin when Ina was born a year and a half after me, my grandparents were taking care of us because my mother had to work, and my father was away at the front. Our grandparents loved us both equally, of that I am sure. On the other hand, my sister is probably right. If you're running from soldiers and other crazies, you probably do have moments in which you wish you did not also have to carry a screaming child covered with boils oozing green and yellow puss. In that way, my sister was one of the millions of the casualties of war that no one counts.

It is definitely true that I did not want her around. She was a wet blanket, afraid of everything, and I wanted to go on adventures. Also, since she was carried cross-country while rest of us trotted along on our feet like homeless dogs, she did not like my long-distance forays. She wanted to stay home to play with dolls, and I hated dolls. I sometimes made doll clothes for her with my grandmother's help. But that was not really for Ina's sake. I loved the colors, the patterns, and the shape of a sleeve never failed to amaze me when it was cut out of flat fabric and then described a three-dimensional object when it was stitched together.

I was much too young to feel any sort of compassion for my sister and her misery. And she could be exactly as nasty and as wicked as I could be. When she did not get to go with me on some outing, she knew how to push my buttons until I flew into a rage at her, and then she would smile smugly and tell my grandmother I had scratched her. Then I would be punished. Sometimes I did scratch her. Hard enough to draw blood. Sometimes she scratched herself, and then I would get punished for that, too, while she smiled triumphantly, and I learned the political concept of false flag operations. Other than that, my life was great.

***

And now, here is how Klara and her baby arrived out of the blue. Just before Christmas of 1945, not long after my mother had managed to smuggle him out of East Berlin, my grandfather was still sick, but well enough to sit up in bed and make me memorize the "Christmas Story" from the second chapter of Luke, so I could recite it to everyone on Christmas Eve under the Christmas tree. Which I did for seven straight years of my life. I remember once asking my grandfather, "Grandpa, why do I have to memorize stuff from the Bible when all the words are golden bowls and silver threads that will be broken anyways?" He said, "So you'll have something to break."

The Christmas tree, in those days, had real candles on it. And the tinsel, being made of lead, rather than aluminum, had real gravitas and a mysterious way of shimmering darkly among the branches, rather than glittering cheaply like the tangled and weightless modern stuff. I thought I was the only person in the world who remembered tinsel like this, but I recently saw a movie, The Book Thief, and it does a great job with the tinsel.

When I was a child, you never got to see the Christmas tree until Christmas Eve, and waiting for it was excruciating. We could not afford a tree, nor did we have space for one, although we did have a green wreath and four Advent candles on the table. But my Aunt Editta and Uncle Walter, the Asshole of Sillenbuch, always had the best tree whose topmost angel almost touched the ceiling and who cast both shadow and light against it to serve as its meta-halo that moved like a living thing. That angel was the most beautiful thing I had ever seen, but my mother said it was pure kitsch. And if you liked kitsch there was something contemptibly wrong with you, so I never let on how much I loved that angel—not that my secrecy helped all that much. My mother, Klaus Bach and Anni Lilo were the ones whose opinions about kitsch mattered, and although they did not know that I secretly loved the angel, I knew it. So, while loving it, I also (and equally secretly) felt contemptible because of it.

"OK, start at the beginning," said my grandfather to me one day in the winter of 1945. And I began, "'And it came to pass in those days that a decree went out from Caesar Augustus,' Grandpa, who's Caesar

Augustus; do we know him?"

"Right now," said my grandfather, "Caesar Augustus happens to be the president of America, his name is Harry Truman, and his soldiers are all around us, as you can see for yourself, just as they were in ancient Israel—things, my Rabbit, don't change all that much. I want you to remember that."

"Yes, Grandpa. But Grandpa, this is now, and God wrote the Bible a million trillion years ago."

"No, Rabbit, the story you are memorizing happened only about 2000 years ago, but it is a story for all time. It's a story that is happening right now, December first 1945, and right here at Friedrich Zundel Street Number Four, Apartment 2, in Stuttgart, Sillenbuch."

"The exact same story, Grandpa?"

"Yes, Rabbit, the same exact story."

"You mean that exact same story has been happening all over the world for 2000 years?"

"Yes, my Rabbit—that's it, and for all Eternity as well."

"Grandpa, you're being silly. That's not even possible."

"Anything is possible, Rabbit, and anything means anything. What does anything mean?"

"Anything means anything, Grandpa."

"Good."

"But Grandpa, if this story is happening all over all the time, then how could any other story be happening, and I know for a fact that there's a million trillion stories."

"Yes, that is a fact, Rabbit—in fact, there's more than a million trillion, there's no end to the number of stories."

"But Grandpa, if there's so many stories, then how could there ever be enough space in the world for all of them to be happening at the same time, and if there's so many stories, how can there be only one story that's for all time?"

"All stories begin with the birth of light, Rabbit, you'll understand it all someday when you're bigger. Do what Mary did with words. Now again let's take it from the top."

"Do what Mary did with words" actually turned out to be more than just a cop-out on my grandfather's part every time he could not or did not want to answer a question. "Do what Mary did" was a constant refrain of his. And here is where it came from: His quotes from the Bible were often his own translations into German from Russian or into Russian from German, and then he also considered what things would be if they were said in Bashkir, Kasakh, or Kyrgyse, as these were all places he had lived. And in that way, my grandfather's Bible became entirely his own.

What Mary did according to most English Bible translations is that "she kept these things and pondered them in her heart." In Luther's German, she did not keep things; instead, she kept words. But by the time my grandfather got through translating into this and out of that, "Do what Mary did" became "Guard these words in your heart, give truth to them and life, give them paths to travel until they become spirit."

So I was memorizing the Christmas Story as my grandfather was recovering from hunger typhus, and just when I got to the words, "… for there was no room at the inn," there was a knock at our apartment door. "Can I go see who it is, Grandpa?"

"Run along, Rabbit," he said, "And bring me a full report."

There were often knocks at the door. Sometimes it was somebody who needed a place to sleep out of the cold, but usually it was somebody who said he or she had not eaten anything for three days, did we have a crust of bread or something, anything…anything. My grandparents never said 'no' to a hungry person—after all, they had survived World War I and the Russian Revolution because kind people had not neglected them when they escaped from Siberia and walked through Russia at a time when 28 million people starved to death all around them. There are better ways to manage a planet's population, I am sure.

So they did not say, 'no,' even if we were having stale bread soup, which I thought really embarrassing to serve to guests, especially since guests were God according to both my grandparents. It is just basically stale, moldy bread boiled in water. If we were lucky, there would be an onion to help hide the taste—extra salt helped also. Bread soup is the most disgusting stuff in the entire universe—crocodile snot would be more appetizing, and I sincerely hope and pray neither I nor anyone else ever has to eat it again, though the probability is not good, as I see it at the moment.

But it did not matter to my grandparents what we were having, if someone said they were hungry, they were invited. If lunch or supper was a ways off, my grandfather would read the Bible to them, or they would swap stories that would mostly be about the miraculous ways everybody had survived the biggest war in history, who the political forces were that made it all happen, and the post-war atrocities of Eisenhower. Sometimes it would turn into a contest about who had suffered most profoundly or who had lost the biggest kingdom. And then, when the meal was ready, my grandfather would thank God (the Guest) for whatever we had to swallow that day.

So that day, when I had just recited the passage from Luke, "…for there was no room at the inn," and there was a knock at the door, I ran to see who it was. My grandmother was just opening it, and I snuggled under her left arm, looking up expectantly. A handsome young man stood there and said, "*Guten Abend, gnädige Frau...* my name is Wagner, Joseph Wagner. I am asking for my wife and newborn baby; they need a place to sleep for the night. I've been all up and down every street in the village. I can survive the night out there, but I'm not sure they can, and there's no room at the inn …"

I bolted and ran back to my grandfather's room. "Grandpa, Grandpa, it's Joseph and there's no room at the inn and he wants a place for his wife and baby and…." That is as far as I got, before my grandmother and Mr. Joseph Wagner came into the room, and my grandmother formally introduced him to my grandfather. I was jumping up and down, too excited to hear what was being said, and before I knew it, my grandmother and Aunt Kellermann had thrown on their coats to go with Mr. Wagner to get his wife and baby, whom he had left at the inn's dining room.

In fiction, a coincidence like this would never fly. In life, stranger things than this have happened; but I suppose even swearing here that Klara and Gaby really did come to us exactly like this would not make any doubter believe. My grandfather, on the other hand, did not seem overly surprised, though he did say, "Well, my Rabbit, that is pretty amazing. That is even more amazing than I usually expect God's ways to be…Herr Wagner knocked at the door, just as you were saying there was no room at the inn. This kind of thing, when things kind of match up without you planning it, is called a coincidence. What is it called, Rabbit?"

"It's called a coincidence, Grandpa."

"Very often a coincidence is a sign from God, in fact, you'll find that as you get older, there are more and more coincidences made by the life of intelligence itself—and didn't we have an amazing coincidence just some weeks ago? Do you remember?"

Of course, I remembered.

"Tell me what you remember, Rabbit—my memory is just about gone," said my grandfather.

"Grandpa, that was so amazing how could you ever forget? We got that care package from Canada."

"So—we get lots of care packages—well, not exactly lots, but still, a lot."

"The one from Canada. Grandpa, you're just pretending you don't remember."

"You're getting good, Rabbit—how could you tell this time?"

Care packages came from America and Canada. But in either case, each item inside the care packages was always wrapped separately in newspaper, and we always un-wrapped everything very carefully so as not to tear the paper. Then, when my mother came home, she would read all the newspapers we had saved for her. Sometimes she would translate a story for us, but more likely than not, a story would leave us hanging because it would be continued on another page which was probably in a care package sent to the Schmidt family in Munich or Frankfurt, and then my grandfather and I would have to invent our own endings. We would look at the English words and laugh about their strangeness when we tried to pronounce them according to German or Russian rules of pronunciation, and sometimes those weird sounds would help us guess at the most unexpected endings.

After my mother was done reading, my grandfather would cut up the paper into small pieces to use for toilet paper. If you crumple up the paper and then pull its edges up and down in opposite directions, it becomes softer and more absorbent. That part was my job. That one time, when the care package arrived, my mother happened to be home, which was another coincidence. And while she was reading the newspapers, she suddenly said, "Mama, Papa, this is absolutely unbelievable—look, there's a poem here by Lena Zeitner—it has to be our Lena." The newspaper came from a small town in the Canadian province of Saskatchewan, and my mother wrote to the newspaper in that town.

And that is how my family was able to find my Great Uncle Sasha and his family after losing track of them during the last terrible years of war and famine in Siberia and Russia.

When my grandmother and Aunt Kellermann came back that evening so close to Christmas with Joseph Wagner and his wife and baby, I was a little disappointed when the mother's name was Klara, rather than Mary, and the baby's name was Gaby. Could it not at least have been a boy? But my grandfather said the names did not matter and neither did the gender, the names were always changing along with the languages and other incidental details—the Bible made it very clear that to turn them away, to turn any woman and baby away, is very exactly the same as turning away the woman and the baby in the story I was memorizing.

And so that is how Klara and Gaby came to stay with us, not just for a night, but for six years. As it turned out, Joseph and Klara were not married, and this had been why a neighboring village had kicked her and her new-born baby out into the cold, but my grandfather said that they were married in God's eyes, he was sure of that, let the neighbors say what they pleased, he would remind them that Mary and Joseph in the Christmas story were not married either—they were only betrothed.

I did not know what any of that meant, and any time I had questions my grandfather did not want to answer or could not answer, he would say either, "Do what Mary did with words," or "This is a question for the women," and sometimes a question was important enough to wait for my mother to come home, and of course, any question that had to wait like that, tended to grow in importance.

Klara and the baby slept in the garret room upstairs under the roof. Joseph stayed the first night, but after that, he lived somewhere else and came to visit regularly for a year or two, but then he just quit showing up. Klara and the baby were doing just fine by then, and eventually, she did find a good husband who was also a kind father for Gaby. But Joseph stayed around long enough to show me how to weave baskets and mats out of straw or willow branches or cattail leaves. He was an artist at it. And Klara was a great addition to our survival band because she was Swabian: she spoke the local dialect, and so she was a huge help in the food department (in more ways than one, as we shall see) because the locals did not want to sell what food they had to foreign refugees like us who spoke some weird and strange form of German. Klara took over the kitchen, which freed my grandmother to do more sewing for a little extra income or, sometimes, black market food, rather than money.

Now, before closing and saving this chapter, there is something else to mention about the pantry and the shelf that served as my bedroom and bed. It was the best possible space the gods could have devised to be my space for sleep and dreams, because, as I mentioned above, that shelf was next to a very small octagonal window. It was just big enough for me to wriggle through and arrive on the garage roof under the sky with its infinite stars. No streetlights until the German economic miracle brought them back a little later. This extra darkness was a special gift to me that made the stars bigger, brighter, and far more numerous as well as miraculous.

And that octagonal window was every bit as good as the famous wardrobe with the witch and the lion in it, if not better. In fact, for sure better. For one thing, it was real. You could in fact climb over the garage roof and down to the top of a wall that went across the back of the farm next door and from there to the ground via a small tree for nighttime adventures in the village or the surrounding fields and woods. Or you could lie on your back on the garage roof and listen to the stars make their music. Or do with words what Mary did. And no implicit racism, fascism, and stupid religiosity informed my garage roof, while Narnia suffers from them all.

CHAPTER TEN

Brother Bühler's Spit

Aunt Lilo's and Klaus Bach's black-crow-style decimation of my grandfather's religiosity was strangely helped along by one of his friends, Brother Bühler. Brother Bühler was the pastor of a Baptist Church my grandparents attended occasionally on the West Side of Stuttgart. I never went because that would have bent my mother out of shape, but Brother Bühler came calling on my grandfather quite often for a time, and Ina and I dreaded his visits. He liked for us to sit on his lap, and there was something cloying about it that made us call him "Uncle Hold-Me-Tight" behind his back—not that he ever went too far by anyone's standards, but he was nevertheless an unpleasant experience for my sister and me.

One time, when my grandfather was telling one of his stories about Siberia, Brother Bühler took issue with him at a point in the story where the Zeitner boys added some Arabic to their vocabulary, Brother Bühler asked, "Didn't you feel like a traitor to Our Lord?"

"Why would I?" asked Grandpa, genuinely surprised.

Well, you're talking about Allah instead of our Christian God."

"It's just the Arabic word for God. I also use the German word and the Russian one—how does any of that make me a traitor? 'Allah Hafiz' just means 'God keep you in His care'."

"Well, but they are Muslims, not Christians."

"The word 'Muslim,'" explained Grandpa, "Means 'one who surrenders to God.' To a Mohammedan, an animal is a perfect Muslim because an animal's surrender to God is perfect."

"This has nothing to do with animals. Their God is not our God."

"Their God is the God of Abraham, same as ours."

"Is that a fact? The God of Abraham?"

"It is a fact," said my Grandfather.

"But they don't believe in Jesus Christ." Brother Bühler was determined to win this argument one way or another.

"They believe He is a great prophet," said my grandfather.

"Well, that's not exactly the same thing as accepting Him as your Savior, is it?"

(He didn't become a 'personal' Savior until American fundamentalists personalized him in their own image).

"Jesus said, 'not only those who have called me Lord, but those who have done my Father's will'," answered my grandfather patiently.

"I think you're misquoting the words of our Lord," said Brother Bühler, "The text is, 'Not everyone who says to me, Lord, Lord will enter the kingdom of heaven, but only he who does the will of my Father who is in heaven.' Matthew 7:21."

"Maybe we are reading different translations," said my grandfather.

Brother Bühler was getting a little hot. "It doesn't make any difference about that text anyway because Jesus said very clearly, 'I am the way and the truth and the life. No man comes to the Father except through me.' John 14:6."

"Well," said my grandfather, "I've been puzzling about that. What exactly did He say? Our Lord spoke Aramaic. I know Russian and I know German. I learned Bashkiri pretty well and also one of the Kazakh dialects and some Kirghiz. Not all languages distinguish between a way, the way, and just plain old way. And then, what did He mean when He said 'I and Me?' Certainly he didn't mean his flesh and bones. He would have meant the Christ who is one with the Father, John 14:10, and the Holy Spirit, rather than the man, Jesus, and in that case 'I am way and truth and life is just as....'"

"Brother Zeitner, Brother Zeitner" interrupted Brother Bühler, "I do believe you are on very dangerous ground here. In the first place, you are supposed to accept on faith, you're not supposed to puzzle."

"Puzzling is prayer to me," said Grandpa, "Don't you ever ask for clarity and understanding?"

"I do, I certainly do, Brother Zeitner, but I don't doubt that He is the Way."

"I don't doubt it either, Brother Bühler, I know it for a fact, but I do think it's possible by the infinite grace of God to find the Way without calling it by the name we use—I lived among the Bashkirs and have found them to be a God-fearing people."

"It was your duty to bring them to Christ, Brother Zeitner," said Brother Bühler."

"Indeed it was," said my grandfather, "And I did my duty, but I can't fix what isn't broke."

"Well, they're not following the Bible in all its detail."

"I don't follow the Bible in all its detail either, Brother Bühler."

Completely outraged, Brother Bühler, loosened his tie and unbuttoned his shirt and blurted out, "That...that...that is...that is sacrilege! You can't just pick and choose which parts to follow!!"

"Well," said my grandfather, "the Bible sanctions genocide, slavery, and rape. And child abuse," he added as an afterthought. I can't go along with those things."

"You just show me where the Bible says these things," said the Brother with drops of his spit accompanying his words as they flew out into the room. I wiped my face.

My grandfather started to leaf through his large print Bible, and I could see he would really find what he was looking for, so I wriggled out of Brother Bühler's hold and asked to go out and play.

"That's a good idea, Rabbit, you and Ina go play, what I'll read isn't for children."

CHAPTER ELEVEN

Klaus Bach

You could just talk to Michael Ende and feel normal, but Klaus Bach was not like that. I knew there was something wrong with Klaus Bach the minute he showed up with Aunt Lilo and a letter from my mother. For one thing, his skin was way too white. And then, he did not look like a sixteen-year-old boy; he looked like a grown up, a miserable grown up—the kind of person that can bring darkness into a sunny room and kill all the laughter.

The day after he came, he was sitting at the table reading, and my grandfather was just being nice and asked, "What are you learning from that book?" He was always interested in what people were learning from any book that was not the Bible.

Klaus Bach came out of that book like a cold demon and hissed, "Englishsh. So I can get out offf Gerrmany."

It hurt to hear him say it like that, and I could tell that everyone else in the room felt the pain of it too.

Often he would come home late, usually after my bedtime, and sometimes he would be gone for days and nights together. Other times, he was around on a Sunday or he would come home earlier than usual, and then he would teach me how to play chess.

Klara and my grandmother and Aunt Kellermann and Aunt Lilo said they did not have time for games. But I taught my grandfather and Uncle Kellermann how to play and was getting good enough to beat both of them sometimes. Michael Ende already knew the game, and I could sometimes get close to beating him maybe. But I could never beat Klaus Bach, and it was not just a matter of skill—he did not play fair. When it was his turn, I was not allowed to talk, so he could think. But when it was my turn, he would ask the dumbest questions like, "How do you know you have a soul?"

"How could you not know?"

"Well, what is it you think I mean when I say 'soul'?"

"When I close my eyes and put my hands over my ears and wait to see what will happen, the waiting is alive and just waiting in my heart, and that's my soul, so there."

"It's your move."

"What did you move last?"

"You should pay attention."

"Well, I would if you didn't ask dumb questions."

"It's not a dumb question. I moved my rook."

"It is so. Everybody that's alive knows it.

"Do they?"

"Well, of course. How can you be alive and not know it?"

"How can you know anything about what other people know or don't know? You can't possibly know what I'm thinking or even if I'm thinking."

"I've seen lots of dead people. They don't look alive and they don't look like they're thinking, but you do."

"Do you think those dead people know they're dead?"

"If they know they're dead, then they're not really dead."

"So that waiting-that's-alive-and-just-waiting that they had inside their body when it was alive, what happened to that?"

I was stumped. And not only that, I got stumped all over again every time I remembered the question. I got so I liked the feeling of being stumped. In fact, that is the only reason I even remember this question after more than sixty years. What is there after a question that has no answer? There is the waiting that is alive and just waiting.

"Well?"

"Well, what?"

"What happens to the waiting-that's-alive-and-just- waiting when you die?"

"How could I know till I die?"

"It's your move and your time is almost up. Any waiting that's alive and just waiting stops when you fall asleep, doesn't it?"

"So?"

Although I got so I liked what Klara called my useless conversations with Klaus Bach (except when it made me lose chess games), he got under my skin and on my nerves sometimes, and worse, seriously into my hair. Sometimes he was mean in a weird way, and before you knew it, he got you to be mean right back. Then you could see that he really liked it that he had made you be mean, which made you feel like being even meaner. My sister could be like that too.

One day when he had really made me feel murderous, I devised an evil plan for revenge and spent a large part of the afternoon chewing up a bunch of my grandfather's used up blotting paper with the help of my best friend, Inge Breuniger, the daughter of Sillenbuch's only hairdresser.

Since blotting paper has become extinct, I should explain that this was very absorbent thick paper, thicker and stiffer than a paper towel, and when you had written something and wanted the ink to dry quickly, you could press the blotting paper down over the writing to absorb the wet ink—the writing would still be there, but you could always tell blotted writing from naturally dried writing. Anyway, Inge and I chewed up a lot of blotting paper to make it into a pulp—it is a wonder we did not swallow enough of the ink the paper had soaked up to make us sick. Then, for good measure, we soaked that quantity of chewed-up blotting paper in more ink we had managed to steal, and then all of that slimy, inky stuff went into Klaus Bach's shoes.

Everybody got really mad at me—and everybody was a lot of people in that small apartment. I could not figure out how they all knew I was the one who had done it. My sister always ratted on me, so Inge and I had done our chewing up of blotting paper in the neighbor's hayloft to make sure nobody but the barn swallows saw us doing all that prodigious chewing and spitting.

The next day my grandfather went for a walk with me to one of the most beautiful places I have seen on this earth—part of it was that forest of oaks I have mentioned—oaks that were each more than five centuries old and some were maybe a thousand years old. At the southern edge of the oak forest and down a slope, there flowed a brook with wildflowers all along its banks, and pollard willows. Their big heads looked as old as the oaks, but of course, willows do not live that long. Still, they were old for willows, old enough so that many of them were either hollow or had little gardens of grass and wildflowers in their crowns where the wood had rotted to form rich soil to which birds and the wind brought seeds. Once, I climbed into one of those small, wild gardens and found a magpie's nest full of all the shiny things she had stolen, including a ring with a real emerald, and my grandfather sent Michael Ende to sell it on the black market for food and firewood.

And on the eastern edge of this oak forest, there were sloe thickets. Sloes are late-ripening, almost black berries with silver frosting on them. My grandmother made medicine and liqueur from them. They grow on thorny bushes that form large, irregular clumps of interpenetrating spheres to look like abstract topiary. In winter they are silver grey with silver lichen on the branches, lichen which looks like strange flowers clinging to the bark. In spring a white veil of flowers covers the thorny, tangled branches, and in summer the bushes looked like big spheres covered with green-leaf damask. The clumps of bushes are so thick and tangled as to be entirely impenetrable to creatures the size of humans, even those as small as I was then. But if you went close to the bushes in summer and peeked through their leafy covering, you could see that birds and rabbits and all kinds of other small creatures called that silvery network of branches within a green summer skin their world.

These clumps of bushes covered a vast territory and formed a natural maze, although there was a central path straight through them that led to the neighboring village. People never strayed from the central path because they were afraid of losing their way in that maze of thorny thickets, but I knew all the nooks and crannies in it by heart.

And part of the amazing magic of the whole place was this: The oaks and the sloe bushes seemed almost images one of the other: the sloes were a miniature version of the world that the oaks made. White owls and ravens flew through the oaks, just as wrens and finches flew through the sloe thickets. Rabbits sat under a sloe bush just as my grandfather and I sat under an oak on soft moss to talk about Klaus Bach.

And it seemed to me that someone big was looking through the oak leaves that made the green skin of our world in just the same way as I looked into the smaller world of the sloe bushes.

"You should be especially patient and kind with Klaus Bach because his life has been much too difficult for any human being to bear, my Rabbit. It is a miracle that he is even alive."

"What happened to him, Grandpa?"

"I think maybe you are a little young to understand; in fact, it seems even I am too young to understand, so you'll just have to take my word for it."

"I am not too young to understand—did he almost get killed in the war?"

"It was much worse than that, Rabbit."

"If you tell me, I promise never to be mean to him again."

"Do you really think you can keep a promise like that?"

"Yes, I can, and you know it, Grandpa—I've kept all my promises to you."

"Yes, Rabbit, you have, but this promise will be much harder to keep than any of the others so far."

"Let me try, Grandpa, please?"

"Well…well…all right, I'll tell you, but you have to promise more things."

"Sure."

"Don't say, 'sure,' till you know what they are. You have to promise never to tell Klaus Bach you know his story."

"OK."

"It will be difficult. You'll want to ask him questions. You'll want him to know that you know. You'll think he'll be your friend if you tell him you know—even then don't tell him. Sometimes you'll think if you tell him, you'll never lose another chess game. It will be a really difficult promise. Can you keep such a difficult promise?"

"Yes, Grandpa."

"You also have to promise you'll tell none of the women in our house that you know—because they'll want to chop my head off for telling you. But you will hear about these things sooner or later—it's best you hear it from me."

"Can I tell Uncle Kellermann and Michael Ende?"

"You can't tell anyone at all; you can talk to me about it when no one else is around. But you can't talk to anyone else about this. No one else means?"

"No-one-else-but-WHY, Grandpa? If it really happened to him, why does it have to be such a big secret?"

"Because he is not finished being in pain about it, and he wants that pain to be his alone for now. In a way, it's all he has. That's one of the reasons I'm not sure it's wise to tell you. On the other hand, if you knew, maybe you would not put chewed up blotting paper and ink in his shoes. His story is really the most terrible story that I have ever heard in all my life, and I have seen two world wars, a revolution, and a couple of famines. So can you promise to keep his story a secret?"

"OK, I promise I will keep his story a secret from everybody except you."

"God help me," my grandfather sighed, and said it again, "God help me," and then he told me the story of Klaus Bach:

"Evil men came to his home in the middle of the night and took him and his parents to a terrible place, a killing place, and there they killed his mother and his father and made him watch. They didn't even let him close his eyes. He was only thirteen years old, but he wished that they had killed him too. Instead, they made him work hard and for too many hours each day in a cruel and dark factory underground for three long years. For three long years he never saw the sun, never even saw the sky. And because they made him work so hard and because they didn't give him enough food or sleep, he stopped growing. And then, after three years were gone, they could see that he was not producing enough work for the little bit of food they gave him no matter how much they beat him. So they sent him, and many others like him, to another place where they were going to kill them all."

My grandfather sighed and was silent for a whole minute. I looked at the moss growing between the oak tree roots, as if moss was all there was to see in the world, and yet I did not really see it, but was alive and just waiting. Then he continued:

"The way to the killing place was very long. They had to walk many hours to get to the train that would take them the rest of the way.

"I would have run away, Grandpa."

"They couldn't because there were men with guns making sure they couldn't. But then, before they got to that train, Klaus Bach's life was saved by an attack out of the air. Your grandmother tells me you were attacked from the air in that same way. Do you remember?"

"Yes, Grandpa, an airplane that had a glass bubble underneath, and there was man inside the bubble and he had a gun and he tried to kill us."

"There were many such planes and such men that attacked the boys and girls Klaus Bach was walking with, and they all ran for cover, like you and your grandmother were running to find somewhere to hide. Do you remember?"

"Yes, Grandpa, we crawled under some hazel nut bushes, and Grandma asked God not to let the man in the glass bubble see which way we were crawling."

"Well, Klaus Bach jumped into a ditch full of water. You know where the cattails grow on the edge of the swamp?

"Yes, Grandpa."

"The water was like that—very black. And very cold. It was February. Klaus Bach stayed under that water until the attack was over, and all the boys and girls who could be found and who could still walk had left."

"Grandpa, how could he breathe under the water?" I remembered my first swimming lesson that gave me the name "Rabbit."

"He breathed through a hollow reed, said my grandfather and continued, "I'll show you sometime."

"When he thought it was safe to come out of the water, Klaus Bach saw some of his friends dead and dying on the road. And there was nothing he could do to help any of them. He was shivering so violently from the cold water that he couldn't even talk. None of the other boys and girls who were still alive could walk, and so he left them there. He would have liked to stay with them, but there was nothing he could do, it was too dangerous, and he wanted to live. He found a haystack where he got dry and warm—you know how warm a haystack can be. He stayed there all night."

"Grandpa, why didn't Klaus Bach just go to find his relatives?"

"Ordinarily that might have worked, Rabbit, but not in this case. The men who had killed his parents and who were going to kill him and his friends—those men wanted to kill all the Jews in the world. And these men owned the government of Germany. The army obeyed them, and the police obeyed them...."

"Some Jews don't look very Jewish, but for Klaus Bach there would have been nowhere to run. Klaus Bach looks Jewish. There is no way not to see that. And Klaus Bach had no way of knowing if any of his relatives were still alive. Maybe the men who killed his parents had also killed his relatives."

"Grandpa, what are Jews and why did those men want to kill them?"

"The Jews are the people of ancient Israel. They are the people who wrote the Old Testament of the Bible. And Jesus of the New Testament was a Jew. They are a great people, and your mother tells me that Germany has killed millions of innocent Jews for no reason at all. I knew they were being sent away to camps, but I did not know they were being killed and I didn't know there were millions. I cannot understand it, Rabbit. I have asked God to explain it to me. Is it that our world has become so evil that crucifying one man is not enough—we have to crucify millions?"

"I don't understand, Grandpa."

"Neither do I. But we should never give up trying to understand."

"What happened to Klaus Bach after that?"

"In the morning, a big dog found him and barked at him and then the dog went to get his mistress. Klaus Bach was sick with shock and with fever, but this lady had a kind heart. She nursed him. Even so, he almost died of pneumonia. By the time he was well again, the war was over, and so was winter, he was sixteen years old and he got to Stuttgart somehow. And he decided to learn English as fast as possible and leave Germany forever. He'll go to America as soon as he passes his high school exams. Your mother met him in the library because he stayed there all day long to study and she caught him sleeping there as well because he didn't have a home to go to. So she sent him to live with us until he can pass his exams.

"Now do you see why you should give him extra kindness?"

"No, Grandpa."

"Why not? I made everything very clear. Explain it to me, Rabbit."

"It isn't my fault that terrible things happened to him."

"Well, but you did promise you would never be mean to him again. Will you keep your promise?"

"Yes, Grandpa. And Grandpa, do you think he will ever finish being in pain about it?"

"I don't know, Rabbit. Maybe his whole life will be unhappy because of the cruelty of the people who killed his parents and who made him suffer so much. And maybe he will create a lot of unhappiness for the people around him. A lot will depend on how kind people are to him, whether his pain is their fault or not. Kindness isn't like money, you know—you don't wait for someone to earn kindness and you don't refuse to give it just because someone else's need is not your fault."

"Why are there wars, Grandpa?"

"Because some people make a lot of money in a war."

"That doesn't make any sense, Grandpa. How can you make money killing people?"

"Well, somebody has to make the guns and the bombs and the air planes and the bullets and the tanks and so on. And then they sell all those things and make money."

"But Grandpa, that still doesn't make any sense."

"Why not? It makes perfect sense to me."

"Well, what if they make a lot of guns, and nobody buys them—then there wouldn't be a war, right?"

"Yes, I see what you mean. It gets complicated."

"Can you explain it, please, Grandpa?"

"I think you're too young to understand."

"I don't like it when you say that."

"I'm sorry, Rabbit. I'll think about it and I'll try to find a way to explain it. War crimes are not easy to explain."

"Promise not to forget."

"OK, my Rabbit, I promise."

"Grandpa, why does Klaus Bach want to leave Germany?"

"Because the people who were so cruel to him were Germans."

"But all Germans aren't like that, Grandpa."

"Klaus Bach really doesn't know that, and when you put chewed up blotting paper and ink in his shoes, he had no reason to feel that you aren't like that."

"But putting chewed up blotting paper and ink in his shoes isn't the same as killing his parents."

"No, it isn't. But it comes from the same impulse."

"What's an impulse?"

"The thing inside you that made you want to get even with him. You are still a child, and so your impulses to hurt others are still small. I'm sure you don't want to grow up to be like the people who killed his parents."

"But Grandpa, the thing that made me want to put chewed up blotting paper and ink in his shoes was Klaus Bach—he was mean, and he wasn't playing fair, and then he said I was stupid for losing the game."

"Well, my Rabbit, there are some things that take a long, long life to understand, and this is one of them. I saw how he made you angry and took pleasure in it. It was unkind of him to do that. But he is not the one who got angry enough to hurt somebody—you are."

"But I couldn't help it, Grandpa, and it hurt me when he said I was stupid."

"Yes, I could see that, but it must have taken you a very long time to chew up the blotting paper—by the time you finished, you could help it, and when he said you were stupid, you didn't have to believe it."

"I still think he had it coming, Grandpa."

"Well, that's why I said that some things take a very long life to learn, and this is one of them. Neither you nor Klaus Bach has had that much time. So I can't really blame either one of you. But I expect you to be stronger than I expect him to be, even though he is older. Your life has not been as terrible as his has been. One of the people who was cruel to him in the factory was a man he'd known when he was growing up. His family had bought vegetables from that man—can you even imagine such a thing?"

"Yes, Grandpa."

"You can? You can imagine such a thing?"

"Well, yes, Grandpa, you just told me, so now I can."

My grandfather was silent for a very long time. Then he said, "You might forget that we had this conversation, Rabbit. When you get to be old, you will find that your memory goes—although another kind of remembering gets better and better. I want you to remember this conversation, and so I'm going to tell you something to make sure you can't forget. I'll remind you now and then.

"You know how much I love the Bible. You also know that your mother thinks it's stupid to be reading the Bible all the time. And you know what? She's right. But so am I. There are things in the Bible that seemed dead wrong to me when I was young, and they made sense when I got older. And there are also things in the Bible that will never make sense as long as I live. For instance, the Bible says it's OK to own slaves. That can never be right."

"What are slaves, Grandpa?"

"Klaus Bach was a slave in the underground factory. He had to work for no pay and he couldn't run away. It is very wrong to do this to people even if the Bible says it's OK. So even if it's the Bible, you can't just believe everything it says. And you can't pick and choose either. So the Bible has taught me to believe everything and nothing. You still have to think about it and make your own decisions. What do you have to do?"

"Think about it and make your own decisions, Grandpa."

"Good. There is something Jesus said that never made any sense to me, and it still doesn't, but I can see the time coming when it will. I can feel it coming like something you forgot that's vaguely coming back. Jesus said if someone slaps you across the face, you should turn the other cheek. Does that make any sense to you?"

"No, Grandpa."

"OK, let me make sure you understand what the words say. If Inge Breuninger slaps you across the face, what would you do?"

"I'd punch her in the nose, Grandpa."

"Very good. Now, what Jesus seems to be saying is that if she slapped the left side of your face, you should turn the right side to her, so she can slap you again. Does that make any sense?"

"No, Grandpa, it's the dumbest thing I ever heard."

"Good, that's just how I feel about it too. So, 'Turn the other cheek' can't mean 'Invite that person to do it to you again.' If that's what it means, then Jesus is an idiot. If that's what it means then what is Jesus?"

"Jesus is an idiot, Grandpa."

"Very Good. Remember that. I'll remind you from time to time. But what else could 'turn the other cheek' mean? Do have any ideas?"

"No, Grandpa, do you?"

"No, but like I said, I can feel an answer coming. Or, maybe, it's a translation problem. Any way, here's our golden opportunity to practice faith and patience and doing with words what Mary did. It has happened that I was the one who turned out to be the idiot. Never be afraid of being an idiot, Rabbit. And now I think we should take a shortcut through the hops field and get a beer."

"Grandpa, you know I hate beer."

"Well, if you really insist, my Rabbit, I'll get you a lemon soda."

CHAPTER TWELVE

The Geese and the Shepherd

Late in February of 1946 my grandfather took me downtown to get weighed. "Is it like Mary and Joseph going to Bethlehem to get weighed?"

"Yes, Rabbit, something like that—except they got taxed not weighed, but, yes, in essence it's the same thing. One way or another Caesar Augustus wants to keep track of how rich you are."

I was going to be six years old by the end of March, the German school year began then, and it was time for me to go to school.

Here is the reason I had to get myself officially weighed: this was the first year after the war that schools were to be in session once again—obviously, school is not possible if you are drafting 12-year old boys into combat zones while also getting carpet bombed and invaded from all sides. But all that was over now, and life had to get back to normal. Yet, due to Eisenhower's policies, there were too many children who still did not have enough to eat and were therefore too weak to go to school. And so, a decree went out that a child had to have a certain body weight in relation to age and height before being allowed to enter school.

I flunked the weigh-in and thus, according to my grandfather, was given the gift of another year of glorious freedom for which I was to thank God. In my opinion, I was not weak, just small for my age and had gotten plenty of exercise since I was roaming all over the countryside most days and practicing the fine art of tree-climbing as I went. There also was more food than the ration tickets allowed for reasons soon to be confessed. But, my opinion notwithstanding, when I got to America at age twelve, I was severely undernourished in a doctor's opinion and my growth had been stunted. Imagine: I could have had stature! And with stature, you can be elegant. If you are too short…well, "cute" is the best you can hope for.

That evening of the weigh-in, the whole *ménage*, except for my mother who was out of town on some secret mission, was helping me to celebrate my extra year of sweet liberty (*dolce far niente*, as my other grandmother put it in Italian), and we were all singing a German folk song about the gusto and freedom of a gypsy's life at the top of our lungs and to the accompaniment of Michael's lute. Klaus Bach, of course, did not sing. He sneered. For he was an intellectual and disdained such populist entertainment as folk songs. The song ended as the farmer's wife from next door called on us.

This was a miracle, according to my grandfather. As far as the local Swabians were concerned, we were foreigners and therefore hated. Germany had been a unified country only since 1871, and so while we may all have seemed like cookie-cutter Germans to the rest of the world in 1945, seventy-five odd years had not been enough to make us all Germans together. We were Swabians, Hessians, Saxonians, Westphalians, Bavarians, Rhinelanders, Thuringians, Pomeranians and so on. (The latter, obviously, are not a breed of dogs in this case.) Note in this context that Germany is just slightly smaller than Montana.

Because my family had fled from Berlin, which was plain to hear in the way we spoke German, we were Prussians, and to other Germans, Prussians were probably the worst kind of foreigners: military, imperious, if not downright fascist, bastards, all of them, with measuring rods for spines and, moreover, programmed to impose that measuring rod on everyone else. Swabians, on the other hand, were poets—pastoral poets at that.

One of everybody's favorite stories in Swabia (immortalized in song) is the one about a singing contest the emperor of Germany held every so often. This particular time, every one of the German "lands" sent their best bards, and each bard bragged poetically and melodically about his own home territory: Schleswig-Holstein, Baden, Friesland, and so on. They told of the rich monasteries they had, the silver mines, the sumptuous vineyards, the vast forests, the cosmopolitan harbors, the fabulous architecture, the great art, the heavenly music, and the deepest poetry.

The bard from Swabia came last. His land had no wealth at all, he sang, but his king, Eberhardt, a man with a famous beard, did not need bodyguards, or cumbersome armor, or highly paid tasters. His king could lay his head in the lap of any of his subjects and peacefully fall asleep. And the emperor, though a Prussian (of course), had nevertheless had the good sense to declare King Eberhardt's bard the winner, as his king was clearly the richest if not the wealthiest.

Swabia was a democracy, even though it had a king, because the king allegedly always did what the people wanted, which is not that hard to do when your population is homogenous and your kingdom is not much bigger than your average Texas ranch. The capital city of Swabia is Stuttgart, a garden city famous for its roses. The word "Stuttgart" can be translated as "Horse Ranch," though the poetic flavor of it is better rendered by "Mare Garden."

I first heard that story of the singing contest from Michael and his guitar and heard it many times after that—each time followed by a far-reaching and in-depth discussion of who, really, should have won that contest the king or the bard. Even the question could be asked in many ways. "The king and his poet" makes for a whole different thread in the damasked fabric of discussion and its weavers than does the "poet and his king."

Anyway, the Swabians have been well pleased with themselves ever since winning that contest back in the Middle Ages. Everyone born in Swabia now takes the credit that should clearly go to the bard (or to his king).

So to those well-pleased Swabians, we were foreigners, and not only foreigners, but Prussians—we ruined the local flavor is the way the Swabian dialect puts the situation by way of a culinary metaphor. Actually, we had been foreigners in Prussia also. Moreover, we had been foreigners in Russia as well, and before that, we had fled from Germany. I calculate that this makes me a fourth or fifth generation refugee.

But even though we were the enemy of all that's holy (in the local Swabian mind), the Swabian farmer's wife came to our house and brought some geranium cuttings for my grandmother. Michael Ende offered her his chair, and our whole household full of refugees waited in breathless anticipation of what our Swabian neighbor would have to say.

"I really appreciate how Klara and Gaby found a home with you," she began. "And me and my Karl was thinkin'," she continued, "We see your Unshellah roamin' all over the place by herself, and Klara, why, she told us that your Unshellah wouldn't be going to school and all, and so my Karl and me was thinkin' she might as well have a dozen geese to mind as she goes along."

"That's a great idea," said my grandparents in unison while my heart soared.

"We can't pay her, you know, but since our Paul and Lisl are grown and gone, why, our Gertie gives more milk than we really need, but even so it's not enough to sell to Möller's store neither, so we thought we could send our surplus over to you."

"That would be a real gift from God," said my grandfather.

And my grandmother said, "Ina, our little one, you know, has rickets."

"Yes, Klara was saying, and me and my Karl was thinkin' the milk would sure help—the milk rations these days are sure not enough to keep a little one alive."

"We would be so grateful," said my grandmother, and Aunt Kellermann said, "Are the goslings hatched then? I just love to see just hatched goslings."

"Not yet. Our Lisl used to love watching them hatch, and I loved watching her, so I thought your Unshellah might like to watch too. I keep them in a box under my kitchen stove. Why don't you come over with her every day until they come out? If I see 'em rock a little like they do, I'll send our hand Gustav or somebody to fetch you. They'll come out any day, you know, and it's best if they see Unshellah right away so they follow her."

My grandmother read to us every night, and often even after lunch. The American occupation government had banned Grimm's Fairy Tales because they were too violent, but my grandmother did not care about that—and so we got them all—unexpurgated with Rapunzel getting pregnant and the evil Queen rolling down the side of a mountain inside a barrel into which long, sharp nails had been hammered. My grandmother also read the Tales of a Thousand and One Nights, Aesop's Fables, Hans Christian Andersen's stories, Russian folk tales, and other fairy tales, especially the so-called *Kunstmärchen*, those written by German Romantic writers. I loved intrepid souls who sat, fearless, under the gallows tree at midnight just waiting, waiting just to see what might happen at midnight under a gallows tree. I adored Harun

Al Rashid, the wise ruler of Baghdad, who wandered the streets in disguise at night to learn about his people and their needs, desires, and dreams. I longed to meet an animal whose German name is *Murmeltier* —"murmuring animal." Now, *that* would be an animal to channel. On second thought, though, it would only work in German. In English a *Murmeltier* is a most prosaic groundhog.

That night, the story my grandmother picked to read to my sister and me by some cosmic coincidence was about a princess whose twelve brothers were changed into geese by an evil witch, but the princess figures out a way to re-humanize them—I forgot just how she did it exactly. Re-humanization would be a very handy trick in our world right this minute, as I hear the drums of war once again or still. Anyway, given a bedtime story like that, it should not come as a surprise that later that night, when I crawled out onto the garage roof to do with the words of the day what Mary did, I saw my future geese, made of starlight, in the cloud shapes of the milky way.

Next morning, my grandmother, Aunt Kellermann, Ina, and I went over to our neighbor's kitchen to see the goose eggs. Bedded in golden straw, they lay in a blue box advertising Morton salt—the box probably having arrived in this Swabian neighborhood as a care package from Kansas. Back then, of course, I could not read the words, "When it rains, it pours," but I remember the blue and gold color scheme, the little girl with her umbrella, and star dust pouring out of a box under her arm. And then there were the eggs with their miraculous shapes. Not long ago, it was through the online Xinhua News Agency that I learned that the universe is egg-shaped, according to evidence assembled by NASA scientists—a thing William Blake knew also, though his means of knowing took a different path. And according to Vedic literature, the universe is the womb of the Divine Mother; golden and egg-shaped, it is called *Hiranyagarbha*.

And the geese, of course, were indescribable from beginning to end. First came the endlessly lovely and innocent life, as, with infinite trust, they broke their eggshells to see the world. And then came the seemingly bottomless betrayal, horror, and grief when, by the following winter, I learned that every last one of them had ended up, featherless, mutilated, and ignominiously stuffed, on somebody's table for Christmas dinner.

But that spring, summer, and fall they were my best friends every day from just after lunch until sunset. I secretly wondered if maybe my geese were more than they seemed. After a while I was sure of it. I counted them swiftly and surreptitiously: there were indeed twelve. They were geese, but something more intelligent seemed to live in them behind the goose disguise.

"Are you really my brothers maybe?" I asked them and looked into their eyes so I could see if they were telling the truth. "yeh, yeh, yeh," they said, looking intelligent, truthful, and nibbling affectionately at my ears, nose, eyelids, and hair. I was not sure if "yeh, yeh, yeh," really meant "yeh, yeh, yeh." Of course, I reasoned, if they've been enchanted, they can't talk sense like a person. Their mouth is different.

In America it is the turkey that shows up on the holiday table and is reputed to be the dumbest creature in the world—in Germany, it is the goose. I have no idea how that piece of slander can be upheld by a people who think themselves as cultured as Germans are pleased to do. About turkeys, all I have is hearsay, though I must note that thinking a turkey dumber than a brick might well be a suspiciously convenient fiction. But I do know geese: geese are as brilliant as Einstein at being geese. They are kind and loving and very protective. If they had ever thought anyone would hurt me, they would have attacked fiercely. So, of course, geese can think. They like to snuggle up and have you put your arm around them and nestle your hand under their wing, and so, clearly, they can love also. No one who has observed a flock of domestic geese with clipped wings call to wild geese flying south can ever again think of a goose as stupid and insensitive. Of course, they talk to each other, and they also had plenty to say to me, though I did not always understand what they were telling me. They certainly expressed a forceful opinion the first time they saw me climb a tree.

***

The morning after we had visited the eggs nestled in straw in their blue and gold box, my grandmother and I were out scooping up molehills to use for potting the geranium cuttings our Swabian neighbor had given her. If you get your molehills in a cow or a sheep pasture, or, even better, if there is a rabbit warren in the immediate neighborhood, then molehills are a hundred times better than anything you can get at Walmart by way of potting soil. So we were busy—we were also gathering wild greens while we were at it, and the sun was climbing. Cloud shadows and stained-glass-bright sun patches raced each other across rolling fields and meadows more smoothly than Olympic skiers. And then, just as my grandmother stood to straighten and stretch her back, a herd of sheep broke over the crest of a hill like sea foam and flowed into the valley right by us as smooth and silent as any cloud. I know the sheep must have bleated, and the black dog, racing, dancing, and defining the perimeter of the cloud of sheep, must have barked with the joy of his work, but I remember only how silent, how self-contained, and singular they all were, including the shepherd who, after a small gap, came striding behind them with his hooked staff and his long, black cloak.

They flowed past us and up the next hill, disappeared over its crest, and the shepherd's cloak, round with wind, looked like the moon setting at dawn, as the morning sun lit up his back. And we went back to scooping up molehills like a herd of antelope goes back to grazing after the lion has taken one of them.

What was this? Just a shepherd with his herd of sheep—an ordinary sight. There had been another time I remembered that should have been noisy, yet seemed smooth and silent instead. And even in the breath of the wind, I remember that same self-contained silence and singularity that I had just seen in the herd of sheep and its shepherd crossing the valley.

I remember it as if I'd seen it from the air or a distant hilltop. And I am sure of the compass directions.

I saw the shepherd and his sheep often after that first time. Most of the time, he had a cow with him also: one of those little grayish brown, furry, almost curly Swiss cows that give the sweetest milk, especially if you let them graze where they can eat wild thyme and if you let them see their calves at milking time.

With my geese, I circled whatever field he was in, but I did not dare go closer. It was as if an invisible glass bell covered him and the whole meadow where he stood, knitting a sweater or socks.

One day, I told my grandfather about the shepherd at lunch and about how impossible it was to enter his field. My grandfather listened quietly—this is one of the things I loved about him: when he listened, you could tell he was listening. My grandmother might not hear a thing you were saying, but she would say "uh-huh" anyway—which was an advantage when you wanted permission for something. You just talked about something inconsequential until you could see her mind was elsewhere, and then you slipped in the thing. She had suffered way too much.

But my grandfather listened—always and especially this time. And then he told my grandmother in Russian that he was going out to find this shepherd and learn whether or not he was a man of God.

At suppertime my grandfather came home and said, "Well, Rabbit, I don't understand why you don't just go up to him and say, 'hello.'"

"We've never really been introduced," I told him. "I can't just talk to a stranger like that."

"This will never do," he said. "This won't do at all. One day God will say, 'Come to heaven,' and you will say, 'Sorry, can't do it; haven't done it before; the place looks kind of inaccessible, and on top of that, we have never really been introduced.' That," he continued, "Is no way to live at all. You talk to the streetcar driver."

"That's different. Everybody talks to him."

"It's not different. Besides, you and the shepherd are colleagues."

"What's 'colleagues' Grandpa?"

"People in the same business are colleagues—it's a kind of brotherhood that sticks together and speaks as one when there's a need. You've got geese, he's got sheep, but it's the same kind of responsibility. If anything, you're better at this business than he is because geese are a lot harder to mind than sheep."

"Why are geese harder to mind, Grandpa?"

"Because geese have a mind of their own; sheep don't. And then, he's got an assistant—that black dog of his. Can you imagine how he'd have to run around all over the place to keep them together if he didn't have that dog? You keep your geese together and safe from the fox all by yourself."

"I don't know, Grandpa, I'm really scared about that. What would I do if a fox comes and wants one of my geese?"

"All you'd have to do is stare at him like this." And he demonstrated by giving me a cold hard look with his little blue pig eyes and white lashes, all hugely magnified by the thickest lenses a pair of glasses ever had. "In fact, that's how you handle any fears you've got. You stare at them hard. They can't bear it; they just melt in a puddle on the floor. Tell you what, my Rabbit, we'll go practice talking to strangers tomorrow."

"Maxim," said my grandmother in Russian, "I'm afraid to ask what you've got in mind."

"That *Krolick* (Rabbit) can't grow up thinking other people are too high and mighty to talk to," he said, "It's idolatry is what that is—it'll end in Popery or Hitler-worship of some kind." And that was that.

My grandfather was determined that I, like him, would be afraid of nothing. And so the morning following our conversation about the shepherd and just before the noon hour when there would be lots of people getting off the streetcar, my grandfather stationed himself mostly out of sight in a convenient store front and watched me ask strangers what time it was. "Just go up to a person and say, 'Excuse me, would you happen to have the time?' And when you get tired of that, you can say, 'Excuse me, could you please tell me what time it is?'"

After collecting this information from about five people, I got to feeling pretty comfortable about it. I guess my grandfather noticed and came out to tell me the next thing would be to ask for directions to get to the inn. "I know how to get to the inn, Grandpa," I told him, but nothing doing, I had to ask three or four people before he was happy.

Then we actually did walk to the inn together, three blocks east, half a block south, and there it was on the left, just opposite the farmer's house that was our neighbor. "Well, my Rabbit," he said, "How was it?"

"Interesting," I said, "Everyone said it was a slightly different time."

"You'll find that's pretty much the case for everyone and everything," he said, "The whole world is a little different and sometimes a lot different for everybody, not just the time on their watches. Now we're going to the inn, and you'll go up to the counter and you'll order a beer for me and a lemon soda for you. Do you think you can handle it?" Then, as we were having our drinks, he wanted to know if I thought I could go say hello to the shepherd after lunch if I happened to find him, and I was pretty sure I could. "I expect a full report at suppertime," he told me, "Leave nothing out."

It turned out to be no big deal and not much to tell. The shepherd stood knitting at the top of a meadow that sloped down to the brook. It may seem a little odd for a man to be standing around and knitting, but for German shepherds (and I don't mean dogs, obviously) this is exactly what you would expect. They are avid knitters, and all German school children see them in their picture books busily knitting and still wearing the clothes that had been fashionable for shepherds in medieval times. Last time I was in Germany in the eighties, a man dressed like that and knitting was minding sheep in the grass next to the runway at the little airport of Bayreuth. I shed two or three sentimental tears about it as the plane took off, and the shepherd became a small black dot on the landscape, a dot that expands to infinity whenever I think of it.

I left my geese in the ditch between the edge of the meadow and the dirt road, where they were munching on snails and slugs, walked straight up to the man, and, by way of "hello," I said with six-year-old bravado, "I can already read."

"Can you read the stars?"

"I didn't know you could read stars."

"You can read anything. People who read books forget this."

"Can you read stars?"

"No. I read plants mostly—and sheep, of course. I read people pretty well. Would you like some milk?"

"Yes, please."

"Sybille, come over here, will you? We've got a guest." The cow, who was grazing near the hedgerow, came as slowly as cows come with a yellow buttercup hanging from her mouth. "This is Sybille," he said, and your name?"

"Angela Mailänder" I told them.

"Sybille, this is Angela. Is it OK if I give her some milk?" The cow nodded once but so vigorously that she would have knocked me out had I been close enough. Then he milked her—just a couple of good squirts into a tall blue and white-speckled enameled cup—and gave it to me to drink, warm and foaming and sweet and rich.

"I'm Hannes," he told me and, petting the dog, a black German shepherd, "This is Wolf. Sybille generally takes a nap after lunch. Would you like to join her? She likes being used as a pillow. I'll mind the geese for you."

So I took a nap under Sybille's sweet breath. I was pretty tired, having crawled out of my pantry window and put in a long night with secret activities to be detailed in another chapter. Maybe Hannes had seen my fatigue. And that was pretty much all there was to report to my grandfather after all that dramatic build-up.

Next day, I went to see him again at my grandfather's urging. Maybe it was even March 29th at 5:20 in the afternoon, the exact time of my birth according to official documents I had to get out of East Berlin on some bureaucratic occasion. But I'm not sure that this is exactly right. It was wartime, and the nurse had the presence of mind to record my birth time accurately? On the other hand, she was German *and* Prussian—and we know about how anal they can be about bureaucratic details like that, even in the canon's mouth. My mother claims I was born at 6:30 in the morning.

Today is my birthday," I said to Hannes, "They say I am six, but when I asked what that means, I didn't really get it."

You've noticed that there are old people and babies in the world?"

"Uh-huh."

"Well, the babies get older slowly and then, before you know it, they're old people."

"I know that too, except it takes a really long time, but how does it move and what's moving?"

"You mean time?"

"Yeah, what is that, what does it mean?"

"I'm not sure anybody knows in words, but you can get an idea. Come."

Hannes tucked his knitting away under his cloak and took up his staff. Wolf, who'd been snoozing, jumped to attention like a jack-in-the-box and gathered up the sheep. We walked slowly (for Sybille's sake who did not like going fast) over three hills and valleys to a place where the brook flowed through a stand of trees, a tiny forest really, and there the stream made a pond in the middle of a clearing. The sheep didn't really like tree country, but Wolf kept them together anyway.

Hannes took up six rocks and threw them into the pond one by one. "See the waves they make in patterns like growing rings? See how the waves of one cut into those of another? See how everything on that pond rocks on those waves? That is your time and its patterns. Now tell me, do you feel any different today than you did yesterday? I mean, you were five yesterday; today you're six. Does it feel any different?"

"No."

"But today has a different pattern than yesterday. Yesterday you took a nap with Sybille—today you walked to this pond with me. The patterns of the days are different but you feel the same, don't you?"

"Yes."

"That will never change. The patterns on top will be changing always, and feelings, the underside of waves, will be changing too, but if you want to know what anything means, follow the rocks to the bottom. And if you have a question, just leave it there. The answer will come, sometimes right away; sometimes it takes years."

As metaphor must be trained out of children before they will let go of that lifeline, I knew he did not mean, "Jump into the pond and dive to the bottom to follow rocks." Even so, I asked, "How can I follow the rocks to the bottom?"

"Sit down and be comfortable, close your eyes, and pretend you're the pond. A very quiet pond. Nothing moving. Now imagine a rock falls in. Leave the waves on top and follow the stone to the bottom where it's even more quiet. Stay there."

Evening birds sang in that silence, and, after a while, I opened my eyes.

"Well," said Hannes, "What happened? Could you stay at the bottom?"

"For a while, and then I started thinking stuff."

"Whenever you realize you're thinking stuff, imagine another rock thrown, and follow it to the bottom. It will be a good idea to practice."

When I gave my grandfather the full report that evening, he said, "That is the peace that is even deeper than understanding. I knew he was a good man the minute I laid eyes on him. Practice just as he told you. It will be good for you, considering what you have already seen in your young life." And I wonder just what the two men, my grandfather and the shepherd, had said to each other about me, a conversation that resulted in this practice for me, a practice for which I had no name other than the absurd and counterintuitive notion of "throwing rocks."[25]

---

[25] Much later (in 1971), this "practice" became one of the reasons I came into contact with

There was something mysterious about that shepherd, no doubt about it. It was generally accepted in the village that he was just a shepherd, but, in retrospect, I do not believe it. He did not have the air of a simple country person. On the other hand, he also was not like anyone in my mother's entourage of intellectuals.

In the years from 1946 to 1952 when he was my friend and teacher, I learned about medicinal plants from him, learning in ways that are just about the exact opposite of the way scientific training is conducted. And the simple beginning with the rock-throwing metaphor-as-meditation-technique was just that: there was more in the six years we had together. Yet he remained a teacher-friend, never assuming the pose of a guru.

While it is perhaps normal for a shepherd to be knowledgeable about medicinal plants, that he would also be a teacher of meditation is far from the usual thing. In 1946, many Germans were not who they said they were for many obvious reasons. I met Hannes again in 1957. But even at age seventeen, I was still too young to ask him all the questions I can think of now.

Transcendental Meditation (as taught by Maharishi Mahesh Yogi; 1919-2008) and had two interesting conversations with him via telephone.

CHAPTER THIRTEEN

The Man in the Sun

One more person showed up to live with us in our ménage, but he did not stay long. Wolfgang Gottschalk appeared in August.

It was towards the end of the day, I was on my way home with the geese, when a sudden thunderstorm said, "Watch out, I'm as big as they come." The sky all around turned dark in nothing flat, but the whole horizon to the west stayed a luminous color unknown on earth, and waited for the sun to step down from behind the indigo storm clouds. The geese and I dove into a rhubarb field.

The huge leaves had ribs of translucent jade, and the stalks changed from jade green at the top to silken and deepening reds with subtle stripes and tiny spots of pink, pale green, silver, and gold. Since rhubarb is a perennial plant, moss and a small flowering vine were established there and covered the ground all around the rhubarb stems and the furrows between the rows of plants, making a carpet of a perfect velvety shade of green in a green light.

On the other side of the field was a greengage plum tree, and the plums were ripe. The tree was behind a fence, and so the fruit was inaccessible, unless you wanted to risk being caught stealing. But today no need to take risks: the rain would down them, and we would get the sweetest ones free for picking them up off the road that went right by that fence. So we crept towards that tree along the furrows under the luminous green cover of the rhubarb leaves, the geese with their necks stretched forward and parallel to the ground.

When the sky broke, and the thunder roared all around us, we got hail, not rain. Hailstones jumping and rolling everywhere as they did when the queen rushed to the palace anger room and tore apart her strings of pearls. The hailstones were big enough to have hurt us, but the green umbrellas broke their fall and funneled them down the stalks to roll and tumble, harmless, among the rhubarb stems.

Imagine pearls bouncing all around us under that luminous green canopy held up by a forest of red and green translucent pillars, and it is easy to see that there was such magic in the air that I was sure something impossible was about to happen. By the time we came out from under the leaves on the other side of the field, the hail had stopped, and the sun was just coming down from behind the dark cloud cover. In the slant light, the earth was brighter than the sky, all greens were golden, reds glowed, and a perfect double rainbow stood in the east.

The hail had brought down plums, leaves, even small boughs with leaves and fruit. Among the melting hailstones plenty of ripe and sweet golden plums lay on the wet and blue-black asphalt with their deep reflections under them, and some were ringed with little rainbows made by thin films of gasoline. The geese and I ate our fill of the plums. They preferred the ones that were squooshed and had worms in them. I preferred them whole and without worms. We ate quickly before cars would purée them, and bees and wasps, and bumblebees would show in their thousands, shift after shift, for days and days until you could smell the plum wine in the air, and every creature in the neighborhood knew of it. Soon the hedgehogs and the foxes would come to get drunk on plum wine and dance under the moon.

After I had eaten as many plums as I could, I picked up the hem of my skirt to make a large pocket and collected more. Then the geese and I sat down on the edge of the asphalt, which was still warm. Before the storm, it would have been too hot for the geese and me to walk on in our bare feet. But now we sat soaking up the warmth and watched little vapors rise from the asphalt and dance in a light, warm breath of wind.

We watched the sun move toward the horizon where it became huge, and its shape flattened out, and the edges became wavy and liquid and deepest red. "It's impossible for nothing to happen," I told the geese. They said, "yeh, yeh, yeh," and nibbled affectionately at my earlobes and hair. "You watch," I said.

At the horizon the black road became a mirage of mirror-bright water so you could not tell where earth ended and sky began. Half the sun was below the horizon, but the bright mirror of road reflected the half sun and made it whole. I stared into it, as I still like to do so I can watch the colored spots dancing everywhere afterwards. And as I stared, a wavering black dot appeared in the middle of the sun.

The spot wiggled and grew bigger. Gradually, it resolved itself into a black and wavy stick figure, unstable in the warm and moving air above the road. It was walking towards us straight out of the liquid sun. It came through the evaporating vapor trails rising from the wet and shiny asphalt, and as it came, it got larger and more stable until what seemed to be an ordinary man was walking down the road. He was wearing black tails, a top hat and he carried a huge flower wreath on one arm.

My grandfather always took me to all the funerals in the village, so I knew that the man in top hat and tails was on his way to a funeral because of his get-up. Since there was none in our village, I figured he had quite a walk in front of him before dark. He was extraordinarily tall and skeletal, and I was still sure that this was no ordinary person on his way to an ordinary funeral somewhere. "Told ya," I said to the geese as they began chattering and several spread their wings, making them curve down toward the ground so they would look three times bigger than they really were, dangerous and hulking. Soon all of them were doing it. They lowered their necks, again parallel to the ground, and stretched towards him. Then, imitating snakes about to strike and hissing fearfully, they surrounded him. They would have scared me to death had they ever done it to me, but then I was barely taller than they. And I knew that they were doing it to protect me. The man gave them no mind and said, "My Lady, can you tell me how to get to Friedrich Zundel Street Number Four?" "*Gnädiges Fräulein*" (merciful little lady) is what he actually said, of course.

This was stunning. The tall man who had come out of the sun stood on the black asphalt wearing black shoes and a black funeral outfit and surrounded by my white geese in full battle stance, the whole thing looking like a giant flower with white petals and a black pistil which had just asked me how to get to my own address. He spoke standard German with a Silesian tone in it like Aunt and Uncle Kellermann. So I knew he came from a magical place of mountains and deep forests, silver mines, giant forms, and beautiful ladies who lived underground and gave precious gifts to the men who found them there—a land of gnomes, and enchanted caves, and wolves.

I also knew that the place no longer belonged to Germany, and all the Germans who had lived there had been asked to leave at gunpoint in the middle of the night and had been allowed to pack only whatever you can pack at gunpoint in the middle of the night.

I answered him cautiously in the local Swabian dialect, "Yeah. I live 'round there. I'll take you 'cause it's time for me and the geese to get home anyways."

"Mind if I have some plums first?"

"Help yourself," I said and offered the ones in my skirt. The geese relaxed and settled down again by the edge of the road.

He ate like I had seen starving men eat. In fact, as I remember it, I am amazed that he stood talking as long as he did among plums, when he could have just immediately picked them up and gorged himself. When he was done, we filled his top hat, replenished my skirt, and then we set out for Zundel Street. "What's your name?" he asked. "Angela Mailänder," I told him. And he said, "Well, I'll be—it's your mother that sent me—I have a letter here for your grandparents."

"There's no funeral at our place," I said.

"Oh that," he said, tossing the funeral wreath into the ditch. "The funeral outfit is just my cover. Now that I'm here, I don't need it any more." He laughed and added, "Did you know that laughing for ten minutes gives you exactly the same nutritional value as one egg? Science has proved it." It was a popular joke in the starving country.

I was instantly his friend and dropped the Swabian dialect, which had been my cover. "Really?" I said.

"Yeah," he said, "but it can't be fake laughter."

"What's your name?" I asked him.

"Oh," he said, "How rude—I should have introduced myself. Wolfgang Gottschalk at your service, my Lady." He bowed.

I repeated the name and then slowly took it apart: "Wolf…Gang…Gott…Schalk." Normally, people would just have accepted these sounds as his first and last names—common enough German names, both of them. But I was breaking the two names down into four syllables, which all happen to be monosyllabic words in German with their own meanings: Wolf…Walk…God…Mischief-maker, Jester, or Fool. He understood what I was doing.

"Yup," he said, "That's me: I walk like a wolf and I'm God's fool. And you'll be the Angel from the Land of May?"

"I've been wondering about that," I said. "I am not an angel plus I'm from Berlin, not Milan, but my daddy was born in Milan—that's why he named me Angela."

"So then that's why you use the Italian pronunciation of the name instead of the German?"

"Yeah; Mom said Daddy had to fight for my name because Hitler didn't allow any babies to have names that weren't German."

"Well, then, how do you know you're not an angel? Have you ever seen one?"

"I've seen pictures and I've heard about them. I don't think the pictures are really real because people don't actually have wings, but the angels in the Bible sound real."

"You read the Bible, my Lady?"

"You can just call me Angela."

"OK, you can call me Wolfgang. So, you look a little young to be reading the Bible."

"My grandpa reads the Bible out loud all the time, well, almost loud, and anytime there's angels, they talk like people who know what's going on, and everybody always knows right away that they're angels and not just people. But my grandpa said they don't really have wings."

"Do you think the angels know they're angels?"

"Well, they're not stupid."

"Then there's hope," he said, "You might be an angel some day. Sometimes it takes years to grow into your name and have it feel natural."

"That must be why then," I concluded a private train of thought of my own with satisfaction.

"That must be why what?"

"I'm minding the geese for this farmer named Smith (Schmidt), and we have a painter down the hill in the old village, and his name is "Bauer" (Farmer). Maybe they'll grow into their names later."

"Do you have a smith named Painter?"

"No," I said, "The smith's name is Betzler which doesn't mean anything."

"Is he a good smith?"

"Grandpa says he is."

"Then he'll give a meaning to the name. Inevitably."

"What's inevitably?"

"It means something has to happen and you know it."

"Like you coming out of the sun just now?"

"I came out of the sun? You want to explain yourself, my Lady--I mean Angela?"

"Explain myself? How can I explain myself? I've never heard anybody explain their self."

"I mean, what makes you think I came out of the sun?"

"I saw you." I told him and described exactly what I had seen.

"Well," he said, "That's pretty amazing. You know what things looked like to me?"

"No, what?"

"You and your geese looked to me like you were sitting in the middle right under a perfect double rainbow. And you looked almost like one of the geese in that white silk dress. Do you know how to write? You should write that story."

And why is a goose girl in post-war Germany dressed in silk? Well, my grandmother made dresses of any material that could be found, and right after the war for a couple of years that included old Nazi flags and parachute silk. My mother and my aunt Ruth both wore underwear made by my grandmother out of parachute silk. She also once took the fringe off a red plush sofa, unraveled it, and then made sweaters for my sister and me. They were scratchy as hell and dyed us bright pink. But they were warm.

"Well, I know my letters," I told Wolfgang Gottschalk, "and I can read, but I can't really write anything except words."

"Well, if you can write words, you can write the story. Stories are made of words, you know."

"That doesn't sound right."

"It doesn't?"

"Stories can't just be made of words."

"I'm sure they are. I am a writer by profession."

"Well, if there's just words, what keeps them together to make sense?"

"Oh my God," he said, "Your mom did warn me about you and your endless questions."

By the time we got home, I knew he was a person who knew me

as a person—not that I put it to myself that way. Children often think without using words, a skill we train out of them to our cost individually and collectively. As a child, I never misplaced my trust, as I did later when I became a woman.

Wolfgang Gottschalk gave his hat full of plums and the letter to my grandmother. She read it and called my grandfather,

"Max, could you come in here for a minute?" He showed up from Aunt and Uncle Kellermann's room, his huge, large print Bible, as always, in hand. Handing the letter to my grandfather, my grandmother said to Wolfgang, "I'll go get you something to eat," and went to the kitchen.

My grandfather read the letter and said, "After you've eaten, the best thing would be for you to go and look like you're leaving town and then come back after dark and make sure nobody sees you.

"You're right," he said, "I guess I got rid of my wreath a little too soon.

"Your wreath?"

"I was carrying a flower wreath like I was going to a funeral."

My grandpa smiled his funny little smile, "How long have you been traveling like that?"

"All the way from the Polish border. I had to get a new wreath pretty often, but other than that, the military police and the border guards always believed that I was just going to the next village to my father's funeral." He smiled a very big smile, "I buried my father all over Germany that way. I got a good map and avoided cities where there'd likely be trouble." He shrugged, "But in the villages everyone believed my story and let me go. I've been lucky, I guess."

"God was with you," said my grandfather. "I once escaped from Siberia, walked through the Ural Mountains alone in winter—well, I had a donkey for part of the way—and then I traveled down the Volga River on a river boat dressed as a Russian priest and playing cards with three real priests, cussing out the Germans the whole time. Won a ton of money, too."

"Well," said Wolfgang Gottschalk, "We'll have stories to swap."

There is probably no way to survive a war without an amazing story to tell and I am all those stories.

My grandmother came back from the kitchen with a plate of boiled new potatoes and onions, which my grandfather thought were a gift from God, but I knew exactly how those potatoes and onions had mysteriously arrived at our place, and God had nothing to do with it. At least, that was my opinion at the time. You'll hear more about it soon enough.

Wolfgang Gottschalk thanked my grandmother for these magical onions and potatoes, and as he was eating, my grandfather pulled me onto his lap and said, "Listen well, my Rabbit, and remember what I tell you. When Mr. Gottschalk has eaten, get the wreath back and then take him to the sloe thickets. Since the sloes aren't anywhere near ripe, chances are you won't run into anyone that far from the village especially not this time of day. People will see you in the oak grove, but they'll think I sent you to show Mr. Gottschalk the way to Heumaden, and I happen to know they really are having a funeral there tomorrow, thank God."

To Mr. Gottschalk he said, "It will be easy to lay low in the sloe thickets. And the path Angela will take you will be easy to remember so you can backtrack after dark—she'll point out all the landmarks you'll need. When you come back, the oak grove will be empty—you can depend on it, because most people in this village know it's haunted after dark. But make sure nobody sees you anyway because we do have a growing segment of the population that doesn't believe in ghosts or anything else either. A very inconvenient development," he added.

Then, turning to me, he said, "And Rabbit, this is important: Do not mention Mr. Gottschalk to anyone. Not anyone. 'Not anyone' means?"

"Not anyone," I answered.

"You have never seen him or heard his name. Understand?"

I did not understand, but I nodded. My grandfather put some money in a blue and white speckled enamel can with a lid. It looked like a small bucket but thinner and taller—it held about two liters, I think, and had a wire handle with a wooden grip. He did not have to say anything because I knew the routine. After getting back the funeral wreath, I took Wolfgang Gottschalk to one of my own favorite hideouts in the sloe thickets close to the creek guarded by pollard willows that actually did look like ghosts on a foggy night in a poem by Goethe that my other grandmother had made me memorize. Then I ran back to the village, taking a short cut across the poppy field and straight through green tunnels of the hops field. I stopped at the inn and gave the can to the innkeeper.

Taking the money out of it and filling it with draught beer for me he said, "Your grandpa's having company."

Protocol demanded that you always said "hello" by asking a question as if it were an affirmation. Here's a typical greeting between two villagers that have known one another all their lives. Joseph is splitting wood in his farmyard, and Hans-Jochen is coming down the street.

Hans-Jochen: "You splittin' wood."

Joseph: "Yup, splittin' wood."

No conversation between Swabians in the village where I grew up was possible unless this ritual greeting was observed. If the answer to the question cannot be stated in the form of its repetition, Hans-Jochen has to guess again until he gets it right. I had been instructed to keep the true purpose of the beer a secret. So to the innkeeper's statement that my grandpa was having company I said, "Nope," and the innkeeper had to guess again: "Him and your grandma is cellabraiding."

"Yup, cellabraiding." I was dying to tell him he would never guess that God's fool who walked like a wolf had come out of the sun, and was hiding in the sloe thickets, and would come back to my house later, and that he and my grandfather had promised stories. But I restrained myself.

I also restrained myself from swinging the can around in big circles to see if I could figure out why the beer did not fall out of the can when it was upside down. Klaus Bach had told me the reason was called centrifugal force, but those words did not say a thing to me, and when I asked him what a force was, he could not tell me—and, if the truth were known, nobody has been able to tell me to this day. Of course there are plenty of people who think they know what a force is, but most of them confuse words with what words say—if you question them closely, you will find that they really have no clue about it. There are lots of items like that. Try questioning somebody about instinct, just for example. If you question closely enough, you will learn that nobody knows what it really is. There are lots of words like that. They're just a cover for not knowing.

I got sent to bed that night before Wolfgang Gottschalk came back and shared the beer with my grandfather. But I crawled out onto the garage roof and made for the oak grove. Spirits were traveling. Change was in the wind. Low clouds raced across the moon's face, leaving vast spaces between them, through which you could see higher clouds and even higher, golden clouds around the moon and a single star. Down on the ground and under the motionless oaks, hardly a breath stirred and when it did, it was warm and soft.

I climbed the oak that stood guard at the western entrance of the grove and waited for Wolfgang Gottschalk—forever, it seemed. A nightingale had begun his crescendos, trills, and warbles by the time Wolfgang showed. I dropped down from a low branch to the soft moss on the edge of his path and said, "We could take a short-cut through the poppy field and the hops—what do you think?"

If he was surprised to see me, he did not show it. He just stuck out his hand, and I took it as if we had done it every day as far back as I could remember. We talked of all I knew. The war behind me, and my life now in Sillenbuch, Stuttgart, and environs. We parted where our paths diverged. I swore him to secrecy, and he went to our front door, while I climbed up the garden wall, then onto the garage roof, and to my closet window.

Right under the peak of the roof of our apartment building lay two hallways at the top of a central stairs, one to the west and one to the east. Along these halls, each tenant had the single room that was intended for storage, and one of these rooms was where Klara and her baby slept. Klara's room was at the end of the hallway toward the east, and if there had been a window in that wall, anyone leaning out would have seen me on the garage roof three stories lower, but the room did not have windows in that wall, which never made sense to me. But it was a design feature in my favor, so I did not lodge any complaints with the body of forces that designed the building. There were mansard windows on both sides of the roof. Klara's room had a window opening to the north. And she must have leaned out of her window at night and seen me climb from the garage roof to the top of the high wall that enclosed the farmer's courtyard, but I could trust her to keep it quiet because we were in league.

Now here is the crucial part of this account of the architecture of our apartment building. Klara's room had access to a space where the roof met the walls of the house. That space was fairly big. Wolfgang could almost stand up straight in it, and that is where he lived secretly for maybe almost a year.

I do not know why he had to be hiding like that. Even on her deathbed my mother did not tell me. When I was a child, there was a tacit understanding that Wolfgang Gottschalk was not discussed. And then, I was a child and accepted countless things without question because, in spite of asking why about seemingly everything, you really never can ask about all there is. For a while, the only thing I could think of that made any sense was that he might have been accused of war crimes. But would my mother harbor a war criminal when the Nazis had kicked her out of school? And the whole country was crawling with Nazi war criminals who did not have to hide. I even had relatives whose hands were far from clean—my uncle Walter, the Asshole of Sillenbuch, just for example. Knowing Wolfgang as I did, war criminal does not make sense.

More recently, and after years of researching what my grandfather told me about Wall Street and the Vatican, my guess is that, as a writer, Wolfgang Gottschalk might have know things, things that would have made him dangerous to the occupation government and, therefore, also a wanted *persona non grata*.

But back then, I knew Wolfgang Gottschalk beyond time, place, or condition, because like me on the garage roof, he did not have to be anybody in that attic space. There, I spent long hours with him in long conversations about the life outside. He would also read to me from books I would bring, and in that secret space he taught me how to write stories about my life.

Klara brought him his food hidden in baskets of laundry. And, just in case there is a question about mundane details, all the bed linen and towels were kept up there—none of the rooms in the apartment had built-in closets, as you would expect to see in all American apartments. So Klara on the stairs with laundry was a common enough sight. He and she each had a chamber pot. People in Germany still had chamber pots in those days. But Klara emptied only one pot into the toilet in our apartment every morning, and it was, perhaps, unusually full, but chamber pots had lids, so no one noticed if they saw her on the stairs with it.

Wolfgang Gottschalk was a secret and a secret sharer of my life just as the secret sharer in the novel by Joseph Conrad. Or like the story of the German nineteenth century cat named *Kater Murr* (Tom Cat

Murr) who lived in the attic and wrote memoirs about his life with the family that owned him. He was not an extremely wealthy cat, so he used what paper he could find in the attic, which happened to be the galley proofs of a novel one of the family members, a musician, had been writing. The stupid publisher never did get it straight as to which story was which, so he just combined them any-which-way and printed them out together. When I first read the story as a child, I could never tell which story I was in, the cat's or the musician's. I must have read the book at least a hundred times.

Then, as suddenly as Wolfgang Gottschalk had come, he left. My mother came home one weekend and brought an American traveling pass to Bilbao for him. I remember that everyone was amazed and asked how she had managed it since, under American martial law, no German was allowed to travel, never mind leave the country. Earlier, you could not stay in one county longer than twenty-four hours, but then one day the American occupation government had had enough of folks walking everywhere in droves and issued a sit-tight-or-get-jailed order.

So how had my mother obtained travel papers? "Easy," she said and explained that after working for the Americans for as long as she had, she was sure that they do not know geography, and so it was a piece of cake to make them think that Bilbao was a village in Germany rather than a city in Spain. Wolfgang Gottschalk was once again going to his father's funeral in the next village—at least as far as the official filling out of papers was concerned. And just like that, he was gone.

CHAPTER FOURTEEN

The Ménage Schools Me

My grandfather had promised a year of glorious freedom when I flunked the weigh-in, and that is what it felt like, too. But I was the proper age to be in school, and so everyone in our ménage talked about my education. Should I not be doing something? Learning something? Just about everyone decided to do something about my schooling, and even if they did not volunteer directly, they made an inevitable contribution—and then, what is not schooling for a child among adults? Michael Ende continued to teach me music. Klaus Bach improved my skills at chess, epistemology, logic, and philosophical discourse. Aunt Lilo taught me more manners than I wanted to learn, as well as how to sit and how to walk like a lady. I definitely did not like having to sit with my knees touching each other. Wolfgang Gottschalk taught me to read and to write. Hannes taught me medicinal plants. My grandfather did not exactly teach me religion, as that was not allowed, but I learned the Bible from him by default, and he began the process of teaching me geopolitics beginning with the criminal nature of modern warfare and its profit motive.

He also taught me the magic of cogwheels. A bit of his life needs telling for context. At fourteen he had been apprenticed to a foundry because, like a mountain woodland gnome, he had the build for it, short, but powerful. Back then, farm machines were imported to Russia from England, and when they broke down, spare parts took too long to arrive, so the foundry began making those replacement parts. And then, after he married my grandmother, she would say, "Max, why are you making parts, when you could make the whole machine?"

"You talk like any fool of a woman would talk," he would say. (That was before he had granddaughters who taught him otherwise.)

My grandmother did not give up, and, one day, his brothers, my uncles Sasha and Otto, heard him talking, and Uncle Sasha said, "You know, Max, she might have something there."

They wrote to German industrialists, Krupp and Thyssen, and before they knew it, they moved from the Dnieper River in the Ukraine to the Volga River where they had found suitable land and soon were making farm machines for the entire region. At the Old Threshers' Reunion in Mount Pleasant, Iowa, I saw exactly the kind of machinery he made—fantastic constructions, whose mechanisms were pretty much open to view, of levers, of wheels within wheels, of fly wheels, and of that unsung hero of the industrial age, the cogwheel. My grandfather could wax poetic about the cogwheel—*Zahnrad* in German, which means "tooth-wheel"—and he made me wooden ones to show me that they can change the direction a rotation circles; they can change the plane on which a rotation circles; they can add more (or reduce) torque in a rotation, thus reducing exponentially the effort required to lift or propel heavy objects.

"The cog wheel is central to all machines, my Rabbit. Here, look at the inside of my watch. And while we're thinking of cogwheels, let's get on the streetcar, and I'll take you to see a really interesting use of the cogwheel." And we rode to the Westside of Stuttgart, Germany to see a streetcar that pulled itself up a steep hill by means of toothwheels that bit into the ground. Had he seen the Antikythera mechanism recently discovered, he would have been ecstatic.

My grandmother taught me to sew. She had worked for a big fashion house in Berlin while my grandfather was saving souls and watching as well as documenting, and researching the political scene along with his buddies from church. My grandmother was an artist with her sewing machine. She could design a dress, or look at a picture of a model wearing one in a magazine and draft a perfect pattern for it that fit you to a T. And the more complicated the pattern, the more she loved dealing with it. She taught me lessons in sewing, in geometry, in color and design, and in love. My first job as her assistant was to put pins into her hands, head first and at the proper angle, so she could use them without having to reposition them. And later, when I was getting really good at sewing, she said, "Never let on that you know how to tailor a man's suit."

"Why not Grandma?"

"It takes forever to tailor a suit; it's the most boring job alive; men don't respect your work and never pay you enough for your time and skill. Stick to women's and girls' clothing."

When a person came to have a dress made, she would let me take their measurements. So I was measuring humans! It seemed such a mystery. I did not make words about it then, but, much later, I remembered my first tailoring lessons as I read St. Augustine: "I measure it, but what it is I measure, I do not know."

One time, a very small woman with a huge asymmetrical hump on her back came to have some dresses and a suit made. My grandmother proceeded with her usual perfect results. Once we had measurements, my grandmother would show me how to transfer these onto a flat surface, cut the resultant shapes out of fabric (first laying them out so as to waste no cloth and adding seam allowances and wearing ease), and then sew the pieces together so as magically to fit over a three-dimensional form.

The first time I made a jacket for my sister's favorite doll, I noticed that the armhole pretty much described a circle. But when I attached a tube to that circle, the sleeve stuck out at right angles to the jacket, instead of hanging straight down, as a proper sleeve should. And when the doll wore it, the fit was just not right; there was far too much stress at the top of the shoulders and too much loose bunching under the arms—not only did it look wrong, it would have been very uncomfortable to wear.

"Rip the seam where you see stress," my grandmother told me, "That will show you the shape you need to add to relieve that stress. Where there's too much fabric under the arms, leave it attached."

When I did as she said, I could see for myself what needed to be done. The armhole describes a circle, but for a sleeve to hang straight down, the top of the sleeve needs to describe a bell-shaped curve, rather than a straight line.

Another thing I did, almost compulsively, was to make paper cuts. It began when I wanted to paint, but paint was neither affordable, nor anywhere to be found. So my mother brought me book covers from the America House Library, where she worked when she was not on some secret mission. These covers would be thrown out since books have to sit on library shelves naked, and I was happy to get their colorful "clothes."

At first, I used them just as I would have used paint: if I wanted to paint a green tree, I'd find green shapes on the book covers, cut them out, and glued them down to make the shape of a tree. Soon, I discovered that if you folded a paper in half, then whatever shape you cut out, it appeared as itself and its mirror image. Soon, I was cutting out the most intricate shapes and leaves, flowers, and birds. No one taught me how to do this, nor did I ever see any examples of other artists doing this sort of thing. When my mother noticed what I was doing, she brought me a pair of iris scissors (intended for eye surgery) and some scalpels from a military hospital somewhere. She also brought black paper, and this became my favorite kind to use for these paper cuts or silhouettes. They all had almost a Chinese feel to them, which is one of the many mysteries of life. I made hundreds of them—silhouettes (as everyone around me called them), and, also, mysteries.

Learning any art or craft is such a perfect way to teach a million-and-one things to a child, especially a sense of accomplishment and the knowledge that work can be pleasure. And, in apparent self-contradiction, learning a craft teaches abstract levels of thinking, as is evident in what I learned about pattern drafting. I went to the "Merz Schule," a year later, and its founder Albrecht Leo Merz understood these principles perfectly and organized his whole school around them.

Just yesterday in the mail I got a small book he wrote back in 1947. It is truly prophetic. He said that a people that mechanizes, stereotypes, and normalizes everything is doomed, and that a people remains viable and capable of evolution when human nature is allowed to be at its most varied. The truth of this is self-evident to me after watching the depressing decline of the American school system for the last sixty years. He would have been horrified at how narrowly America defines "normal" and then medicates everyone who falls outside those bounds, even children.

But Albrecht Leo Merz was later. My next most important teacher was Uncle Kellermann.

The gods arranged for Uncle Kellermann to teach me arithmetic. Who else would have been as perfect for the job? He was small and round and grey. His hair was grey, obviously. And orderly—every part of him was nothing if not orderly. Each grey hair on his head was combed so that it lay as close to parallel as lines on a sphere could be. Lots of men in the mid-nineteen-forties wore their hair that way, including Uncle Walter, the Asshole of Sillenbuch, who was tall and gaunt and grey. But, more important than size, there was a geometrical difference in the way each of these uncles wore his hair, a difference which would strike most people as utterly inconsequential, but to my mind, it was hugely telling, although I could not have said what it told exactly. But the hair of two uncles definitely occupied my mind for a significant time of my life.

Both uncles wore a grey suits with a grey vest. However, Uncle Walter, the Asshole of Sillenbuch, wore ties of various subtle colors, but Uncle Kellermann's tie was always grey with darker grey stripes. He also had a set of grey pajamas and a bathrobe of thick, grey flannel with thin white stripes. Furthermore, he had a grey and orderly wife, who, somehow, contained the deepest grief in her dark eyes. He was a little sad for her sake because of it, but, unlike her, he had a life apart from sadness.

Due to my grandmother's pattern-drafting lessons, it was easy to see that straight lines have over-all three choices in configuring to a sphere: they could accommodate the sphere and describe orderly curves with all the lines meeting at two points opposite each other, like the lines made by the sections of an orange. Or they could refuse to do this and, instead, describe concentric circles all around the sphere. In other words, the hair of two uncles had shown me the difference between longitudinal and latitudinal lines. A third way reveals itself when you peel an apple with the infinite care Uncle Kellermann gave to the task to produce a perfect spiral. I had tested my understanding of these things by asking Uncle Kellermann if I could comb his hair for him (the Asshole of Sillenbuch would sooner have died than have anyone touch him, especially his hair).

And it was clear: Uncle Kellermann preferred a more or less longitudinal arrangement of hairs, while Uncle Walter compelled his hair to lie along latitudinal lines that nevertheless curled slightly around each ear from back to front. Uncle Kellermann then suggested that I should volunteer to help Klara peel potatoes and slice them. Cuts along latitudes resulted in circular slabs of graduated sizes; longitudinal cuts resulted in sections *à l'orange*, just as I had envisioned, and I reported my findings to him. Longitudinal lines were not really parallel according him, but I maintained that in spite of the fact that they did not exactly look parallel since they obviously converged at two points on the sphere, they were parallel in spirit. And spirit was more important than appearance, as my grandfather had succeeded in teaching me in spite of Aunt Lilo's efforts to the contrary on behalf of my mother, the formidable empiricist.

In addition to his longitudinal hairstyle, Uncle Kellermann had a grey mustache under his round nose, and this mustache was trimmed in such a way as to make his upper lip look like a miniature hedgehog. Now, a hedgehog is a most wonderful and intelligent animal whose geometry is also nothing short of divine, since he knows how to lay his needle-pointed spines in longitudinal lines along his back, or he can roll up into a ball and make them radiate from his center like a star. Uncle Kellermann's mustache hairs could perform both of those amazing hedgehog tricks. In short, Uncle Kellermann was miraculous in my eyes.

I loved Uncle Kellermann because of the way he had taught me to write my letters with love and care for each curve in the sinuous path of a pen trailing wet ink. And now I loved him even more because he let me play with his hair, and I made such outrageous hair sculptures on Uncle Kellermann's head, that even Aunt Kellermann had to forget two world wars. Two sons and a daughter killed. And she smiled a fleeting smile.

At supper, Uncle Kellermann announced that I had great talent for mathematics, and I announced that I would be a hairdresser when I grew up.

"You can forget that," said Aunt Lilo, "Your mother will never allow that; you are going to university. Maybe you should spend less time playing with Inge Breuninger." (Inge, if you remember, was my partner in the crime of chewing up blotting paper, and she was subversive on a number of counts, besides being my best friend and the daughter of the only hairdresser in Sillenbuch).

My grandfather said, "If you go to university, look out: maybe someone will carry you off as his prey..." and he gave me his famous ravenous wolf look.

"Herr Zeitner! What kind of nonsense are you putting into the child's head about universities?" asked Aunt Lilo, scandalized.

"I'm quoting a Bible verse," said my grandfather with a face that once won him tons of money as he, dressed up as a Russian Orthodox priest, was going down the Volga on a riverboat and playing poker with three real priests.

"Oh, the Bible has something to say about universities," she said, her voice dripping with sarcasm.

"Let's hear the whole verse," said Klaus Bach.

"'Look out'," quoted my grandfather in his best biblical voice, "'Maybe someone will carry you off as his prey through the philosophy and empty seduction according to the traditions of men and according to worldly precepts rather than Christ.' Colossians, Chapter Two, Verse Eight."

Klaus Bach laughed outright. "That is so perfect—from what I can tell, that's exactly what universities are like."

"If that's what universities are like, I don't want to go," I said.

And Klaus Bach said, "You don't have to be a sheep in a university—you can be a wolf instead—that's what I'm planning to be."

"I don't want to be a wolf; I want to be a hairdresser," I told him.

"Well, that does it," said Aunt Lilo, "You are not to play with Inge Breuninger any more."

"Inge Breuninger has nothing to do with it," said Uncle Kellermann, "The reason why Angela wants to be a hairdresser…"

"This subject is closed," said Aunt Lilo, "Inge is not a good influence. Period."

Next morning, Uncle Kellermann and I were both ready, both freshly scrubbed with morning faces, and willing. He had combed his hair and glued it to his head with pomade, and my grandmother had parted mine in the middle and plaited it into two tight, wet braids, one just behind each ear, and so Uncle Kellermann and I both had more or less longitudinal hair arrangements, with all that this implies and which perfectly predisposed us for the study of mathematics.

First he taught me to count. Not much of a problem there since I already knew how, but he insisted on formalizing things. I did not like counting. Hannes and my grandmother both had a thing about counting, as I learned when I came to show off and practice counting sheep or dumplings. My grandmother said, "You don't count the number of dumplings, matching them to the number of guests. You cook enough; you cook with all you've got."

Hannes was even more radical about it: "If you count your sheep too much, they die." And I remember how horrified he was when, in a neighboring village, they started to stamp red numbers on the backsides of sheep. And then, when they all got hoof-and-mouth disease, he said it was not any wonder. "A sheep is not a number," he said, "It may seem contrary to all appearances, but it is a fact: every sheep and as unique as you and I." And I believe he would have maintained that position even after Dolly, the first cloned sheep, was born. "The stars," he would have said, "Stood in a different position when she was born than they did when her mother was born; the weather was different, the world was very obviously different." And of course I would have to agree that a world in which there are cloned sheep is very different from a world in which a cloned sheep is virtually unimaginable.

Despite some queasiness, I was good at counting, though in the long run, endless counting turned out to be terminally boring. Then, finally, Uncle Kellermann thought it was time to move on to addition. "One and one is two," he told me.

"No way," I countered. "One and one is one."

"That's absurd—how do you figure?"

"One…and…one…is…one." I told him with slow emphasis.

"You are not making sense. One and one is two."

"I don't think so. How can one be two? One and one and one and one and one is one." My mother had instructed me that if I felt something was the truth, not to let anyone talk me out of it—herself excepted, of course. And in this case, I felt very sure I had a handle on the truth.

"Can you explain how one and one is one?" asked my wonderfully grey Uncle Kellerman.

"It doesn't matter how many times I say one, it's still one," I told him, "An apple and an apple is still an apple."

"You are not making any sense at all; one apple and one apple are two apples." (In German, the difference between "an apple" and "one apple" is even fuzzier than it is in English—in fact, it is non-existent. In Chinese the whole thing is the profound philosophical problem that it actually does appear to be).

"But Uncle Kellermann," I explained to him patiently, "If Grandma yells 'Angela' out the window for me to come in for supper, it doesn't matter how many times she yells—only one Angela will show up for supper. Angela and Angela is Angela. One and one is one."

"Then, according to you, two and two is two?"

"Yes, of course."

"You amaze me," he said and then tried to show me with pebbles: "Here's a pebble. And here's another pebble. How many pebbles do you see?"

"Two."

"Good! Very good. So one and one are two."

"But Uncle Kellermann, I don't see what the pebbles have to do with anything, and anyway each pebble is still its own self."

He threw up his hands at that point, and so the story of my learning arithmetic is somewhat analogous to my grandfather's throwing me in the Neckar River to teach me to swim: I was a howling failure as a student of arithmetic, and Kellermann the Grey was a commensurately howling failure as a teacher of arithmetic. My grandfather said, "Well, there is some sense to what she is saying; we should just leave this for professional teachers when she finally does go to school." It would be twenty-five years before I understood again what I had understood very well when I was child.

"She will need arithmetic if she's ever to handle money," said Uncle Kellermann, and I was a little disappointed in him since that seemed the statement of a sore loser to me.

CHAPTER FIFTEEN

The Lord Works in Weird Ways

In disgust over the stupidity of arithmetic, I went next door to visit my other grandmother, my father's mother, who lived with her daughter, my excellent aunt Editta and her husband, my uncle Walter, the Asshole of Sillenbuch. Now, to visit my "other" grandmother, I first had to get past my Uncle Walter, and this takes a little explaining.

In spite of being the undisputed Asshole of Sillenbuch, my uncle Walter was not the ultimate boss in his family. His only son (or maybe it was just my aunt Editta's son), my absolutely wonderful cousin Gert-Dieter who was just past his mid teens—he was the boss in the family. I adored Gert-Dieter and wanted to be just like him when I grew up. And it was not just because he had the authority to lock his father in the guest bathroom when the latter got too vile to be tolerated. I also adored Gert-Dieter because he had so much hair on his legs that he looked like a furry animal, which I found completely enchanting. My cousin Gert-Dieter was a faun! My grandfather told me I could always ask God for anything I wanted, and what I wanted more than anything was to have legs like Gert-Dieter when I grew up: I would be a hairdresser with furry legs.

Whenever my cousin the faun locked my uncle Walter the Asshole of Sillenbuch in the bathroom, Uncle Walter changed magically from being the complete Asshole of Sillenbuch to being one of my very best friends. I thought maybe Gert-Dieter had magical powers. Or maybe the bathroom had magical properties. It was long and narrow and it had a long and narrow window with bars in the short wall opposite the throne at the other end of this very constricted space. That window faced a cherry tree that I loved to climb any time of year, but the only time I was allowed to climb it was when Uncle Walter was locked in the bathroom. He would holler out that window for me until I was around to hear it, and I then would climb the tree, make myself comfortable on a branch just outside the bars of his prison, and the two of us had a lazy time, a philosophical time, or a crazy time talking about village gossip, while I hung upside down from a branch or sat on it cross-legged.

But when my Uncle Walter was not locked in the bathroom, I had to watch my back any time I opened the gate to his fenced-in property because he would throw rocks, serious rocks, with a deadly intention, though, somehow, he just about always missed me; yet there was quite a row once when he did hit me between the shoulder blades hard enough to draw blood, and my grandfather paid him a visit. Uncle Walter, the Asshole of Sillenbuch did not stop throwing rocks, but he always missed me after that. However, I did not know what the two men had talked about, so I watched my back.

Since the front door of the house did not face the garden gate that opened onto the street, there was a choice among several combinations of dangerous and circuitous routes to get to the entrance. And you could not assume Uncle Walter was not in the garden just because it was raining cats and dogs—he could suddenly rise roaring to his full, gaunt height from a crouching position behind a bush, his hair re-arranged by the rain along longitudinal lines converging on the top of his head and pouring over his face like water weed over a rock with a very large craggy nose and wild eyes.

Sometimes I could fool him by climbing the fence rather than coming through the gate, but if he caught me, there was a storm full of evil words like black hail stones. We had an unspoken agreement, however: if I made it to the stone steps leading to the door, I was home free.

Triumphant for having got there without injury, I rang the bell. The housekeeper told me to wait in the library, while she went to inquire if Grandmamma were receiving company.

She was a formal "Grandmamma (*Großmamma*) My mother's mother, in contrast, was just "Grandma" (*Oma*). The difference between my two grandmothers made me wonder how such a big dissimilarity could obtain in the same species. Other animals (except dogs) looked pretty much like each other, but not humans. On the other hand, I thought, maybe, if I were an ant, other ants would look wildly various to me.

In the library, which was also my uncle Walter's study, I visited all the pieces of sculpture and other works of art and craft that crowded the place. My favorite was a bronze bull who was only pretending—really he was the king of all the gods. On his back and lying on her stomach with her chin resting on her crossed wrists was a naked woman whose name was Europa. Did she know? She looked very relaxed, so she must have known. Besides, no bull would just let you lie on his back like that...an ox maybe, but not a bull. And then he went swimming in the ocean. If she had had any doubts before, *that* should have clinched it: bovines do not like to go swimming, whereas with gods, anything is possible.

Waiting in the library, I was trying to guess what Grandmamma was doing right then. There were only four things she did in her rooms when she wasn't sleeping:

She read old, leather-bound books with the best pictures in them. The most amazing thing about these pictures, though, was what I learned about them when I returned to Germany after two years in America. They were engravings, woodcuts, lithographs, pen and ink drawings—all black and white, but I had remembered them in glorious Technicolor. "Are you sure, Grandmamma," I would ask again and again, "You have no books with colored pictures in them?"

She played solitaire with antique decks of tiny cards from the eighteenth century, cards with reproductions of eighteenth century paintings of lords and ladies doing what lords and ladies did on decorous and more or less public occasions in the eighteenth century, showing off fantastic clothes and wigs. Sometimes she took the part of one of the gentlemen, and I would take the part of the lady, and we would have long and very polite conversations guided by the chance fall of the cards we were playing with. Or a long conversation about the duties of a lady-in-waiting and the duties of a queen. Through family, Grandmamma had some obscure connection with Queen Olga, the last Swabian queen.

Grandmamma made intricate lace and embroideries, wearing thimbles that would have made any silver or gold smith shine with pride. She had learned from her mother, who had learned from Queen Olga, who had valued needlework enough to become the patroness of a well-known school of needlework in Stuttgart in 1883.

And on unlined onionskin paper, Grandmamma made exquisite handwritten copies of poems in the old Gothic script that had been outlawed by the American Occupation Government. Then, she would give these to me to memorize.

Grandmamma was so old, she looked as translucent to me as the onionskin paper, and I imagined that when people died, they simply became more and more transparent until they became completely invisible. She always wore black—I thought at the time to make herself more visible and solid, but of course, she was a widow and not only that, she was grieving for her son, my father, although, as you have read, I now believe she was actually his grandmother. And, thus, my great grandmother.

I dropped her a perfunctory curtsey at the door, "Good morning, Grandmamma, are you feeling quite well?"

"As well as can be expected at my age, thank you, Child. Do you have a poem for me today?"

"The Sunken Crown by Ludwig Uhland," I told her.

"Let me hear it," she said and added, smiling, "Slowly, but slo-o-ow-lee-ee, with care for each word."

> "The Sunken Crown
> by Ludwig Uhland
>
> Up on yonder hill
> There stands a simple hut,
> And from its humble doorsill
> You see the lovely land spread out.
>
> There sits a farmer, who is free,
> Evenings, on his bench,
> And, dangling his scythe idly,
> He sings to heaven his thanks.
>
> Down in the valley below,
> Dusk hides the deep pool,
> And sunk in its watery shadow,
> There lies a rich crown, golden and proud.
> At night it lets ruby and sapphire play
> By the moon and the stars gently lit;

It's lain there for many a long, grey
Year, and no one looks for it."[26]

"Ah, Uhland," said Grandmamma, "No friend of monarchy, but a fine poet. Not as good as Mörike, though. There is no one like Mörike for clean, limpid sound—except Rilke, of course."

She loved poetry and had me memorize scads of it, mostly from the German Romantic period—Schiller and Goethe, naturally, but she loved Uhland and, especially, Mörike because they were Swabians. I may not remember what I had for breakfast today, but I can still recite at least ten poems by Mörike. Moreover, I knew that Mörike had a cat named Weissling and a dog named Joli. Of Uhland, on the other hand, I remember one of the very worst rhymed couplets purporting to be poetry ever written by the hand of man—worse even than the one by Wordsworth, which tells us about his child's grave that he "measured it from side to side, 'twas four feet long and two feet wide." At least Wordsworth had the sense to edit it out. Uhland tells us of a Swabian crusader who, with one stroke of his mighty sword, sliced a Turkish warrior in half from the crown of his head down to the saddle and deeply into his horse's back. As a result of this great "Swabian stroke,"

---

[26] Here is the original. The translation in the text is mine. Die versunken Krone (1834)

Da droben auf dem Hügel,
Da steht ein kleines Haus,
Man sieht von seiner Schwelle
Ins schöne Land hinaus;

Dort sitzt ein freier Bauer
Am Abend auf der Bank,
Er dengelt seince Sense
Und singt dm Himmer Dank.

Da drunten in dem Grunde,
Da dämmert längst der Teich,
Es liegt in ihm versunken
Eine Krone, stolz und reich,
Sie läßt zu Nacht wohl spielen
Karfunkel und Saphir;

Sie liegt seit grauen Jahren,
Und niemand sucht nach ihr.

To the right and to the left
A half Turk fell of life bereft[27].

The German word for "stroke" also means "prank." And this is why Swabia is as full of stories about "Swabian strokes" as America is of redneck jokes.

"You look a little down," Grandmamma said as I finished Uhland's poem.

"I hate arithmetic, I hate it, and I really hate it," I told her with passionate emphasis.

"I see," she said.

"It's really stupid, but Uncle Kellermann says I have to learn it if I ever want to handle money."

"Oh, with all due respect to Uncle Kellermann, he does speak wisely as an accountant," she told me, "But for you, what he says makes no sense. A lady learns for the sake of learning, never for the sake of money. In fact, a great lady does not entangle herself with money at all. It is simply not her concern, regardless of whether she is rich or poor; and you are a lady first of all. If you learn mathematics, it will be because you see the beauty of it." I nodded gravely and much relieved. Then she added a line from Mörike, "'*Was aber schön ist, selig scheint es in ihm selbst.*'" "Whatever is beautiful shines blessed within itself." The sentiment is much the same as Keats' equation of beauty and truth, with the added suggestion in Mörike that beauty needs no audience, and the thoroughly German romantic irony in the verb "scheinen," which says both "to shine" and "to seem."

I always thought it a special occasion to visit Grandmamma in her rooms, which housed an amazing collection of eighteenth century porcelain figurines of ladies and gentlemen dancing, playing chess, pretending to be shepherds shepherdesses, and some wearing black half masks held up by thin sticks. With her quiet and cultured voice in my ears instructing me in the duties and manners of a lady, which included the exact depth of the curtsey a lady had to drop to all manner of personages and, also, what kinds of persons one might expect a courtesy

---

[27] *zur Rechten sieht man wie zur Linken,*
einen halben Türken heruntersinken.
In my opinion, *"niedersinken"* would scan better than *"heruntersinken."* But what do I know. I am not Uhland: My dog is RuDog and my cat is Greymir.

from. How to treat a servant so as to get loyal and intelligent service was another thing that was important to her. And, as a background to these conversations, I learned my first stitches in crewel- and white work when I was not yet six. "The world," she said, "Is not normal now because of the war, but soon it will be again the way it was before Hitler came, so learn what I tell you, so that you will be at home in that world to teach your daughter."

***

The world was not normal—she was right about that. Nor did the world ever return to what Grandmamma would have called "normal." As if to prove that it would not, the gods arranged for Klara to call me into the kitchen when I returned home unharmed through the magnificent garden of my uncle Walter, the Asshole of Sillenbuch.

"Can you keep a secret?" she asked.

"You know I can keep a secret—you know we've got Wolfgang Gottschalk," I said, whispering his name.

"I mean, can you keep a secret from him and from everybody else in the family—and in the whole world?"

"Sure."

"You didn't even think about it before you said, 'sure.' I can't trust nothin' like that. I want you to think about this, 'cause this is important. Sleep on it, and lemme know in the mornin'. It'll be a really big and secret secret that you have to keep forever." She spoke a thick and wonderful Swabian dialect, which I wish I could render. And I learned it quickly despite Aunt Lilo's disapproval.

I didn't think I'd be able to sleep after that promise of such a big, important secret, but in the end I must have dozed off. I woke freezing on the garage roof where I often spent time after I was sent to bed even if I had no plans for going anywhere. I'd "throw rocks in the pond" or do with the words of the day what Mary did. In fact, "Do with words what Mary did," was one of my grandfather's alternatives for, "Good night, Rabbit."

I showed up in the kitchen early. Klara was making breakfast: a watery soup out of leftover mashed potatoes—mashed potatoes without milk or butter. "I'm still sure," I told her.

"Good," she said, "I figured I could prolly count on you. Tonight, when everybody is sleepin', I'll come and wake you 'round midnight. You have to be real quiet and don't wake your sister. Get dressed—wear something dark—and go your usual way over the garage roof…"

"You know about that?" I gasped in a whisper.

"I know everything that goes on in this here house, but don't let that worry you none. You're gonna keep my secret, and I'll keep yourn. So you go your usual way 'cause I don't wanna take no chances us bein' seen together. Meet me in the northeast corner of the Unkauf's hops field.

And all the while she said these amazing things, she kept right on doing her routine kitchen things as if it was just nothing she was saying.

I was in heaven. I could barely make it through the day without telling somebody, and it truly is a miracle that I never told.

When I got to the hops field that night, Klara was already there since she did not have as complicated a path to travel as I did over the garage roof and garden wall. The tall and almost gothic tunnels of a hops field are as easy to hide in as the rows of a cornfield and just as magical.

"Here's the deal," she said, "We're gonna be raidin' fields, startin' tonight, a couple, maybe three times a week. The corn salad in Betzler's field looks real good to me—we're gonna do that field first and then we're gonna get us some winter cabbages from the Kaufmann's. The Smiths send us milk, so we'll leave their fields alone. I tried buying stuff from the farmers 'round here, but them stags[28] wouldn't sell me nothin', so now we're gonna take that stuff for free. And if we have these extra veggies, I can trade in some of our vegetable ration tickets for meat tickets—in fact, I already done that. That weird painter down in the old village, he's a vegetarian, so he was real happy to trade in his meat tickets, but you don't need to know none of that."

"What's a vegetarian?"

"I told you, you this ain't stuff you need to know—vegetarians don't eat meat. You can ask Mr. Bauer about that yourself—you're down there often enough, wasting his paints."

"He don't think I'm wastin' no paint. He thinks I got talent."

"Whatever," said Klara and continued, "Now, here's how we're gonna do it. I'm gonna hide out in the hedgerows and keep watch. You're real

---

[28] The word "stag" or, in German, "Hirsch" is, in Swabia, as terrible a term of disapprobation as is "hog-dog" in other parts of the country.

small, and you're gonna belly-crawl along the furrows with this basket and knife and get the stuff. Get the plants apart some, so there's no bald spots in the field that somebody could notice. If I see anybody coming I'll do an owl's hoot, and you just drop down flat on the ground—keep your face down and your hands and the knife outa sight. And look, I've got this here little wooden thingy that can do a nightingale. And when it's all clear, you'll hear this": She demonstrated the most delicious warble to melt your heart on her wooden thingy. "And then you just keep on going, OK?"

"OK," I whispered.

"Now here's somethin' else. If you're gonna be a thief, you gotta figure you might get caught. We're gonna be real careful and we're not gonna get caught, but just in case, here's the deal: they never put kids in jail. You can trust me on that. So if anybody's gonna get caught, it's gonna be you, and you are gonna keep your big mouth shut. I want you to understand that, 'cause you're gonna be safe no matter what—I wouldn't be 'cause I jus 'turned twenty-one. Is it a deal?"

"Yeah, no problem." Like I said, I was in a state of ecstasy. It seems we come into this world trailing criminal records right along with the clouds of glory that Wordsworth bragged about.

Other than a real owl calling a false alarm once, the whole thing worked like a charm. I crawled down a furrow away from the hedgerow, pushing the shallow basket in front of me, then crawled the neighboring furrow back, and we emptied the basket into Klara's bigger one. "I had Joseph weave these baskets special to be dark brown," she whispered.

The cabbages were not as easy as the corn salad had been. Cabbages are bigger and harder to cut and their stems are woody and tough sometimes. You also have to dig through a bunch of slimy rotting and stinking leaves before you get to the clean head in the middle. And in case you are wondering why that is, here is why: the outer leaves of winter cabbage freeze and then rot in the next thaw, but cabbage heads are so tightly wrapped, the inner part is safe, and so they are prepared for this loss. Klara showed me how to do it at the edge of the field, cautioning me not to cut myself. The knife was sharper than a razor—my grandfather kept all the kitchen knives sharp. It all went without a hitch, and I was back on my shelf in the pantry in nothing flat, sleeping the sleep of the righteous.

For lunch next day we had pork rinds and cabbage and potatoes and onions and corn salad, and if that does not sound sumptuous, just remember stale bread soup. My grandfather said the blessing, thanking God for the abundance, and I started to speak, but Klara kicked me hard under the table.

"Were you going to say something, my Rabbit?" he asked.

"I was just gonna say a verse from the Bible," I said with emphasis, giving Klara a look that said, whaddayatakemeforanywaysyathinkI'mstupidorsomethin?

"Going to say a verse, not gonna," said Aunt Lilo.

"Yes, Aunt Lilo."

"Well, what's the verse?" my grandfather asked me, while Klaus Bach sneered and Aunt Lilo looked bored.

"The Lord works in weird ways."

"Wondrous ways," said Uncle Kellermann.

Aunt Kellermann said, "I think it's mysterious ways, Albert. The Lord works in mysterious ways."

"Weird ways too, in my experience," said my grandfather. And then my heart almost stopped when he asked Klara, "To what do we owe this feast?"

"Our farmers have had a change of heart, I guess," she said. "I got this stuff really cheap."

"My prayers have been answered," he said.

From then on, we had more food, at least by the standards I had been used to, because Klara stuck to her plan: we raided the fields in the neighborhood two or three times each week. When I was out with my geese, I would take really good looks at what was growing and where, getting a thief's view of the lovely land spread out. We discussed these matters when we were alone in the kitchen and made our plans. And just so you know, the kitchen was its own room with a door—so it was a private space. Fortunately, we only did this for one spring, summer, and fall. I do not think I would have been able to raid fields at night and go to school by day. But for that summer and fall, she and I sure had a good time of it.

We never did get caught, and I never told anyone about our nighttime adventures. I am sure a modern teacher would not think that these escapades would be good for my self-esteem and moral character, but I felt pleased as pie with myself when my grandfather said the blessing and twelve people had food to eat.

And from then on, "The Lord works in weird ways" was one of my favorite verses, which I often added to the blessing. My grandfather never found any fault with it. Uncle Kellermann objected one more time, but my grandfather said, "The Bible is a translation. Luther didn't say 'weird,' but another translator might have."

You just cannot be quite as fundamentalist a Christian if you speak more than one language than you can be if you do not. Later, on one of those days I had said it, my grandfather took me aside and said, "I didn't want to hurt Uncle Kellermann's feelings, but you should know that this verse, whether we say 'weird' or 'wondrous' or 'mysterious' is not in the Bible at all, it's just something we say. Uncle Kellermann's feelings are hurt when you say 'The Lord works in weird ways,' so maybe you'll want to consider not saying it."

"Do you think the Lord works in weird ways, Grandpa?"

"I can't even begin to imagine it any weirder than it already is, Rabbit."

"OK, then I won't say it anymore.

CHAPTER SIXTEEN

One Horrible Imagination

Every evening my grandfather listened to the news on the radio, and I was required to listen also. I rarely understood what was going on, but sometimes he would explain—and sometimes not. More often than not, he would say, "Do with those words what Mary did." Sometimes when I questioned him, he would tell me to ask Aunt Lilo or some other member of the household, and occasionally a question had to wait until my mother came home for a weekend. One night the news was about the declining infant mortality rate, which had been twice that of other countries in the immediate post-war years—but now, things were getting better in Germany. And that piece of news led to a question that had to wait several weeks for my mother to come home.

"Where do babies come from, Grandpa?"

He was silent for a whole minute and then said, "That's a question for your mother."

I got impatient and asked Klara because I figured she would know since she had a baby, but she said the stork brings them, which was clearly nonsense. I told her so, too, "Unkaufs up the street had a baby last week, and I never saw no storks near their place. I never see no storks at all in the village."

All the storks lived in a far-away swamp—the only place I was not allowed to go by myself, though, of course, that did not keep me from exploring that most interesting, fecund, and beautiful world.

She did not say anything, so I added, "If storks brought babies, you'd be seeing storks all over town all the time."

"They come at night," she told me.

"Klara, owls are the only birds that fly at night, and you know it."

"Well, maybe owls deliver babies."

"Owls would never deliver babies."

"Why not? They're big, strong birds that can carry a load."

"Owls would eat babies, same way they eat rabbits and frogs."

"You have got one horrible imagination."

"I do not. And if it's storks, where do they get the babies in the first place? Storks can't make babies out of thin air, you know," and added, "It ain't natural."

"It is too. All kinds of things grow in the swamp. The wind and the birds bring seeds." That started to sound a little bit reasonable maybe. Hannes had explained how the wind and bird droppings carry seeds everywhere—but seed for babies?

"I ain't never heard of no seed that grows babies."

"That's 'cause you aint' heard all there is to hear. Why don't you do what your grandpa said and wait for your mom to come home?" Klara was holding out, and I knew it.

"I thought we was partners."

"Well, there's some stuff you're too young for."

I left in a huff and asked Aunt Lilo. She said, "They grow in their mother's belly. Have you seen Giesela Mahler lately?"

"Uh huh."

"Yes, not uh huh."

"Yes, Aunt Lilo."

"Well, doesn't she have the biggest belly you've ever seen? It's called being pregnant. Frau Mahler is pregnant," Lilo said in her best schoolteacher voice.

"Like Mary in the Christmas Story!?"

"Exactly. Frau Mahler will have a baby any day now—in fact, I won't be surprised if it turns out to be twins."

Babies growing in a person's belly sounded even more fantastic than storks, though she was right about Frau Mahler's belly being enormous—that much was plain to see.

"How do the babies get in the belly of a person and how do they get back out?"

"Why don't you ask your mother those questions? She knows for sure because she had you. I've never had a baby." I knew she was lying. Not about never having a baby, but about not knowing.

I went to see my grandmother with this important question.

She sighed deeply and said, "Men," and would say no more except, "It's a question for your mother—she's the one with the scientific knowledge."

My mother did not enlighten me either. She said, "When a man and a woman are married, a seed is planted, and the baby grows from that seed in the mother's belly." I was too young to call it a cop-out via passive voice construction, but I knew indirection when I heard it. The idea of a seed had started to sound pretty solid, though—but how did the seed get planted and where did they get it? I knew my mother well enough, however, and could feel that no further questions would be welcome. Yet I had learned something for my efforts; I had learned that here was no ordinary question. My grandfather would not touch it with a ten-foot pole, two women beat around the bush, one told outrageous bird stories, and a fourth had pain in her heart at the very mention of it. Here was something dark and not allowed.

Then another event convinced me even more deeply that there was something unspeakably horrible about the origin of babies. On those weekends when my mother came home with her entourage, two Russians were often among the group. One was Prince Nikolai Andreyev Azarenko-Zarovsky who was an old and very kind gentleman with deeply sad eyes. His wife was a prisoner in Bulgaria or someplace like that. The other man was the only one of Nikolai Andreyev's children whom he had managed to get out of Russia alive: the handsome and very dashing young Prince Volodya Nikolaievich Azarenko-Zarovsky.

Since they were friends of the family, the son was just called Vova, and the father was addressed as Nikolai Andreyev. My grandfather said he did not have much use for princes, but he also told me you could tell how close the two of them were to the czars of Russia by the fact that the word "zar" appears twice in their names. "Zar" is the German spelling. I am sure that had my future uncle Vova known that his future lay in America, he would have used the most common American spelling for his names: Aczarenko-Czarovsky. Or, maybe, since he had intellectual pretensions, he would have used the more scholarly Atsarenko-Tsarovsky.

There was something about Vova did not like from the start. Maybe it was the fact that he wore his hair combed straight back like Uncle Walter, the Asshole of Sillenbuch. Except that Uncle Walter's hair was glued down and grey, while Vova's hair was chestnut brown and loose and kept falling in his face and had to be repeatedly brushed back with an elegant sweep of the hand. And anyway, I liked my uncle Walter because he never pretended he was not an asshole. Maybe I did not like Vova's mustache and silk ascot ties. Maybe I did not like the way he held a cigarette or a pipe at a certain angle. Maybe it was the way he used soft, gooey, and lingering Russian "L's" that almost melted into a "Y," even when he was speaking German, although a Russian accent never bothered me in anybody else. I could tell my grandmother did not like him much either—same way she did not like Klaus Bach.

Anyway, one day Vova came to visit with a bunch of flowers for my grandmother and a bottle of vodka for my grandfather—which, in those days, had to have been a black market item. He kissed my grandmother's hand in a way that I understand now to have told her exactly what her baby girl was in for. She knew what was coming. And she did not need to wait for Vova to say to my grandfather, speaking in German, "Maxim Pavlovitch, I am kheerr todayi to ask mosst khumblyyiy forr yourr younguest and mosst byootteefulll daughtrr's khand in murritch."

My grandmother said she was going to put the flowers in water, but then she never came back into the room, which was also the family dining room and my grandmother's sewing room as well as the bedroom of my grandparents.

He was honored, my grandfather told Vova, but of course he would have to speak to his daughter about it before he could give an answer. They had a couple of shot glasses of vodka together, and then my grandfather asked suddenly, "Do you love her?"

"Ayiddoo," said Vova, "I llyove kherr deepuhlly, widd all my khearrt, and I wuill churrish kherr forrevrr." You had to have a tongue like a big, fat, slimy, garden slug to produce L-sounds like that.

"I see," said my grandfather.

I did not see. I did not see at all how my grandfather could fall for it like that. Vova had actually not said he would cherish her. He had used a German cliché that amounts to the same thing, "Ich werrrde sie auf Chänden trrraggen," but it says literally, "I will carry her on my hands." I didn't know it was a cliché at the time, but I sure knew him for a big fat phony.

That weekend Ruth and my mother both came home without guests, and things turned into a screaming match immediately, with

Ruth weeping and my mother telling everyone what was and what was not going to happen. It was the same dark and hateful atmosphere that had risen like a vulture and spread his wings over the room when Maria had said she was going to Berlin to take care of Dad. "Are you pregnant?" my mother shot at Ruth in her most hateful and commanding tone. Ruth denied it. Then my mother threw out those ugly dark words again, accusing Ruth of being in a state of sexual bondage to Vova, while Ruth was wailing and screeching about how much she loved him and how much he loved her.

These horrible scenes went on every weekend forever it seemed. My grandfather went for long walks, and I ran away into the fields to find Hannes. My sister sat in a corner and cried.

And then, suddenly, everything was OK. My grandmother grumbled a little about how she did not like where the silk and other stuff came from, but she started sewing an amazing wedding dress of ivory peau de soie for Ruth with lace insets, silk embroidery, and little seed pearls. Ruth was a beauty to begin with and in that dress she looked incredible. My grandmother added a simple veil held in place by a crown made of peau de soie roses that she showed me how to make, and they turned out to be really easy.

Things never go entirely smoothly when you are sewing, so my grandmother would grumble something that sounded approximately like "*yazvitj yevo*," and meant approximately "to the devil with it," but most of the time, she was singing while she sewed. Then she made some even more amazing frilly dresses for my sister and me that looked like clouds made of whipped cream with translucent fog swirling all around them. We were going to be flower girls. And we were going to carry the back of Ruth's skirt because it was so long it trailed on the ground. Nobody was able to give me a reasonable explanation for why the skirt could not be shortened so it would not trail on the ground and sweep up dust and get dirty unless somebody carried it.

Though Aunt Lilo, Klaus Bach, and my mother agreed that it was all a "colossal piece of kitsch," and though my grandmother and a whole lot of other old women cried throughout the whole thing, it was a fairytale wedding in the Russian Orthodox Church in Stuttgart, which was resplendent in the manner of Russian orthodox churches with glass tile mosaics and gold leaf glowing in candle light, with mysterious icons, and a Russian choir taking the soul from deep despair to clear and high jubilation.

It was also a brief moment of glory for the Russian *émigré* and refugee community who had all turned out in their finery. I remember especially an old man in grey. He was wearing a monocle, and his wife wore a dress in a slightly lighter shade of grey and antique silver jewelry inset with marquisettes—they whispered to each other in French. She had a monocle hanging on a long silver chain. Michael Ende was standing next to me saying, "Look, they are all actors and actresses, and the play is over. The person who wrote the play has given them no more lines to say, and they don't know what to do about that." And I thought, "All this is created to hide something dark about the origin of babies, and now we'll soon know what that horrible thing is." I was sure of this and felt it as a painful contraction of myself in my whipped cream dress while clutching a bouquet of white roses and jasmine blossoms in my sweaty hands.

But then their scent and that of myrrh and frankincense drew my attention upward, and I discovered high above us a white dove in the golden sky of the cupola while the chorus sang their brilliant hallelujahs.

I remembered my Aunt Editta had shown me, in the best picture book in the whole world, a painting of Mary kneeling and an angel, just arriving—you could tell, since his feet as yet bore no weight and his skirt was flying in the up-draft of his descent. The angel, Aunt Editta said, was telling Mary she would have a baby. A white dove hovered above her head. I was sure I would never see a more beautiful painting. She said, "That is because the man who painted it had an angel's name, 'Rafael.'"

And in this amazing wedding there was also something of a surprise for our whole family. Just before Ruth was married to Vova with crowns held over their heads as they walked all around the altar three times, she was baptized. The priest announced three times in a deep, sonorous, and hypnotic voice straight out of Kubrick's film, "Eyes Wide Shut," that she was henceforth to be known as the Princess Irina Maximovna Azarenko-Zarovsky.

Then the whole thing was over, everybody went to a big party except Klara who took my sister and me home.

Next morning early I went to find my grandfather and asked him, "Do pigeons bring the seeds for babies?" There is no difference in German between pigeons and doves—it needs a context or a modifier to distinguish them.

"Pigeons? What in heaven's name are you talking about, my Rabbit?" I told him about the dove in the church and in the painting.

"Well, in that case, yes, you could kind of say that. That dove is the Holy Spirit. It is really invisible, but it is always portrayed as a dove."

"It can change itself into a pigeon?"

"It moves through all things."

"Including pigeons?"

"Yes, my Rabbit, including pigeons and rabbits, especially rabbits like you."

I went straight to the kitchen and, smugly triumphant, told Klara, "I know where babies come from."

"Really? I can't wait to hear this."

"Pigeons bring the seed."

"Oh. Pigeons? Is that so?"

"Yes," I said, "So there."

"And how do the pigeons do this?"

"They fly over your head and drop the seed when you get married, and then you swallow it and it grows into a baby in your belly."

Klara almost spilled boiling water all over us because she laughed so hard, gasping out between laughs, "I can't fucking wait to tell Joseph.... P-p-pigeon shit.....I can't stand it......you swallow pigeon shit!"

"You can ask Grandpa," I told her and did not speak to her for the rest of the day.

The first time Ruth, a.k.a. Princess Irina Maximovna Azarenko-Zarovsky, came home to visit after the wedding, even my grandfather got a little hot under the collar. The Russian Orthodox Church was just as corrupt as the Roman Catholic Church he told her. Then he added, "And exactly what is wrong with the name I gave you when you were born, Ruth?"

"I hate that name," wailed Ruth, a.k.a. Irina Maximovna. "You called me Ruth because you hate Germany, and I was born here."

My aunt Ruth had reference to the fact that she was the only one of my grandmother's nine children who was not born in Russia, but in

Germany among the alien corn, and also to the fact that when my grandparents said "us" they meant Russians and when they said "them," they meant Germans. I did not completely figure out that I was not really Russian until I actually went to school. Even then, I preferred Russian because often, in the many discussions my grandfather had with the many Russian friends that came to visit him, these discussion turned around the fact that—and everyone agreed on this fact—the Germans had "nix kultura." The context of the discussion made it quite obvious that "kultura" (or culture) meant "heart." I was convinced of the truth of this, obviously, since my grandfather had agreed. After that conversation, the idea had become memorable because of a conversation with Klaus Bach, who, if you'll remember, thought that everything related to the heart (as a metaphor) was kitsch. I told him once over a chess game that my grandfather had said in no uncertain terms that Germans had no culture. Of course I used the German word for "culture" (*Kultur*), not the Russian one, but that was before I had learned that you don't translate words or even sentences: you translate meaning.

"That is utter nonsense," said Klaus Bach. "We have Mozart and Beethoven and Goethe and Bach—yes, exactly, we have Bach."

"What?" I asked, puzzled, "What do Mozart and Beethoven and Goethe have to do with heart?"

"Heart?? What are you talking about? We're talking about culture, not heart."

I patiently explained the context of my grandfather's statement about "no culture" to Klaus. And he, when he got it, he said, "Your grandfather said 'Germans have no heart'?!"

And when I nodded he was silent, and I thought he was thinking about his move, but then, he forgot to protect his queen, and I, for the first time ever, won the game.

But, let us return to Ruth wailing about my grandfather's alleged hatred of Germany and giving her a name that implied "alien corn."

"I named you Ruth," said my grandfather, more in control of himself than he had been, "So you would find a husband as kind and loving as Boaz in the Book of Ruth. It is not easy to find a good husband in a foreign land where you know nothing of the people and are not one of them."

"Are you saying Vova is not a good husband and he doesn't love me?" shrieked Ruth, a.k.a. Irina Maximovna.

"He doesn't know what love is just yet, but that doesn't mean he can't learn. I learned rather late myself."

Irina put her hands over her ears and repeated, "He loves me, he loves me, he loves me," until my grandfather said, "Oh, grow up, will you? Your ability to be a good wife concerns me as much as his ability to be responsible for one."

Then a few months later, Vova and Irina showed up and announced that they would be immigrating to America. My grandmother cried.

But I was excited. I would have an Aunt and Uncle in America. America was the land care packages came from. America was the land of opportunity and freedom and equality, the land of all possibilities and the best country in the world. America had stores called Sears and Roebuck that made fat catalogues that always began with the most beautiful dresses for little girls you could ever imagine. In fact, the dresses grandma had made for the wedding were copied from what Ina and I had picked out of one of those catalogues. I have no clue how Sears and Roebuck catalogues came into my possession, but they did, regularly. I would look at them and wonder how it was possible for so many things to exist in the world, and one store had them all—dresses and tools and shoes, all in the same store. And I fervently desired dozens of those dresses in every pastel shade imaginable. I knew my mother would hate them and me for wearing them and call them kitsch which is almost as horrible as sexual bondage, but I wanted them. How I would have managed my favorite sport, tree climbing, in one of those insane dresses was something I never considered.

So the prince and his new princess left for America, and my grandfather said, "What's done is done, and if it's done, it must be God's will—time tells the truth; we shall just go on as before."

***

Meanwhile, my grandfather and I had been listening to the news again every night, and one night there was something on the radio that really got my grandfather excited. The radio said that the brick factories could not keep up with the demand for bricks in the rebuilding of Germany. There were no bombed out buildings in the village, but I knew bricks were hard to get because on the rubble piles of all the bombed out buildings in Stuttgart you could see women sitting around with hammers to knock the mortar off bricks so they could be re-used. This decade they did the same thing in Zhenjiang, Jiangsu Province, China. That whole town looked like a war zone since so many buildings were being destroyed in order to build new ones, taller ones, more expensive-looking, more fantastically modern with more glass and more steel. In fact, in China it was going on right under my kitchen window. They took off the roof tiles of two buildings opposite mine one by one and made a human chain down the ladder so that each tile could be saved and reused. Then, when they knocked down the walls, women sat with hammers on the rubble piles and knocked off excess mortar because women's labor is cheaper than bricks.

When my grandfather heard about the brick shortage, he said, "Why that's crazy. We are sitting on a gold mine here in Swabia."

"You mean there is gold here?" I knew what gold was and how precious it was. I also knew that my grandfather had panned for gold in the rivers and streams of Siberia and had traded it for salt, weight for weight. And so his answer to my question was disappointing: "No, my Rabbit, it's just a manner of speaking. The soil here is mostly clay but you can make bricks out of clay."

"Then why don't people do it?"

"They probably don't know they can. I'm going to the next town meeting in Stuttgart and I will tell them."

"Can I come too?"

"Yes, you can, and we'll ask Nikolai to come also."

CHAPTER SEVENTEEN
Grandpa's Excellent Sidekick

Nikolai Sidarchuk ("cedar-CHOOK") was a very different Nikolai from the one who was my new uncle Vova's father. Nikolai Sidarchuk was my grandfather's best friend and excellent sidekick in countless adventures and he was no ordinary human being—that much was obvious at first sight. He looked more Asian than Russian, though he had blue eyes. He was barely taller than my mother, and stronger than an ox. He had high cheekbones, a flat face, a very low nose-bridge, a strong jawbone, a bit of an eyebrow ridge and a sloping forehead. I have seen faces wilder and more resembling our primate cousins than even his in China. Not in the cities, but in some out-of-the-way places you see faces that would give your most hard-line creationist pause and even paws. But then, maybe not—I once taught college seniors in the States, who told me in all sincerity that white people came from Adam and Eve, while black folks evolved from apes.

Though he looked more like an animal than a man, Nikolai was handsome in my eyes, and when I was a child, I was sure he had magical powers. Maybe part of the reason I was so sure about that was that he believed in magic and demons and devils and ghosts and in evil as well as good spirits. When his wife, Nastya, got a little black kitten, he took an ax and chopped off the tip of the kitten's tail to let the devil out of it. He came to tell my grandfather about it and he was still sobbing because of the pain he had caused the kitten—but what could he do? The devil definitely had to go.

My grandfather explained patiently that all angels and all demons and devils live within human beings, not animals.

"But Grandpa, demons can live inside of pigs—I know for sure," I interrupted.

"You do?"

"Yes, Grandpa, it's in the Bible."

"Oh," he said, "Right. You mean when Jesus sends the demons into the pigs. I've never understood that text—it seems completely out of character."

"What do you mean?" said Nikolai, "Can the Bible be wrong?"

"Well, yes, I think it can. Not very often, and you always have to figure that maybe your own understanding might not be big enough. There are texts that made no sense at all to me twenty years ago, but today they're crystal clear. Still, mistakes can creep in. After all, the Bible was written by human beings and it was translated by them also."

"I thought God wrote it," said Nikolai.

My grandfather answered, "He did in a manner of speaking."

"Maxim Pavlovich, He either did or He did not," said Nikolai, and I did not understand the rest of the conversation because it got really confusing about how you could know if it was God or Satan telling you what to write.

Here is the story my grandfather told me about Nikolai:

Originally from somewhere in Ukraine, he had come out of Siberia like Tarzan. He had been sentenced to life imprisonment in a maximum-security facility where life was bound to be brutal and short. Most people who were sent to Siberia were not behind barbed wire and watched by armed guards with dogs and searchlights. Siberia was so big and so wild that nobody could really escape anyway. Where could you go? You would not get far before the guards or the wolves got you. But whatever it was Nikolai had been accused of, it was so terrible that it merited a barbed wire prison in addition to hard labor and severe rations.

But as I think back on the story my grandfather told me, I remember that World War II did not end in 1945 in the Ukraine—it was ongoing, as I heard the story from my grandfather, and it did not end until about 1953, so Nikolai might just have been on the wrong side of some imaginary line drawn in imaginary sand by the boys that run our world.

Anyway, he is in this awful place thinking about escape. Thinking about Nastya back in the Ukraine: young, beautiful, slender like a young birch and strong—a hod carrier by profession. She can climb up ladders in her bare feet, her hands spanning her waist and with a huge load of mortar or bricks on her shoulders, all stacked on a board that curved around her neck. And she inspires a plan. It has to happen in late winter because the guards would not try to follow you for long, as they would in summer. He knows this from the bitter experience of others. No one succeeded in summer; the guards and dogs always found you, and then you died. And in winter it was worse: those desperate enough to try had left easy tracks to follow, and at the end there were always bloodstains in the snow and wolves fighting over a few bones.

Maybe things are different now, but back then, when it was called *the* Ukraine, there was not a Russian[29] man alive who did not equate young girls with birch trees in spring with flowers at their feet. My grandmother often sang a song about such girls and such trees, *beryoshy*, as she was sewing. And Nikolai's prison was in the middle of a young birch forest. Nikolai bides his time watching the birch trees until he sees spring in the branches. He can see it coming long before the guards can: a softness, a slight swelling of winter buds…layers of snow slowly seeping to the roots and rising in the trees, making them supple, responsive… the inside of the bark beginning to be sweet with sap. So one moonless night under a cloudy sky and heavy snow-fall, Nikolai swings into the branches of a young birch…she arches her back, and he swings to the next one that bends willingly, and the next…no tracks in the snow… no scent to follow…nothing…he vanishes like the melting snow.

When he re-appears, having swooped up Nastya on his way, he turns out to be a master builder. My grandfather and I first met him in downtown Stuttgart one day. We had gone to watch work on the reconstruction of the castle that had been bombed to the ground, and I saw him in the crowd and pointed him out to my grandfather who said, "That man speaks Russian or I owe you an ice cream."

"You're on," I said," Because that man isn't from any country I've ever heard about."

"If he speaks Russian, you're buying the ice cream for all three of us," said my grandfather. (I had money back then because this was before my mother had found out that he and I were involved in a small business. She had been paying me ten pfennig—roughly a dime—for every pair of the household's shoes I would polish, and I had turned around and had offered my grandfather five pfennig for doing it.

---

[29] My grandparents both thought of the Ukraine, the Crimea, the Caucasus, Kasakhstan, Kirgistan Bashkortostan, and Georgia—all places where they had lived—as being part of Russia.

This had worked swimmingly until my grandfather said to me at lunch one day, when my mother happened to be home, that I still owed him fifteen pfennig. My mother said, "Why does the child owe you money?" And then the whole thing came out, and my mother said, "I am not nurturing any capitalists in my bosom").

We snuck up behind the man and my grandfather said, "*Zdras'seetyeh.*" Nikolai wheeled 'round, and with tears running down his cheeks, he said, in Russian of course, "Oh my brother, I thank God you found me!"

My grandfather answered with the time-honored greeting in troubled countries: "My brother, have you eaten?"

Nikolai and my grandfather hugged each other with tears running down their cheeks, both of which German men do not tend to do, so we were an instant little piece of street theater. "I have eaten today, thank you Brother," said Nikolai, "But my wife and I, we have no real place to stay and no work, and look, those men, those builders, they are making mistake after mistake, that staircase will fall, and I could help them, but I don't speak enough German, and…"

My grandfather interrupted, "The stairs will fall?"

"I am sure."

"You can build them so they won't?"

"I can."

My grandfather was never one to waste time. He took Nikolai by the elbow and said, "Let's go talk to them," we crossed into the roped-off area and were instantly surrounded by a group of men who were not friendly. But grandfather stood his ground and insisted on seeing the foreman "Because there is a dangerous situation developing here."

Germans can be a little arrogant sometimes, and so, although the foreman did show up to find out what all the fuss was about, his first reaction was, "You want me to believe that this Neanderthal here knows better than our German engineers?"

My grandfather said, "Man, I'll do you a favor, and I won't translate what you just said for my friend here. And in answer to your question I will say only that there are plenty of witnesses here who will remember that I tried to warn you."

To make a long story short, the foreman did not believe my grandfather and Nikolai, but the stairs fell some days later—fortunately during the lunch break, so no one was hurt. And we had been at the building site daily waiting for what Nikolai kept insisting would happen any minute. When it did, the foreman said, "OK, let him write down his ideas for the engineers."

When my grandfather translated, Nikolai said, "Maxim Pavlovitch, I am ashamed to tell you, I cannot write."

"Do you mean you're a bad writer or that you can't write at all?"

"I am so ashamed, Maxim Pavlovitch, but I have never learned how to read and write."

"And you could still tell them how to build this staircase?"

"Yes, I did such work in Russia in Petersburg[30] and in Moscow—I learned from a master."

"You mean you worked on palaces?"

"I did."

"Did you watch closely enough to know what they did wrong here?"

"Yes, I told you, they were making many mistakes."

"Many?"

"Well, one, but many were born to it."

"If you tell them what the mistakes were, will they know how to correct them?"

"No, I will still have to tell them—there is nothing so easy about a free-standing spiral staircase."

"Good," said my grandfather, "We have a bargaining position." And to the foreman, he said, "We will write down some of the mistakes your engineers made, but if you want to build it right, you'll have to hire my friend here and pay him properly for his expertise."

My grandfather wrote in German what Nikolai told him in Russian, and, in no time, Nikolai was a sought-after expert in the reconstruction of bombed out palaces and castles. He could pick up a single brick from a ruined castle and see in it the wholeness of the thing in all its splendor. I watched him build a staircase that floated in air and was made of gold. If you lay on the cool marble floor under it and looked up, it seemed to go on forever in a swirling spiral and then there was a dome of blue sky with clouds and angels and you could touch the golden flowers on the banisters.

---

[30] I have never understood why that place is called "St. Petersburg." It was named after a czar who was no saint.

And so, by the time my grandfather and I heard the news that there was a severe brick shortage in Germany, Nikolai and Nastya were established in a tiny basement apartment in Sillenbuch. Nikolai could have made a fortune traveling all over Germany on reconstruction projects, but he refused to leave town and my grandfather's company. He and I walked over to their place together, and I made my grandfather promise they would not make me eat too much borscht when we got there. "I'll do my best," he said, "But you know how they are."

I did know. You had to fight with them to get to stop eating, even though there was a food shortage. That is the way it is in China, too. There is no food shortage, but anytime you get invited out, the host is never happy until you have destroyed your entire digestive system. And "have you eaten" is a way to say 'hello' in China, as it was in Russia, because there, too, there had been famine within living memory.

The three of us went to the town meeting and my grandfather did get to say his piece about using clay to build houses. People just laughed. But he was used to public speaking and pointed out Nikolai's successes. He said that to his knowledge clay could not be used in tall office buildings or factories, but it made very good houses, even big, luxurious houses. People still did not believe him. But an old gentleman with hair as white as my grandfather's said, "I've got a piece of ground in Sillenbuch. You can build a demonstration project if you want. I can help you with expenses, but I can't pay you."

My grandfather said he would think about it. On the way home on the streetcar, he asked me if I would like to help build a clay house. Of course I said yes. He said that I should think because it would be very hard work. Then he said to Nikolai, "I don't believe I just volunteered to do again what I hated doing years ago at gun point in Siberia."

When we got home, my grandfather broke out the bottle of vodka Uncle Vova had brought, which my grandfather had been saving for a special occasion, and this was it. Soon he and Nikolai were dancing in squatting position like a couple of Kazakhs with their arms around each other's shoulders and their legs flying in the air. Then my grandfather demonstrated that he was not drunk by doing a headstand on the dining room table. And after that the two of them had visions of building clay houses all over Germany and becoming millionaires.

Nothing even remotely resembling those visions ever materialized.

They did build a really beautiful little house for the white-haired old man on the city council, but nobody believed it would last. And by the time it was obvious that it would, the brick shortage was over. Now Germany is the world-leader in the technology of building houses with on-site clay, but back then, it was just an idea ahead of its time.

As for me, the building of the clay house was a huge disappointment. What my help consisted of was the boring and difficult labor of stomping around in a huge and shallow sort of mud pool in order to mix the clay with sand and chopped straw. My leg muscles became so awesome as a result, however, that the neighborhood boys let me play on their soccer team when they were a boy short. My usual position was "*Linker Stürmer*," and I still don't know what that is in English. I was the fastest runner in town and I could turn on a dime. After all, I was called "Rabbit" (*Krolick* in Russian) by a person of substance and consequence.

CHAPTER EIGHTEEN

Learning to Read Plants—and a Greek Tragedy

Hannes, Wolf, and I were lying on the big black shepherd's cloak next to Sybille in a flowery meadow on a perfectly windless day. Wolf was snoozing and Sybille was chewing her cud. The sheep and the geese were grazing lazily—not chowing down on anything they could find to swallow, but looking for the choicest herbs and flowers. Hannes and I were looking up into cloudless, dazzling blue. I have not seen blue like that in years. Now the sky is a silvery blue because of geo-engineering (chemtrails) and most people are too young to remember anything different.

Meadows like ours that day do not exist anymore. Maybe far back in the mountains of Switzerland. These days people use weed killers so that nothing but grass grows in a pasture. I have often wondered if grazing animals really get a balanced diet without those flowers. If a sheep or a cow were ever not feeling up to snuff, where would she find the herbs to fix it? What about special treats like cowslips? And if all the special treats and the medicinal plants were gone for two or three generations, a cow would have nothing to teach her calf. Impoverishment—any way you look at it. And hay smells good, but not as wonderful as it does when flowers and wild herbs are mixed in with the grass. I wonder, too, if some of those flowers I knew as a child are now extinct. I've lived here in Fairfield since 1992 (minus two years in China), and there are many plants that have become extinct regionally in that time because of the use of weed killers. The butterflies are gone, the fireflies are far and few between. And there are at least five species of birds I no longer hear or see. A few tree frogs that once were ubiquitous are left in one small neighborhood only. In the mid-nineteenth century, Indian Chief Wapello said the U.S. Congress, "If the white man continues like this, he will succeed in killing all the animals, and then he will die of a great loneliness." I do understand this grief.

But back then our meadow was replete and resplendent with dozens of different kinds of meadow flowers, and therefore it was also overflown by ten thousand golden bees, their summer humming sweet in our ears.

And the larks were up. Hannes said, "Have you ever seen them play?" We sat up, and not only were they singing joyfully in flight, as no other bird can, they were playing a game with swans' down. That day, our meadow lay next to a fairly large pond that was the summer home of a couple of swans. If there are swans, then there will be swans' down lying so lightly on the surface tension of the water that the feathery fluff does not get wet. During molting season, there can sometimes be so much swans' down on a pond that it looks like luminous mist especially in slant light, when the sun, rising or setting, shines through it.

A lark would come swooping down to the water, pick up some swans' down in her beak and take it aloft as high into the sky as only larks will dare and then drop it. Another lark would catch it in his beak and drop it; the first lark would let it float down a bit and then catch it. They would alternate like this, and the winner was the lark who could pick it up closest to the water without getting the tips of her wing feathers wet. Some of the larks were doing it in pairs and some of them were practicing solo. We watched them and then lay down again on our backs with our hands folded under our heads and watched tiny points of light in the bright yet deep blueness. Hannes said, "It will be useful to remember the larks playing."

"Why?"

"I'll tell you when the time comes. Promise to remember them." I promised while wondering what important lesson could be hiding in the lovely games our larks were playing on that lovely day. Then Hannes asked, "Do you see small points of light dancing in the sky?"

"Uh huh."

"Do you think they're part of the sky or do you think they are part of your eyes?"

"I don't know," I said after a long pause.

"Why don't you watch them and then see if you can tell."

I watched and watched. Finally I said. "I really can't tell; can you?"

"No, I really can't either. What do you see when you close your eyes?"

"Nothing."

"Look again. Close your eyes and put your hands over them. Now look carefully. I'll do it too."

If anyone had seen us sitting at the top of a sloping meadow with our eyes covered for a long, long time as if we were in deepest grief, I wonder what they would have thought about it.

Finally, Hannes said, "Don't open your eyes yet, but move your hands away from them."

I did and said the German equivalent of "WOW!!", which is now also 'wow', but back then, American influence had not yet wowed a lot of German words to the point of fainting out of existence.

"What did you see?" asked Hannes.

"When my hands were covering my eyes, I saw light purple moving shapes against dark purple, but then I couldn't always tell if the shapes were maybe dark purple and the background was light purple. And then when I moved my hands, the shapes suddenly turned two shades of bright red."

"That's pretty much my experience too. Did you notice if there was a pattern to the shapes?"

"I don't know; I'll look again." After a while, I told him, "It's kind of a big circle, and you can see where the middle is, but if you try to look too hard at any shape, it changes." I looked some more and then said, "Grandpa and Uncle Kellermann made a kaleidoscope for us for last Christmas. I don't see a lot of colors when I close my eyes, but I see that kind of pattern, kind of. You know, the shapes change and the patterns change."

Out of one of the immense pockets inside his cloak, Hannes took a handful of square cards held together by rubber bands. Taking the bands off, he handed the cards to me, and I was amazed to see how many patterns and colors could be made from just the basic model of the shapes you see when you close your eyes. "They're called 'mandalas'," he told me.

When I went home with my geese later that day, I started to paint mandalas and cut mandala-like snowflakes out of paper for days and weeks until I realized the inherent endlessness of the project. But that day when I saw the mandalas for the first time, I closed my eyes and looked at the mandalas in the darkness of closed eyes and then again in color and definite shape on the cards.

"What's the difference, do you suppose, between the cards and what you see with closed eyes?"

"I can see it, but I can't say it," I told him. Hannes refused to be content with that, so I asked him what he saw as the difference

"I have the same problem you do," he said, "but between the two of us, we should be able to figure out how to say what we see."

While the sheep and the geese grazed and rested and grazed again lazily, we wrangled back and forth, finally concluding that what we saw with eyes closed were mandalas not yet born, and so characterized by infinity in the potential for manifest shapes. As for the twinkling and dancing spots of light in the deep blue sky, we arrived at no answer to the question as to whether it was the sky doing that or whether it was our eyes. When I first saw the Iowa prairies in the mid-seventies, the sky and the horizon still sparkled like that. But now, all that is gone. The sky, at best is silvery blue instead of deep blue. The sparkling points of light are gone. And crickets are single voices now, no longer a joyful chorus.

I thought about mandalas and points of light dancing in the sky for a while as I watched the deep and boundless sky. Then I remembered asking people what time it was and that everybody's time was a little different. Grandpa had said the world was a little different for everybody. At last I said what had been on my mind for weeks: "Hannes, can you teach me how to read plants?"

"I don't know."

"How come you don't know?"

"Some people can learn and some can't. You can't really teach people to read plants. All you can do is make them aware that they can do it, and then if they can, you can help them become better readers."

"OK, make me aware that I can do it then."

"Have you been throwing rocks into the pond?"

"Uh huh."

"How often and how regularly?"

"Grandpa said that throwing those rocks brings the peace that is even deeper than understanding and that I should practice regularly because of the war. So I get up every morning when the sun shines in my window and I find a spot in the fields or the woods where I'm alone and I do it there before breakfast. And every night when they send me to bed I climb out on the garage roof and do it there except when it's raining. Sometimes I fall asleep and then wake up later wondering why I'm sleeping on the garage roof."

"You should practice sitting up, not lying down."

"I do; I don't notice when I lie down and fall asleep."

"That's OK then. Do it now. After a while I'll hold something under your nose to smell. Don't open your eyes—just enjoy the smell."

After throwing God knows how many imaginary rocks to vanish into the depths of myself, a wonderful smell appeared in the world. Hannes said, "You can open your eyes now and tell me where you felt the smell."

"What do you mean, 'where?'"

"Well, did you feel it in your fingertips or your knees?"

"No, Silly, in my nose."

"OK, close your eyes again and throw more rocks."

Another lovely smell appeared after a while. And there was the same question and the same answer. I do not remember how many times he told me to close my eyes and how many great smells he produced for me by crushing leaves or flowers under my nose, but the last time he did so, I opened my eyes instantly and said, "I feel it in the middle of my chest." It was the same summer smell I remembered from Irredorf when the pears were ripe and the hazelnuts and the creeping charlie[31] perfumed the air.

Hannes smiled, "You felt it in your heart."

"That's where my heart is?"

"Kind of—it means that you can learn how to read plants. Now tell me if the smell was warm or cool?"

"Cool?"

"You don't have to be afraid of making mistakes. If the smell stays in your nose, then you can't trust the information, but if you feel it in your heart, you will never make a mistake."

---

[31] What is called "creeping Charlie" in Iowa is called "Jill-over-the-ground" in Ohio. It is also called Alefhoof, Heymaids, Tun-hoof, Hedgemaid, Lizzy-run-up-the-Hedge, Gill-go-by-the-hedge, Cat's foot, and Robin-run-in-the-Hedge. When I told an Iowa farmer all these names for it, he said, "We should just settle on 'low-lyin' Bob'." The Latin is "*Glechoma hederacea.*" The German name is Gundermann or Echt-Gundelrebe. It has been a useful and effective medicinal herb for 5,000 years.

"OK. For sure cool."

"The easiest thing to know about a plant is whether its effect is cooling or heating in the body," said Hannes, "Obviously, if somebody has a fever out of control, you want to give him cooling herbs, and if somebody comes in out of the cold with frozen toes, you'll want to give herbs that will heat the body. Let's try again. I'll let you throw rocks for a long time because I've just given you information, and so your mind is busy. I'll see when your mind is quiet and then I'll let you smell it again."

I opened my eyes and told him I could feel the smell in my heart.

"Well, what does it feel like?"

"I don't know."

"Yes, you know; if it was in your heart, you know. You might have to hunt for the words to tell me, but you know."

"Let me smell it again."

"No need for that. I'm sure you know."

After a long pause I said, "Like the stuff that's left after they make apple cider maybe—I don't mean the way it smells, because what you gave me to smell wasn't apples, but it feels like squeezed out."

"Dry?"

"Yeah, squeezed out and dry."

"That's really good. I told you if you feel it in the heart, you couldn't make mistakes. Anything else?

"Clean?"

"Of course clean. Very clean. We call that kind of smell 'astringent.'" The German word[32] he used held an image to fit the effect.

"Astringent," I repeated and let the word and the remembered smell meet beyond my mind.

Hannes continued, "The sense of smell is the easiest one to feel in the heart. Taste is next. After a while, you might be able to do it with seeing too. Some smells will make you feel them in the middle of your forehead, but you have to be very good before that happens. Now, the effect of the plant you just smelled is also called 'astringent'—you need such plants whenever there is an infection in the body."

"What does 'infection' mean?"

"Well, pus, for example. Anytime there's pus, you've got an infection.

---

[32] The German word is "*zusammenziehend*" which literally says "pulling together."

The plant you just smelled has been used for thousands of years for all kinds of things: kidney problems, heart trouble and so on."

"Like my sister. She had an infection in her skin. She had boils."

"And what did they do about it?"

"When we got to Stuttgart, Grandma opened them and drained them and tried to keep everything clean and dry—she made a tea with plantains[33] and washed her with it and made her drink it.

"So your grandmother knows plants?"

"Uh huh."

"Well, maybe you got your ability from her. Now about your sister's boils: that infection was just below her skin, but what if the infection is inside the body where you can't reach? In that case, you have to give astringent plants because their effect is exactly like draining an abscess or a boil. It's like squeezing the dirty water out of a wet rag, except that with an astringent the rag would contract and squeeze itself dry. You probably know the effect in your own mouth—have you eaten sloe berries? The effect is cleansing and the name we give to that effect is 'astringent.'" (If he had been in America, he would have used cranberries as his example, but cranberries are not half as astringent as sloes, which will really dry out your mouth until it feels fuzzy.)

When I got home that night and gave my full report on the day's events to my grandfather after supper, my grandmother was even more interested than he was. She said, "I learned herbal medicine from my mother, and she learned from hers, but neither of us could read plants. But my great-grandmother—she could read them. You are lucky to have found a teacher." Then she added, "Tell Hannes I'll come to see him sometime soon because I've seen plants around here that I've never seen before and I've wondered what their uses might be."

So I had the blessings of both my grandparents for anything Hannes wanted to teach me. And I learned from him for about six years—even after I started to go to school. In fact, often, I just did not get on the streetcar to go to school and ran to find him in the fields instead.

***

When my mother came home for a weekend with her entourage,

---

[33] The German name is "Wegerich;" it is antimicrobial, anti-inflammatory, and anti-toxic.

all of us would often go for long walks in the oak grove, and everyone was always impressed with how many plants I could identify by name.

Klaus Bach asked me on one of those walks who had taught me to name so many plants, and I remember my answer clearly: "The plants tell me their names."

"Rubbish—plants can't talk."

"Well, you can know who they are in your heart."

"More rubbish—besides, if the plants could tell you their names, they would tell you their Latin names—the Latin name is the scientifically correct name."

"That's stupid. They know I can't speak Latin, and neither can anybody else around here except the Catholic priests, so why would the plants know any Latin?"

"And how do you know about the Catholic priests? Do you know them in your heart also?" Klaus Bach could never say "heart" without sneering and making me feel like I just said something stupid and full of kitsch.

"I know them because I went to church last Sunday—they speak Latin in church, you know."

"Ali," he called out to my mother who was walking with a group of actors a little ahead of Klaus and me, "Did you know Angela attends the Catholic Church on Sundays?"

They waited for us to catch up and my mother asked me, "Who gave you the idea to go to church?"

"I asked Grandpa why everybody goes to church on Sunday, and he said, 'Why don't you go and find out for yourself?'"

"And you went to the Catholic Church?"

"First I went to the Lutheran Church."

"And did you learn why people go to church on Sunday?"

"No. I couldn't figure it out. I asked grandpa again, and he said maybe a lot of people didn't really have a reason—they just go out of habit. The Catholic Church is more beautiful. There are lots of paintings and statues, and the music is nice. But I couldn't figure out why people would want to go to the Lutheran Church. It was really boring."

"So then you started going to the Catholic Church because of the pictures and the music?"

"Well, no, because it's always the same, so I only went a few times.

When you're not home on the weekend I mostly go to see Hannes or Mr. Bauer, or Uncle Walter, or Aunt Editta, and Grandmamma. They never go to church."

"And how do you even know that there are two churches?"

"Well there's only two churches around here, that's all."

"Then how do you know one of them is Catholic and the other one Lutheran?"

"I asked Grandpa, and he said that there are many kinds of churches in the world, not just two, but here in Sillenbuch we only have the Catholic Church and the Lutheran Church. He said all the different churches believe different ideas—he said that was the trouble exactly because God is not an idea."

"I don't think there's anything to worry about," my mother said to Klaus. Then Ursula, one of the actresses, said, "This is really a romantic spot, let's rest here for a while. Come sit by me, Angela."

I went over, sat down next to her on the short grass and told her, "I think your eyes are romantic, not the spot."

She got all excited and yelled at everybody, "Listen, listen, did you hear what Angela just said? She said that my eyes are romantic and the spot isn't."

Klaus Bach asked me, "Do you even know what 'romantic' means?"

"Yes, 'romantic' means 'in love,' and so I figure Ursula must be in love because the spot isn't."

Everybody asked Ursula who the lucky guy was, but she would not say. Then she changed the subject and said, "Ali, what about your two kids in the play?"

My mother asked me, "How would you like to act in a play?"

"What's that?"

"It's a kind of pretend game—like opera, only people don't sing all the time."

One of the actors said, "Why don't you take her and Ina to the Schiller production—then they'll know what a play is."

"That's a great idea," said my mother, and so the following weekend we got to go to the Stuttgart State Theater and watch a production of "The Robbers" by Friedrich von Schiller—it was breathtaking and even intoxicating, although I could not really follow all that was happening on the stage. We had seats in the first row of the balcony. I could not sleep that night thinking about how much the two brothers in the play were like Ina and me and about how they could make something so real, and I was excited at the prospect that I would get to be in a play myself.

* * *

But then the reality of being an actress turned out to be really horrible. My sister and I got haircuts and we were supposed to be the two sons of a lady named Medea. I never got to see the whole play because I was always backstage when I was not on stage, but my mother had told us the story, and there was not that much to it. Some guy named Jason went to some other country across the ocean in a ship and he wanted the fur of a sheep that was golden. I could not see what was so special about that because all the sheep I had ever seen were pale gold on top and deep gold underneath. He had trouble getting the fur, so a lady named Medea helped him to get it. I liked the part about sowing dragons' teeth and harvesting soldiers. Then Jason and Medea ran away together on Jason's ship, and when her father came after them, she killed her brother and cut him to pieces so that her father had to pick up the pieces, and Jason and Medea got away. I had a hard time understanding why Medea's dad had to pick up the pieces of his son, since the boy was dead anyway. Then, when Medea and Jason got to his place, Jason decided to marry another lady, and Medea killed her by poisoning her wedding dress. And after that it was not exactly clear to me what Medea did or might yet do.

Medea was a really scary person. And, as a child, I was not entirely able to separate what was real in that play and what was not—this was never a problem in the stories my grandmother read to me. Her voice, though lively and responsive to her text, was always calm and kind and detached no matter what she read. But Medea was really crazy. On stage, she asked my sister and me if we were scared. And I answered her. I told the truth; I said, "YES."

Then a guy stopped the whole thing and said, "I already told you twice, Angela, you and Ina do not have any lines in this play. When Medea asks you if you are scared, I do not want you to say anything—just be quiet. OK?"

I said, "OK."

"OK," said the guy, "Let's start that scene from the top."

Medea went crazy again, but this time the guy stopped her almost right away. He said, "Listen, Ursula, you are a refugee; for God's sakes draw on that. Remember what you went through; imagine you went through all that for Jason, you established his power for him too, and then he dumps you for an insipid girl who's never seen anything but parties and servants."

So this time Medea went even crazier, and I just could not stop myself from saying, "Yes, yes!" when she asked if we were scared. I was beyond scared. I did not really know of what either, because Medea was not making any sense to me, but something in me responded to the utter sense of desperation and absolute abandonment and rage that she let loose into a voice that commanded the whole auditorium. She would have scared anybody. I could smell the terror in my heart and taste it, and yet, at the same time, part of me wondered why anybody would come to see her go crazy like that and pay money for it.

And why did the guy call her Ursula? Ursula was a blonde woman. Medea had black hair and wore too much make-up.

The guy stopped us again. "Angela, didn't you promise that you wouldn't say 'yes?'"

I started to cry, "I'm…r…r…r..really…s..scared."

Medea said, "Why don't we show the kids how the fire works in the wagon so they know it's not a real fire and then they'll know I can't burn them to death in it."

That did it. That gave a focus to my fear. She was going to burn me in that gypsy wagon of hers that she had sitting on stage. I was sure of it. It did not help when she took off her hair and she really was Ursula underneath all that make-up and fake hair. And it did not help when Jason and Medea, looking like really good friends all of a sudden, showed Ina and me how the wagon was going to look like it was burning to the audience, but really it would not be burning at all. Who could trust her after her hair was not even real?

That night, after we got home, Mr. Smith, the farmer next door, slaughtered a pig. And the pig screamed in mortal terror and pain, then moaned loudly forever, and gasped out his final agony. I could not eat, and grandma said I had a fever and put me to bed. I wanted to crawl out on the garage roof where it was cool and the stars would sing to me, but I could not move.

I saw the burning wagon, and suddenly it was the big van with a red cross on it that arrived on the muddy field at the Elbe River. A doctor and a nurse got out of the van, and he said, "My God, what can we do? We need a thousand trucks full of supplies. What can we do?" And the pig screamed and soldiers came up from dragons' teeth and screamed, and I could not help it, I screamed too, and the director said, "Angela, you don't have lines in this play." Then my grandmother said, "Max, get her down off that shelf for me and carry her into our room—I have to get that fever under control."

And then the truck was empty and the doctor was crying and he kept repeating. "I'm a doctor, I'm a doctor," and the nurse said, "Not now, not any more; there is nothing you can do." It was warm inside the van and dry and I played a game with my sister. I would give her a push and she would run laughing from one end of the truck to the other. It was parked on a slope so she ran downhill. And my grandmother said, "If you keep this up, there will be tears." But we did not stop, and then Ina ran into the pot-bellied stove in the truck and cracked open her head.

Grandma called me, and then a bomb exploded and the truck burned, and I was afraid I had killed my sister, and they would put her under the tarp with white powder eating away her face. Then the doctor looked like Hannes and he said to my grandmother, "I think you're right, it is a cathartic fever, so we should just let it run its course—the linden flowers I brought should keep it under control."

CHAPTER NINETEEN

Dynamite

The winter settled in not long after we finished the "dirt house," as the villagers called it, even though it was a lovely place whose walls were white, inside and out. Not big, but airy and full of light; there really is something to walls that can breathe. I have seen such houses since then, and nothing would please me more than owning a dirt house like that, although where on the planet I would put it is another question.

In the winter months the sheep stayed in the barns of their owners, and the swans stayed in farmer Smith's barn—he had no sheep. Hannes, Wolf, and Sybille always disappeared in the late fall. "Remember all you've learned. And especially remember the swallows playing with swans' down." And then he was gone until spring came again. I never asked where Hannes, Wolf and Sybille went—I knew they would be back as soon as the sheep could leave their barns, and then Hannes would gather them up from every farm in the village and take them out into the fields. Sybille would lead the procession, wearing a garland of early spring flowers round her neck with sweet and dignified indifference.

During that winter I spent a lot of time with my grandmother showing me how to sew dolls' clothes, and with Michael just listening to him practice his music. My grandmother and the Kellermanns were always willing to tell or read stories.

I wished I had a guitar to play, and Michael Ende would have taught me, but it was not affordable, and his was much too big for my small hands. But he did let me strum while he changed his finger positions, or he let me press down the strings at the right places to produce the right sound. We discovered together that I had perfect pitch. If a chord was not exactly right, there was an extra vibration that would need to be resolved. I saw the same kind of "extra vibration" at the boundary between two colors sometimes.

Often I went exploring on my own. It was still fall; the silver beech trees had shed most of their leaves—leaves a shade of light golden brownish pinkish tan meant to make silver look more polished, and the woods looked downright elegant. And somewhere deep in a forest, I found an old bunker that was well-hidden. I came home excited to tell my grandfather about it, and he and Nikolai came with me to take a look. "My Rabbit," said my grandfather, "Promise me you'll never come here alone again—it is really dangerous. There is dynamite and all kinds of stuff in that bunker left over from the war."

"What's dynamite, Grandpa?"

"You'll see—Nikolai and I will make good use of it."

My grandfather and Nikolai brought out box after box of dynamite and then transported the boxes secretly under the cover of night to hide them in the sloe thickets where they hammered together a box in a really thick and hard to find spot. They covered it with a tarp, tying down the four corners so the wind could not blow it away—if ever a wind could even get through those tangled and thorny bushes.

A section of the beech forest had been cleared to make way for apartment buildings, and my grandfather had somehow managed to get the right to dig out the tree stumps to use for firewood. It was impossibly hard labor, even with Nikolai's help, so when I found that bunker, my grandfather was sure the dynamite was another gift from God. He and Nikolai set to work at once to blast out all those tree stumps, and then they hacked and sawed them up into usable pieces that were stored in the garage along with an unbelievable collection of junk grandpa and Nikolai kept there as well. I guess if you have been through two wars, you throw nothing out. Every piece of thread might come in handy some day. My grandfather's junk collection was legendary.

No sooner had they stashed all the fire wood, well-pleased that we would all be warm this winter, than two American army jeeps pulled up in front of our apartment building, and four huge MP's got out, came to our place, and arrested my grandfather for possession of explosives.

He was cheerful as they were leading him away in handcuffs. I was running with them to the jeep. "Don't worry, Krolick," he said in Russian, "And don't ever tell anyone where that bunker is. Not anyone means?"

"Not anyone."

"That's my swift Krolick. I'll be home in no time, you'll see. Your mother will make sure of that. Tell Klaus to find her to tell her what's happened. Tell him to find her tonight, even if he has to go to Frankfurt on the night train."

I stationed myself at the next to the last streetcar stop where Klaus Bach would get off. He was spending most days at the America House Library to learn English and to study on his own for his high school graduation exams.

When Klaus Bach got off the streetcar, I told him "Grandpa got arrested, and he said you have to find Mom and tell her."

"Who arrested him?"

"Amis" (German slang for American soldiers).

"Military police?"

"Uh huh."

"Do you know what for?"

"Uh huh."

"Goddam, tell me already."

"He had dynamite."

"He had dynamite?!"

"Uh huh, and he wants you to find Mom and tell her."

"Oh my God. He had dynamite! Where did your grandpa get dynamite?"

"I dunno."

"'I dunno.' I know that tone of 'I dunno,' I bet you do know. The two of you are thick as thieves."

"I don't even know what dynamite is," I told him.

"Well, I bet you know what he used it for, 'cause he must have used it, otherwise they wouldn't have known he had it."

"Yeah, it works like a bomb except it comes up instead of falling down, and he blasted tree stumps out of the ground so we wouldn't be cold this winter you included."

"Then you know what it is."

"Do not."

"If you know what he used it for, you know what it is."

"Do not. If I turn the switch, the lights come on—that doesn't mean I know what electricity is, and you couldn't explain what it is either, so there." Actually, I knew very well what electricity was—it was the Blue Fox of Siberia about whom my grandmother told endless stories, but I also knew that this was not an explanation that would work in Klaus Bach's world.

"You'd make a good Jewish lawyer or a Talmudic scholar," he said, "But you're not fooling me. We are not talking about what it is; we are talking about where your grandpa got it. I'll tell your mother you know."

"Then you'd be lying 'cause you're just guessing I know."

"Well, I don't believe you; and you had better tell her because your grandpa could get the death penalty for possession of explosives."

"Grandpa said not to worry; he'll be back in no time."

"That's because he's even more of a child than you are, and the combination of the two of you together was bad enough before Nikolai came, but now it's downright dangerous. You don't know how worried sick your mother is about the three of you and your crazy doings all the time." Then the streetcar came back from turning around at the last stop, which was only a stone's throw away, Klaus Bach went back downtown, and I was rescued from an unpleasant conversation.

When my mother came home a few days later, she did give me and Nikolai a merciless grilling, but she made the mistake of questioning us together. Alone, she would have been able to break either one of us, but together we kept insisting that we had no idea where the stuff came from and we sure had not known it was illegal. "Well," she said, "I believe Angela didn't know it was illegal, but you, Nikolai, how could you not have known that?"

"Forrgive me, Alexandra Maximovna," he said, "But khow can anyone know vat Amerricans arre sinking? They are verry, verry strrange people, verry, *verry* strrange. They don't look like us. They'rre giants. Sometimes theirr childrren khave skin you can see srrough, and some of zem arre the colrr of darrk ood."

"That's right," I put in my two cents worth in support of Nikolai, "Some of their children have transparent skin, and some of them have dark brown skin, and they cut their hair so it looks like a brush—so how can we know what they are thinking?"

"The way people think has nothing to do with the color of their skin," said my mother, "Or their haircuts."

"Forrgive me, Alexandra Maximovna, but khow can zat be? Is theirr skin not parrt of zem?"

"Their blood and their brains are the same color as ours," said my mother.

"Sank you, Alexandra Maximovna, I vill sink on zat," said Nikolai and would say no more. I thought about the hair sculptures on Uncle Kellermann's head and Grandmamma's 18th century figurines with white and complicated hair styles, and it seemed to me plain as day that a hairstyle would influence your thinking—it was beyond obvious, but I knew better than to argue the point with my mother.

About a week later, my grandfather came home with another four gigantic M.P.'s, and my mother as their translator. He showed them the field where he had blasted the tree stumps out of the ground, he showed them the stacked up wood in the garage and the box of dynamite in the sloe thicket. The M.P.'s confiscated the remaining dynamite. My grandfather asked them to leave the wooden box, and they obliged him. He did not tell them about the bunker.

And then, another week later, he was home for good. He had gotten a really good, long rest in jail, he said, and the food had been pretty good except for the fact that Americans put sugar in their pickled herring—"It is a sin to do that to herring," he said. They had even brought him his big print Bible to read when he had asked for it. My mother had talked to the judge, and he had appointed a lawyer who had argued that Maximilian Zeitner never possessed any explosives—he had simply found some that the German army had left behind, he had never really taken possession of it, disposing of it instead in a peacefully useful manner. When my grandfather told me about it, I said it was a stupid argument, and I did not understand how the judge could have fallen for it. "God works in weird ways," he told me.

"Grandpa," I asked, "Why didn't you tell them you found it in the bunker?"

"Because there's more dynamite there and all kinds of other stuff that might come in handy some day, so never mention it to anyone and never go there alone because that place is really dangerous."

And so we all settled in for winter, and that winter was the beginning of the stories of how my grandparents had lived in Russia and Siberia. Though I knew the general outline by the spring of 1946, these stories, which came to me piecemeal over the years, were as real to me as my life around me, and like my grandfather, I believe that Odessa is the most beautiful city on earth, though I have never seen it. Like children everywhere, I could not get enough of stories, and asked for them to be told and retold and told again until they became part of my blood and somehow deflected my own terrible memories, giving them the shape of a story as well, human and meaningful.

***

We acquired a kitten somehow that winter, and I was so enchanted with him that I have rarely been without a cat since. His name was Mohrle (German for "Blacky"). Mohrle and I often had the same conversation over and over. I would crouch on the ground before him with my elbows on the ground and my chin resting on my fists; Mohrle would sit on his haunches, his front paws neatly side-by-side, and look at me waiting, and purring. After a while, I would say, "*Katze?*" (German for "Cat"). Mohrle said nothing. Then I would try Russian "*Koshka?*" Mohrle still did not say anything. I tried again with the diminutives: "*Kätzchen?*" Silence. "*Koshinka?*"

Finally Mohrle spoke and said, "Mmmrrraow?"

"I don't understand it either," I would tell him, "German sounds like claws and hisses; Russian sounds like warm fur and purring. But you're not any of those words."

CHAPTER TWENTY

Albrecht Leo Merz

By the time the early spring of '47 and the old winter fought for ascendancy, I had put on enough weight to be allowed to go to school. I had had a rich education in our survival band, in the village, and the fields and woods around it, and in frequent trips across the city in the yellow streetcar number ten and, when luck would have it, with a poetic driver. I still marvel at it: a streetcar driver who spoke only in rhymed iambic hexameters. What a gift!

Other children, though, were virtual strangers to me. I had played soccer with the village boys, but that was somehow impersonal—I did not really know them outside of the game, and I only played when they were short a "man." And Inge Breuniger was my friend, but we did not spend that much time together, especially since Aunt Lilo had to be kept in ignorance of our continuing friendship.

Except for my grandfather's cogwheel creations, I did not have any toys and did not really miss them either; though there was one set I did long for every long, long year of childhood until Christmas time. Then, on Christmas eve I could go over to my Aunt Editta's house where the Christmas tree was always the most magnificent thing I had ever seen, and then, after reciting the Christmas story (Luke: 2-20), I was allowed to play with some exquisitely carved and painted wooden animals with movable joints that had belonged to my father when he was a boy, and his father and grandfather before him. All imaginable animals were there, especially those that lived in Africa. I handled them lovingly and maybe I could feel the warmth of my father's hands.

So, on the whole, I was almost never around other children. There was a brief exception. The farmer next door, whose geese I had been minding, had a grandson who sometimes came to stay for longer visits.

Helmut and I became friends for a brief time until he offered to show me his boy parts if I showed him my girl parts—and we both knew enough about adults to hide in the hayloft for the mutual exploration of parts, which turned out to be no big deal and left me even more completely mystified than I had been before about the darkness surrounding sexual bondage and the horrible origin of babies.

"You're gonna have a baby cuz we're married now, and you have to do what I say," Helmut informed me.

"The hell we are," I shot back, "You have to do this marriage thing in a church or it ain't legal, and if ain't legal, it won't work."

"If you don't do what I say, I'm gonna tell."

"Go right ahead, they'll punish you more than me—they'll cut your thing clean off."

I guess my threat worked, because Helmut avoided me after that little anatomical adventure, and I never heard another thing about it.

And again, I spent most of my time alone or with adults. I had no wish to go to school and said so. Life was just fine as it was. It was, in fact, heavenly perfection. "School will be good for you," my grandfather told me, "You have to get to know people your own age sometime."

"They don't tell good stories and their games are stupid," I told him and saw no reason at all why I should go somewhere just to be with other children.

"There will also be teachers. Good teachers."

"I've already got good teachers. I've got you and Hannes and Uncle Kellermann…"

He interrupted my epic catalog before it really got good and started, "You don't have a choice. There is a law that children have to go to school. A decree from Caesar Augustus."

"He makes laws for children? I thought laws were for grown-ups."

"Yes, of course he makes laws for children."

"Why?"

"So that you grow up more or less useful to him and to society."

"I could be useful without going to school."

"What could you do?"

"I could be a shepherd like Hannes."

"Well, he went to school when he was a boy, you can be sure of that. Even if you want to become a shepherd, you still have to go to school until you are fourteen years old at the very least. But you can go ask him. I know for a fact that he had more schooling than any other shepherd in the world."

"What happens if I just don't go? I could hide in the attic," I whispered, "You know, with Wolfgang Gottschalk."

"They will put your mother in jail if you don't go to school."

"That's blackmail and it stinks; I hate the law. And I don't want to be useful to Caesar Augustus."

The hint of a smile appeared in my grandfather's face and vanished in the same instant. He said, "You don't have a choice unless you want to send your mother to jail, and you know her—she would not be pleased about that, so you might as well give school a chance. You don't even know what it will be like—you might actually like it; and it wouldn't hurt if you accepted change a little better than you do. Life is change."

"Well, would you like being forced to do what you don't want to do?"

"No I wouldn't, but I'd make the best of it. And I wouldn't judge something before I know what it's like—it's not as if you're being sent to the mines in Siberia—in that case you'd know ahead of time you're going straight to hell—life expectancy in the salt mines and the lead mines was about two years, extremely miserable years, making you wish you'd die as soon as possible—but in this case, you are judging something you don't know anything about. There are children everywhere in the world who'd give anything to go to school and they can't."

"Well, I'm not them."

"Someday God will say, 'Come to heaven,' and you're...."

"I'm tired of hearing that, Grandpa. And school is definitely not heaven. Inge Breuninger and the soccer boys—they all hate school. A lot."

"Tell you what, my Rabbit, you've got almost a whole month before school starts. We can go right now and take a look at it, and then you won't be sulking around here and poisoning everybody's atmosphere."

There was then another small and contentious conversation about whether or not it was appropriate to go to visit the school barefoot. "It's not winter," I told my grandfather. He said, "You have to get used to wearing shoes, Rabbit; everybody wears shoes to school." I did not see the sense of it. "I don't like shoes, Grandpa. I never want to wear shoes."

"Do you remember the woman who knocked on our door wanting something to eat? The woman who was barefoot?" I nodded, and he went on, "Well, did you see her feet? Do you want feet like that?" I did remember and I still do see the very thick, yellow, hard skin that made her feet look like something other than human and three times bigger than they should have been. These days, you hear a lot about the benefits of going barefoot, but I do not think that they mean for you to walk barefoot from Silesia to Wuertemberg-Baden. So, in the end my grandfather persuaded me that if I wanted to take a look inside the school, I would have to wear shoes.

To my surprise, we stopped to wait for the streetcar instead of walking further down a block to the village school.

"I'm not going to the same school all the other children are going to? I'm going to get to ride the streetcar to school every day through the Silver Wood?"

"Yup," said my grandfather, well pleased with himself.

"I hope it will be the streetcar driver that makes poems. Mom says it's crazy to make poems. Do you think it's crazy to make poems, Grandpa?"

"She didn't say it's crazy to make poems. She said the driver is crazy because he speaks *only* in rhymes."

"Do you think he's crazy?"

"I don't know...." As he was speaking the streetcar passed us to turn around at the next and last stop, and we could see it would indeed be my favorite driver. My grandfather said, "Why don't we see if what he says today makes sense? If it does, he's probably not crazy."

As we got on the streetcar and my grandfather paid the fare, the driver said:

"Wie geht es der gold'nen Prinzessin der Sonne,
Vom Grossvater würdig betreut und begleitet?"

(How is the sun's lovely and golden-sweet Princess
Attended with honor in grandfather's trustworthy care?)

"Not so good," said my grandfather. "She doesn't want to go to school—I'm taking her on a tour of the Merz Schule in hopes of changing her mind."

The streetcar driver smiled at me and said,

*"Die Schul' ist gut, und bringt den Kindern die Wonne,
Lern fleissig; nur so wird die Weisheit verbreitet."
Und ohne Weisheit gibt es den Frieden wohl nicht.
Dann leiden wir, sind grausam, entbehren das Licht."*

(That school is good—even gives the children much bliss.
Learn well, my child, and thus guard and spread wisdom fair.
For peace cannot reign in the land without wisdom bright;
Then we suffer, are cruel, and bereft of light.)

We managed to get seats in the back, and I whispered in my grandfather's ear, "School can't be bliss—that's crazy."
"We'll see," said my grandfather.
We rode through the Silver Wood, and, at the second stop on the other side, where we got off, the driver called out its name:

"'*Frauenkopf*,' *meine schönen Damen und Herren,
Seht licht die Gartenstadt; könnt euch nie verirren.*"

("Woman's Head, ladies, gentlemen, enjoy the sight.
Never get lost: see the city with gardens bright.)

He had reference to a lovely little terrace from which you could see almost the whole city of Stuttgart, a garden city indeed, with roses on all its slopes, like a giant bowl at your feet. The terrace was called "*Frauenkopf*" (Woman's Head) because two magnificent stone sphinxes looked out over the city on either side of it.

From that terrace, it was just a few steps to the school—in fact, this terrace was often the Merz playground at recess. Just beneath the low stonewall, there were low growing junipers that hung their bonsai-gnarled branches over the precipice. There were places on those branches that were flattened and polished to a high sheen by generations of children sitting and rocking on them and seeing the city spread out at their feet.

Being no ordinary person, my mother had chosen no ordinary school for my sister and me. The Merz Schule is now big and successful: Here's the introductory paragraph of their current website if you click on "English:"

> The private educational institution Werkhaus / Werkschule Merz was founded in Stuttgart in November 1918 by Senator Albrecht Leo Merz. Shut down by the national-socialistic government, the school was reopened in 1945 under the American military administration. Merz School was recognized and recommended as a model school by the UNESCO. Albrecht Leo Merz introduced the method of 'Recognizing and Creating' as a concept of learning and teaching.

And here is a lovely thing I learned, poking around in their website: The oak grove, which was part of my magical world when I was a child, was protected by law shortly after I left Germany, and it is now what the Merz School considers one of their classrooms. It was certainly one of mine.

The Academy now specializes in film and media; back then, however, it was simply an art academy married to a series of crafts shops in the German guild tradition: a master craftsman in each shop, assisted by journeymen and apprentices. There was a wood shop that made fine furniture, bowls of all shapes and sizes as well as other wood carvings; there was a metal shop which produced candle sticks and other items made of brass or bronze or copper; there was a pottery, a shop for spinning and weaving, a leather shop, and a book bindery that bound books by hand as useful objects and as objects of art. I still have a book I bound back then. The art school and all these shops were on the grounds of the Merz's home and gardens.

As I recall it, the Merz Art Academy and workshops were going strong by 1947, but I think my class starting first grade was the first one after the war. They were planning to add a grade each year until they again could offer twelve years of schooling of unequalled quality. Truly. I have been a teacher for almost sixty years now (teaching my first class of English Language Learners at age 15). I have since taught in five different cultures and at every level of instruction from kindergarten through graduate school, and have never seen a school as good as the Merz Schule was when I attended it. I hope they are still as good.

Albrecht Leo Merz, his wife, and his three sons, Volker, Helge, and Siegurt, were some of our teachers; though the eldest son, Siegurt, did not come back from a Russian prisoner of war camp until we were in our second year, but I remember his homecoming as if he had been my father: *Frau Merz* found old helmets with gunshot holes in them, hung them upside down from all the trees in the garden and planted violets in them for his homecoming. Aunt Lilo said the whole bunch of them together were a colossal piece of kitsch. "Maybe *Edelkitsch*," she allowed, but still kitsch. There is no English word for that particular variety of kitsch—it translates into something like "noble kitsch."

When my grandfather and I arrived at the school, the old gentleman welcomed us, and in spite of myself, I loved him right away. His name sounds like the German word for March (although it is spelled differently), and I was sure that this was one of those coincidences my grandfather loved so much to see as signs from God that we live in an intelligent world. "I was born in March," I told him, during introductions.

"That is a great sign," he said.

"Yes—but a sign of what?"

"It means something very great will happen."

"Inevitably?" "*Zwangsläufig*"—is the word I actually used.

"Ah," he said, "*Du sprichst ein großes Wort gelassen aus. Ja zwangsläufig.*" (A big word spoken with ease and detachment. Yes, inevitably.)

He was busy with an art class for adults who were all doing charcoal or pencil drawings of different kinds of branches in different arrangements sitting in vases or lying on small tables, and all these branches were alive with swelling buds. "Draw the moment before they burst open," he told his class.

I had visited Mr. Bauer, the painter in the old village down the hill from us, and he had let me use his paints on occasion. I had also watched him paint an oil portrait of my grandmother in which she looks out onto a snowy white and endless Siberian prairie. And I had made collages; I still make them. Paint was expensive (still is), but my mother brought home the colorful dust jackets of books that would then sit drab and naked on library shelves without them, as noted earlier. And those dust jackets gave me endless materials for collages, sometimes mixed media collages. So my first glimpse of my future school as an art school did much to change my negative attitude; the good omen of my future principal and art teacher being of the month of March like me did not hurt either, and getting to ride the streetcar every day was icing on the cake.

Albrecht Leo Merz invited me to wander around and look at the work people were doing. And I could not get enough of seeing how different people drew the moment just before the buds would open. I still see several of those drawings clearly in my mind's eye.

My grandfather talked to *Herr Merz* while I wandered around in the classroom, and when I rejoined them, *Herr Merz* said he would show us some of the workshops. The first one was the wood shop, and here people were busy working on a strange contraption the likes of which I had never seen. A big wheel and a small wheel, both solid and without spokes, connected by a central post with a small bench attached.

"What are these things? Will they be cogwheels?" I asked

"I'll show you, my little dove—come."

He took us to the pottery, and I saw a potter's wheel for the first time—of course, I recognized right away that this is what they had been working on in the woodshop. These were the old-fashioned ones, operated with your feet. The master potter showed me how to throw a glob of clay on the wheel. And then, sitting on the bench and using his feet in a steady rhythm and in opposite directions to make the wheel turn, he closed his eyes, centered the clay by pulling it towards his own center, and then made a vase grow in front of my eyes. I was enchanted. He changed its shape, and I soared beyond heaven.

"Well," said *Herr Merz*, "do you think you would like to learn how to do this?"

"Yes, yes, yes," I said, jumping up and down with each word.

"There will be about twelve splendid little doves like you," he told me. He understood something about children that I learned again when I taught with Li Yong Quan (a.k.a. Brave Heart) at a kindergarten in Zhenjiang, Jiangsu Province, in China. I do believe I owe my success in teaching those children to Albrecht Leo Merz.

He showed us around the other workshops, but there was no need. I wanted to come to this school. I also could not wait to run out into the fields, later that day, to tell Hannes that throwing pots felt a lot like "throwing rocks into the pond." "You could just see it," I told him when I found him, "When the potter closed his eyes and put his hands on the clay."

Before my grandfather and I left the school to go home, Albrecht Leo Merz said, "Your mother showed me some of your writing and your collages and your silhouettes; I cannot wait to work with you. I really like your watercolor of the cat and the crow."

The feeling was definitely mutual. Speaking to me as a colleague, he looked like a combination of Albert Schweitzer, the mad scientist in "Back to the Future," and Albert Einstein with a little Goethe thrown in for gravitas. In other words, he looked like a genius, and he was one. I can never see the photograph of Einstein with white hair and sticking out his tongue without loving Albrecht Leo Merz. The picture they have of him on the website looks like it comes from 1918, but I recall an old man with white hair sticking out all over his head. He always wore a white lab coat spattered with paint. He was an artist teacher. And he knew how to deliver praise and criticism with equal parts of love and loving irony. Like the Great Immortal Patriarch Subhuti in *The Journey to the West*, Albrecht Leo Merz had "found his true nature and let it run free." He was at his best always, dancing and singing among us as we painted. And because he was always completely himself, this is what he addressed in us and therefore brought out, so we could know it. We were all completely comfortable with him. About other teachers, we might have differing opinions on differing days. About Albrecht Leo Merz we were unanimous always. We loved him.

He taught us not only how to paint but how to see. As he went around the classroom, singing and dancing, delivering praise and gentle criticism, he would also sometimes take a brush, add a little dot or a small line, and what had been a shapeless blob of color became a thing of intelligence, a meaningful form.

In the mornings we had the regular academic subjects—reading, writing, arithmetic, geography, and so on. In the afternoons, we were farmed out to the various workshops, for two or three weeks in each one, where the master craftsmen (or women) taught us, while the apprentices and journeymen assisted us. The pottery and the metal workshop were my favorites. There were some children who loved hammering ashtrays and bowls out of metal, but that did not interest me after the first time. What I loved about the metal shop and found completely absorbing was enameling on copper, and I quickly learned how to do *cloisonné*. In the few boxes of possessions I left in my daughter's care before leaving for China, I still have one of the pieces I made back then as a Christmas present for my grandfather.

I was not too fond of spinning or weaving, and carding wool was hard work, though I liked the smooth, clean, soft end product. I also did not like handling leather. But the bookbindery was a great place. We bound some of our textbooks ourselves, and we kept journals that we could bind into books. There was, however, a fly in the ointment: the rest of my class and I really had a problem with one of the apprentices—a horrid teenager, in our opinion, and he had a problem with us, me especially. I forget who did what to whom first, but somehow it got to the point where I had to be extremely careful in that place, otherwise some very hot bookbinder's glue on a large and wide brush would come into painful contact with exposed skin.

On Saturday mornings Albrecht Leo Merz taught a class that all of us looked forward to: "*Erkennen und Gestalten.*" The website translates his philosophy of education as "Recognizing and Creating," and I suppose it would sound pedantic to find fault with that. Still, German words seem to wear their etymologies on their sleeves more than English words do, and for me an etymology is not just an external history of a word going back in linear time, but also an internal evolution from silence through various levels of imagination and thought to audible form. To me "Erkennen" has more to do with "Ur-kennen" or original knowing than with "re-cognition." But the word "cognition" would not work in this context.

Where the website says "creation" the German says "*gestalten.*" And everyone knows that "Gestalt" and its verb "*gestalten*" represent a concept complex and untranslatable enough that English-speaking psychologists simply use the German word. You can create a mess, but you cannot give it a Gestalt without transforming it into something that is not a mess.

What it came down to was that Albrecht Leo Merz took seriously both the English word "education" from Latin "to lead out" and the German word for it, which has a quite different etymology than does the English word. "*Ausbildung*" and its verb "*ausbilden*" would normally be translated into English as "education" and "to educate" without a second thought. But if you look at how the word is formed (German words, remember, wear their etymologies on their sleeves), you would indeed see "*aus*" or "out." But "*bilden*" does not mean "to lead"; instead, the German verb suggests giving a Gestalt to something. "*Bild*" is the noun evident in "*bilden,*" and it means "picture" or "image." And so, for me, the deepest meaning of "ausbilden" is to realize or fulfill the image in which we are created. I am certain Albrecht Leo Merz had this in mind also. And to prove it, he gave each one of us the opportunity to rise to countless creative occasions.

He knew, as did Hannes, that children are naturally capable of great depth and acuity. I remember, for example, my own surprise when my daughter asked me when she was no more than three or four years old, "Mom, is the sky blue because it's blue or because my eyes are blue."

"Cat, everybody knows you have brown eyes."

"Oh, Mom," she said in a tone of incredulous exasperation, "You know what I mean."

So what did Albrecht Leo Merz teach us on Saturdays? For one thing, he taught us to pay careful attention to what we can observe directly and what we might assume. And he taught us to think about *how* we know what we think we know. I remember once we came into the big hall where the adult art classes were taught, and there was a screen. When we were all seated and silent in anticipation, we heard the sound of liquid falling behind the screen: a miraculous sound. When *Herr Merz* asked from behind the screen what we were hearing, I said, "You're pouring water from a pitcher into a glass."

He asked, "How do you know that it's water and not milk or oil?"

"Milk or oil, especially oil, would have a darker and softer sound when it splashes."

"How do you know that?" he asked.

"I get to help in the kitchen."

"How do you know it's a glass and not a tin can?"

"I think you'd hear the tinny sound of a tin can."

"Could I be using a porcelain cup instead of a glass?"

"I don't think so. What you're using is taller than a cup and holds more."

"Could it be a porcelain vase?"

"Yes, but I still think it's a glass."

"Any reason?"

"No reason, I just think it is."

"Great."

Then he asked, "How do you know a human being is involved? Maybe a machine is pouring the water." We all laughed at that. "Well, he said, "It could be Helge pouring the water." We looked around, and did not see him.

"It still feels like you," said a boy named Joachim, who was to become my best friend.

Albrecht Leo Merz took all answers seriously. "It still feels like you" happened to be the right feeling—but in any case, he never discounted feeling, never stuck only to empirical observation. He understood that often when you "just know" your mind could be arriving at an instant synthesis of 10,000 things. And then, who really knows what knowing is?

Once he showed us two glasses filled with water. He put an egg into one glass and it sank to the bottom. He put an egg into the other glass and it floated.

"Can any of you explain this?" He asked.

"That egg is too lazy to swim," offered one of my classmates. Now, as it happens, the German word for "lazy" is "*faul*," which could be stretched to also mean "rotten." Or, maybe, the girl said "*verfault*," I do not remember, but I am sure the ensuing discussion included both rottenness and laziness. In response to a question, the girl said she would have no way of knowing the difference until she smelled the insides of the eggs. "A good answer," said *Herr Merz*.

Olga, a girl from Russia, said: "Maybe the egg that floats has been blown out like they do with Easter eggs."

"Very good idea," said Albrecht Leo Merz as he switched the eggs, "But, as you can see, not the case."

A little boy whose hand had been excitedly waving in the air, put it down.

"Why did you put your hand down, Peter?" asked *Herr Merz*.

"I thought maybe one egg was raw and the other egg was boiled—but you switched them, so that can't be it."

"Good thinking," said *Herr Merz*, "And that's still a great idea that we can test sometime—but as it happens both eggs are raw."

Then Joachim noticed that the water in one glass was cloudy and clear in the other. "It's the water, it's the water," he blurted out.

"Yes," said *Herr Merz*, "You were all thinking about the eggs so much, you forgot the water."

This illustrates perfectly one of the things Albrecht Leo Merz taught us: to observe both point (egg) and field (water), and not only that, to expand a point into a field and to collapse a field into a point. Ask any systems analyst, and he will tell you that this ability is the essence of creative thinking. It is certainly one of them; the use of metaphor is another. Albrecht Leo Merz had that one covered too, as he uncovered it for us.

"Can anyone guess what the difference is in the water of the two glasses?"

One little boy, an American boy, as it happened, blond, with translucent skin and an American haircut (a crew cut), thought he knew. His name was Dennis. And Dennis was amazing. During our first winter in school, we often did not have enough fuel to put in the potbellied stove we had in the classroom, and Dennis figured out a way to steal wood for us. I wish I could remember the details. He got caught, but then, his daddy, an American officer of high rank, saw to it that we always had enough wood that winter. Anyway, Dennis said in halting German that he had swum in the ocean and in a freshwater swimming pool and that his daddy had pointed out to him how much easier it was to float in salt water.

Albrecht Leo Merz invited Dennis to taste the water in both glasses, and Dennis, beaming, reported that yes, indeed, one was salty the other fresh. *Herr Merz* said we would still have to solve the problem with rotten, raw, boiled, and lazy eggs. We were to think about it until next time. He told us testing rotten, boiled, and raw eggs, would not be too much of a problem, but he could see no way to test for lazy eggs—if any of us had a plan, he would give us a prize.

I took the problem straight to Hannes: "Can you read eggs?"

"Eggs? Why would you want to read eggs?"

"To find out if they're lazy or not."

"You mean rotten?"

"No, I mean lazy."

"Eggs can't be lazy or not lazy. You could say they're lazy because they're just lying around; and you could also say the opposite because a bird is very busy growing inside—would you like to explain what you're talking about?"

I explained the situation to him, and he said, "Well, maybe chickens can be lazy or not lazy, and if that's the case, it might be possible for someone to read this even before the chicken is hatched. But I'm sure

I can't and I don't know anyone who can, but that doesn't mean such a person couldn't exist."

"If a chicken is lazy, could you say the egg was lazy?"

Well, I guess you might be able to make a case for it," he said, "We are born with some qualities and we acquire others."

I took my next problem to the kitchen. "Klara, can you tell the difference between a raw egg and a hard boiled egg without breaking them?"

"Of course."

"How?"

"You spin them like a top on the table. A hard-boiled egg will spin easily, a raw egg will try and wobble around lazily, but it won't really do much."

"Is that because raw eggs are lazy?"

"I don't know—it's just the way it is."

"Do hard boiled eggs float in water?"

"Eggs don't float either way. Next time I boil some eggs I'll let you know. Then you can spin them and also try to with a raw egg."

"Can you tell the difference between rotten eggs and fresh eggs without breaking them?"

"No you can't. That's why, when I break eggs, you always see me breaking each one over an empty bowl before I use it." Obviously, after the advent of refrigeration, people no longer have to take this precaution.

Next, I lay in wait for Klaus Bach. "I don't have time for chess tonight," he told me, "I'm going to the theater with your mother."

"Can I come?"

"It's not a play for children," he said.

"Why not?"

"Take my word for it, Jean Paul Sartre would bore you to death. But you can come to the opera next time we go. Your mother already has tickets. 'The Magic Flute.'"

"Well, I just have a question."

"OK, shoot."

"Klara says you can spin hardboiled eggs like a top and raw eggs are lazy and just wobble around. Why is that?"

"Let me think about that for a minute."

"Your minute's up."

"Well, an egg has different things inside: egg white and egg yolk, and there's also a little bit of air—there's a thin membrane too, but that's got nothing to do with the present problem. Now, because of that air bubble that sits near the shell, the egg white and yolk slosh around when you try to spin the egg and they can't move as fast and maybe there's also a problem because the egg yolk might be heavier than the egg white—anyway they all slosh around and keep the egg from spinning properly. It's called inertia, and the air bubble always wants to get to the top. When I have time, we'll experiment with full and half empty bottles of water."

"No need," I told him. "I can see what you're telling me in my HEART." I emphasized the word "heart" because I knew he did not believe the heart could know anything. He was in a rush, so he just raised one eyebrow instead of giving me a speech.

I gave my report the following Saturday. My case for lazy eggs was that if chickens could be observed to be lazy, then this laziness might well be part of the egg even if we did not have a way of observing it. Maybe somebody sometime would find a way to read it. *Herr Merz* said I deserved a prize—some chocolate, as it happened. I refused it though. When he asked why, I said, "I didn't figure this out by myself, I asked Hannes and Klara and Klaus Bach different questions."

"Formulating questions as well as consulting with friends and experts is part of research," said *Herr Merz* and continued, "so you get the prize anyway—you can always share it with Hannes, Klara, and Klaus Bach." I gave the chocolate to Joachim. Because I had eaten raw, unrefined cacao for months on our flight from the Russian army, I hated the stuff, so it was it was not pure virtue that made me reject the prize.

In an earlier draft of this chapter, I said, "The school was decades ahead of its time." What a meaningless cliché! It is a good thing that I learned from Wolfgang Gottschalk and in my first four years of school that all writing is re-writing. The educational philosophy and practice of Albrecht Leo Merz are timeless. All our learning was hands on. We were never considered empty receptacles for information, although we also learned to listen. And I never saw an objective test until I came to America.

Herr Merz taught us to see unity within diversity. That idea certainly was not fashionable when I went to graduate school, and deconstruction was *de rigueur* (stupidly rigid, in fact). "Unity within diversity" sounds abstract, but *Herr Merz* did not teach it as an abstract concepts; instead, he allowed us to experience what, say, a willow tree and a fountain had in common. Then he asked us to paint "that which is falling" (*das Fallende*) or its contrary, that which was rising (*das Steigende*), in various ways—realistically—so far as we could, or as abstract form. All our class work was integrated with every other class. If we learned about dinosaurs in natural history, we painted them in art class.

Maybe, I would never have known the greatness of the Merz Schule, had I not subsequently seen just how bad schools and teachers can get. Maybe, I became a teacher because of Albrecht Leo Merz and his sons. Any good teacher anywhere can do much, but teaching can be a most frustrating task in the context of bad schools and bad educational philosophy. Looking back, I am grateful to have a standard by which to measure and judge. Nor am I the only one who thought it a great school. The United Nations Educational, Scientific and Cultural Organization (UNESCO) had designated the *Merz Schule* a "model school," and we often had visitors from all over the world who observed us

There was coherence and peace in our school. And you could even say that there was bliss.

CHAPTER TWENTY-ONE
My Inheritance

Suddenly, arithmetic, which had been a serious problem, as Uncle Kellermann and I had discovered together, became the easiest thing in the world for me, although that ease did not last long. I remember some of this mystery myself and have some of it from my mother, but my sister Ina does not believe a word of it. I know my mother would not ordinarily believe any stories that had anything "unscientific" about them—she was a dedicated empiricist, a scientist, in the strictest sense you can imagine. And my sister followed in her footsteps. When Ina studied psychology, she believed that B. F. Skinner was the greatest thinker in the field—precisely the one I would have accused of not being able to think at all.

"Well," she said, "You'll have to admit that he's very clever."

"Cleverness makes wars, not peace," I retorted, but she thought of my comment as the perfect example of a *non sequitur*. To me, what is a *non sequitur* and what is not depends on how far you can jump.

Since I was a year late starting school, my sister and I were in the same grade—and we sat next to each other in the first row. She was unequalled in arithmetic—and somehow I always got exactly the same answers on my papers as she did on hers. Not only the same answers, but the same process of working things out. Naturally, everyone assumed I was cheating. I denied it—and I do remember being grilled about it by the person who was best at grilling: Mrs. Merz. They moved me to the back of the room. It made no difference; my papers still looked exactly like Ina's. But if they gave my sister and me different problems to work, I was the glorious failure I had always been.

Albrecht Merz became interested in the phenomenon and put us into separate rooms, as far apart on campus as possible. That is the part of the story I have from my mother because they did not tell my sister and me what they were up to, but they told her. And the result was always the same: if they gave us the same problems, we both got the same answers. If they gave us different problems, my sister performed brilliantly, and I was the clueless doofus.

Then *Herr Merz* questioned me about it himself. Now, he did not grill me, he asked questions. But there was not much I could tell him.

He asked, "Why do you sometimes get the answers right, no matter how difficult the problem is, and sometimes, no matter how easy it is, you can't do it at all?"

"I don't know," I told him.

"Well, do you know the difference between when you get it right and when you don't?"

"Sure. If it feels clear and good, then I know it's right."

"So then, if you don't know the answer, what does that feel like?"

"It feels horrible. I wish I could figure it out, but the numbers just don't make any sense—it's like they stay outside of my mind and don't even come in. Like the door is closed."

"And when things are clear, do you know where the clearness comes from?"

"What do you mean?"

"Well, when you write, you always write clearly. Sometimes I see you change a sentence to make things more clear. What tells you that you should change it?"

"My heart."

"OK, that's what I mean. The clearness comes from your heart. And where does the clearness come from when you do math and you know it's right?"

"From my heart too."

"You say 'your heart'—some people would say it comes from the mind."

"Yes, I know. Klaus Bach thinks your heart doesn't know anything, but Hannes told me you can trust your heart more than you can trust your mind, and grandpa says he's right. Grandpa said Klaus Bach doesn't know his own heart because it's been hurt too much."

"And who are Klaus Bach and Hannes?"

"Klaus Bach lives with us, and we play chess and talk about the heart and the soul and the mind and God and stuff like that. Klaus Bach thinks people don't have a soul."

"Do you think people have a soul?"

"Uh huh."

"And why do you think so?"

"Well, you wouldn't even know you're alive if you didn't have a soul."

"I see."

"And who is Hannes?"

"He's our shepherd in Sillenbuch. He teaches me how to read plants."

"And what do you learn when you read plants?"

"If you can eat them and what they're good for if you're sick and stuff."

My mother was called in for a conference for the second time. The first conference had been about the fact that I absolutely could not distinguish between left and right. That was not so bad, but I could also not distinguish between a thing and its mirror image. I wrote equally well with my right and my left hand, but if I wrote with my left hand, you needed a mirror to read it. Of course, my family had known about this for a couple of years since I had written like this in my notebooks: sometimes I had used my left hand, sometimes my right, and sometimes, just for kicks, both at the same time, starting in the middle of the page and writing outwards. Nobody had ever said anything to me about it. But the Merz School, although it was the best school I have ever seen, felt it was important to train me to use my right hand only. My mother told me later that, normally, they would not have had a problem with left-handedness, but in this case, they thought that writing for which you needed a mirror in order to be able to read it should be discouraged.

So I was forbidden to use my left hand. I did not like it one bit, and felt really lopsided for a long time, but after a year or so, I was used to it. Still, it made the problem of telling left from right and mirror image from the "real" image even harder. Sometimes, when I am really stressed out even now, I write 9 when I mean 6. Or 18 when it should be 81—a disaster in the age of checkbooks. And when I am tired, I sometimes type words backwards.

The upshot for my education in arithmetic was that my mother and the school decided to do nothing. It did not seem right to call what I was apparently doing "cheating." On the other hand, it was perfectly clear that if I continued as I was, I would not learn much arithmetic. What was clear to everyone was that I would never graduate from any German high school unless I passed rigorous tests in mathematics, but, for now, everyone felt it would be best not to bother me. Maybe something could be done later.

Circumstances, however, conspired to keep me from ever being bothered with arithmetic. Moving around among three different cultures during my school years (Germany, the U.S., and France) meant that I had to learn languages first and neglect arithmetic. Then, when time came for algebra and calculus, I found I could function fairly well because they are primarily about thinking, not about numbers.

I was never tested for dyslexia, but dyslexia seems a reasonable assumption under the circumstances. And yet, if I am dyslexic, how did I manage to excel in two Ph.D. programs? Both of them required so much reading that it was physically impossible even for a normal person to read all that was assigned by the deadlines we were given.

Maybe my reading comprehension was as good as it was just because I had to be really slow at reading, so that I did not miss much. And of course, you always see more than there is in print. There is nothing you can really say or write down without layers of underlying assumptions on the one hand and run-away implications on the other, and, on the third hand, there is metaphor leading to unfathomable depths. But, often, I just did not have enough time to read what was assigned. Academic writing pretends to be dense, but, really, most of it is just convoluted and willfully obscurantist. So one trick I used to get around this in academic writing was to read the introduction and the conclusion, and, given these, I could see what had to come in between. Sometimes even the primary reading material assigned was too much for me. So I invented various shortcuts. For example, I scanned Madame Bovary and underlined all the color words without actually reading the work, and then wrote a paper about color symbolism. I discovered in the process that Madame Bovary's eye color changes. Was that an oversight or a plan? Of course, I argued that, regardless of authorial intent, the change in eye color indicated a change in character. Then, one of my professors published this slip-shod work of mine as his own in a professional journal. That kind of plagiarism actually happened more than once, and not just to me. But you'll hear more about the corruptions of academe in due time. Some of it is downright unimaginable, and I will have to see who's still alive in one of those places before I will feel safe about telling the truth.

Back when the sky was a deeper blue with tiny points of light dancing within the blueness, and I was in third grade, my aunt Editta decided she would help me with the daunting task of memorizing the multiplication tables. Together, we climbed to the top floor of her house, and then, with her carrying a bouquet of various sizes of feather dusters, we would work ourselves down floor-by-floor, dusting statues and picture frames, antique bowls, gorgeous vases:

"Five times three is fifteen and three times five is also fifteen.

"Nine times seven.

"Eight times four.

"Six times six is 36, there is nothing love can't fix."

If I got the answer right, she asked the next question. If I got it wrong, I had to recite the multiplication table in question three times. But as careful and as patient as Aunt Editta was, just about the only one I remember is six times six. In the end, she concluded that I had no Mendelian inheritance for arithmetic.

One day as we got to dusting things in the library while my Uncle Walter the Asshole of Sillenbuch was pouring over his stamp collection volumes, my Aunt Editta said, "Maybe we could sell one or two of these things; the children are hungry."

"I'm not selling anything for a sack of potatoes!" he roared. "Besides," he continued in a calm but sarcastic tone, "They'd feed all those stray cats and dogs they're always taking in over there."

"We only have one cat and no dogs," I told him and added, "Cats don't eat potatoes."

"Hmmmm" was all he said.

Later that day, I carefully sneaked through his garden and, after ringing the doorbell, had the housekeeper take me to the library, where Uncle Walter still sat studying his stamps. "What do you want?" he said without looking up.

"Please, Uncle Walter, please don't sell any of your things—they're too beautiful and I would miss them."

"What?!" he snarled, "So you can inherit them when I bite the dust?"

That was a consummation that had not occurred to me, but it was immediately enlightening and sounded heavenly. So I said in the smallest and most polite voice I could create and still be heard:

"May I please, Uncle Walter? May I inherit them?" And the air changed in that instant. Carefully, he put the stamp down he was holding with a pair of tweezers in one hand and a magnifying glass in the other and then, smiling his most wicked smile, he said:

"Well, I'll be…you're not as dumb as I thought. Maybe you're a girl after my own heart."

CHAPTER TWENTY-TWO
Joachim and Vimsie

I tried to play with the other kids during recess, but I just never really got the hang of it. Catty-corner from the *Frauenkopf* with the two stone sphinxes, there was a public playground we also visited often during recess, as the school did not really have much of a playground of its own. The one catty-corner from the *Frauenkopf* was less civilized, not paved, and the same trees grew here all around a playing field—the trees that I had come to love when we lived in the forest ranger's house after we had left Berlin. In Stuttgart, they did not grow in white sand, but in a sort of ochre gold and dusty ground. Their tall trunks, though, were the same rose and gold and orange near the tops. I remember hugging one of those trees and weeping while the other kids played. It was not because they had excluded me from a game that day, although they had. It was the knowledge that I would somehow never really be part of any group. And it was not just that I was a Prussian in Swabia. It was more than that, although I could not have explained it to myself, but I knew clearly and for the first time that I was alone in a sense too deep for words. Who knows why this upset me so much that day. Normally, I would just pretend I was a snail who could pull his eyes on little sticks inward, withdraw into his lovely house and close a small door. Whatever the case, that day, I cried instead.

It was Volker, the youngest of the Merz sons, who came to console me, squatting before me in his traditional Swabian leather shorts, asking what was wrong. But I could neither explain, nor did I feel like giving up weeping. It was too deep an issue not to weep for as fully as possible. He seemed to understand as he squatted there before me, and I, while still crying, studied the small, carved ivory forest and a stag crowned with magnificent antlers on the cross piece of his suspenders.

One of my classmates, Joachim, came over; it was the boy to whom I had given my prize of chocolate. Volker whispered something and left. Joachim stood and watched me sob for a long time. In fact, he watched in silence so seriously and for so long that I started to laugh. "We could be friends," he said simply.

"Yes," I said, and took a deep breath, and when I let it go, it liberated a couple of left over sobs.

"I'll meet you at the *Frauenkopf* tomorrow morning, and we'll just skip school."

"Yes," I said, while Volker called us all together because it was time to go back to school.

"We'll rob a bank," Joachim whispered to me as we were walking back to the campus two-by-two.

"Yes," I said for the third time, and thus our friendship was born and solemnized.

One thing that was great about the Merz Schule that I have not mentioned is that they did not get totally bent out of shape if you were absent occasionally—you could overuse this privilege of course, but I had gone on my own adventures in town or had just taken a day off occasionally to lie around in some fragrant meadow with Hannes.

So the day after Joachim and I had formed our alliance under the rose-gold trees with the dark needles, I got off the streetcar without any intention of going to school.

"I'll tell," said my sister predictably, when, turning into the *Frauenkopf* terrace, I told her to go on without me.

"You do that," I said, "And I'll cut Heidi's clothes to shreds and never make her any new ones." Heidi was her favorite doll, named after Johanna Spiri's heroine in the book of the same name that we had both read.

Joachim came crawling out from beneath the junipers and said, "There's a sort of friend of mine I want you to meet."

We walked to the edge of the Silver Wood together, and a man was standing there, smoking a cigarette. I had seen him there lots of times, wearing a slouchy hat and a trench coat and looking like the detectives that looked out suspiciously from the cover of the murder mysteries of the time.

"This is Angela," Joachim told the man, "She's my new associate."

"You sure you can trust her?"

"Absolutely," said Joachim.

"We'll give her the code name 'Black Hand,'" said the man. Joachim gave him a small, plain, paper bag he pulled out of his pocket, and the man gave him some money for it.

"What's going on?" I wanted to know after we had left the man and walked toward the streetcar stop.

"This guy is my black market contact. He says his name is Vimsie, but I don't think it's a real name. I pick up cigarette butts and some other stuff sometimes, and he pays me. He sells stuff on the black market. I think he opens up the cigarette butts and rolls new cigarettes out of them."

"Well," I said, "I know where we can tons of cigarette butts. I mean tons, and long ones, too—almost as long sometimes as a whole half cigarette, sometimes even longer than that."

"Really?"

"Yeah."

"We're gonna be rich," he said, "Maybe we won't have to rob a bank. Where is this wonderful spot with cigarette butts lying around all over the place?"

"Sillenbuch," I said, "And they're not exactly lying around, but they're not hard to get either."

"Explain, Black Hand."

"We'll get them in the American quarter."

"American cigarette butts? They're even more valuable than German ones; we're gonna be really rich. Where do you find them?"

"Garbage cans."

"Garbage cans?"

"Yeah, and there's all kinds of other good stuff in American garbage cans."

"Wow," he said, "What kinds of stuff?"

"Food, and clothes, and toys, and stuff. One time I found a whole loaf of bread with just a tiny little green spot on one end. Except American bread is really terrible. But you have to be careful when you're getting stuff out of American garbage cans 'cause almost all the Americans don't like you to take their garbage."

"How come?"

"I don't know. It's not like you're stealing cause they already threw that stuff out, but they don't want you to get it out of their garbage cans anyway. Sometimes they have dogs to guard their garbage cans."

"Well, I don't want to get bit."

"It's not hard to deal with dogs—you know that. Besides, not everybody has dogs, so you maybe get some food out of a garbage can where they don't have a dog, and you give it to a dog guarding a can, and then he's your friend. You'll be amazed about how much food Americans just throw out. Really good food, too."

"What if they catch you?"

"They don't. I don't think they really want to catch you; they just want you to get out of there and leave their garbage alone. When they peel potatoes, the peels are as thick as your little finger. They throw out a lot of food."

"Strange."

"Yeah, my grandpa and his friend Nikolai think they're very strange people, but my mom says they're just people like us. There's one lady that's different from the others though. When she sees me, she throws out some really good stuff on purpose I think—like a present for me."

"Really? What kind of stuff?"

"Like a really big piece of cake or a sandwich or something else really good."

"Why do you think she does it on purpose?"

"Well, when she saw me look through her garbage, she came out really slow, and I ran away, but not very far 'cause there's some really good bushes to hide in, and she wasn't chasing me and she was smiling. And she didn't open the garbage can, but she put a package on top of the lid, and then she looked around and motioned me to come—I think she knew I was in the bushes. And then she went back in the house. So then I went to look what she'd thrown out—I snuck up on the garbage can really careful, grabbed the package and ran like hell. Well, guess what it was? It was a perfect ham sandwich with Swiss cheese and mustard—except Americans use mayonnaise instead of butter and they put lettuce leaves in sandwiches."

"They put lettuce leaves in sandwiches? For real?"

"Yeah."

"Really weird."

And so one of the things Joachim and I did together was raid garbage cans in the American settlement. And we did get rich on cigarette butts—at least by our own standards of what constituted wealth. When Vimsie found out we were raiding American garbage cans, he enlightened us as to the usefulness of coffee grounds. "They can be used twice," he said. "But Americans throw them out after using them only once, so if you can find coffee grounds that aren't mixed with other garbage, I'll pay you for those too."

So we could afford all kinds of things: ice cream cones occasionally, even a movie sometimes. They would not let us in without an adult, but we knew an old beggar who would come with us for the price of a movie ticket and some extra change. He would grumble and make outrageous claims about how much money he would have made begging during a two-hour movie, but he was always willing to go with us anyway.

Of course, I introduced Joachim to Hannes, and of course I took Joachim to all the great places I knew around Sillenbuch, the Silver Wood, the sloe thickets, and the Oak Grove. And he took me to all the great places he knew in the city. Toward the end of 1947 we sometimes even had enough money to buy a real lunch in a real and elegant restaurant all by ourselves. We usually went to the same place near the *Schlossplatz*, the square in front of the old castle. The first time we had made that daring move, the waiter dressed in black and with a napkin over his arm had asked, "Do you have any money?"

Joachim showed him the inside of his pocket and said, "Man, what kind of question is that—what do you take us for anyways? It's an insult to the lady is what that is."

The waiter smiled slightly, bowed a little, and said, "My apologies to the lady, Sir, may I recommend the rabbit in sour cream or the *poulette à l'orange?*"

"Not rabbit," I told them.

CHAPTER TWENTY-THREE

Explosion

The following morning, Joachim and I wandered around in Silver Woods, but we decided to show up at school for the afternoon workshops—enameling for me, hammering out ashtrays or bowls for him.

And I guess we had been overdoing our extracurricular adventures; *Frau Merz* was on hand to grill us.

"Where were you?"

"Silver Woods," we said in unison.

"I notice the two of you are always together. What were you doing in Silver Woods?"

"Nothing"—again more or less in unison. And it was true. Just walking around and climbing a few trees, so we could have a conversation from one tree to the other, never seemed like doing anything to either one of us.

"Nothing?" said *Frau Merz* with a tone that promised trouble. "Joachim, I'll talk to you later. Go to your workshop." Joachim left, and I was left standing in the middle of the small playground in front of our classroom.

"Now," said Mrs. Merz, after Joachim had left. "What were you doing in Silver Woods?"

"Nothing."

"Angela, you know that's not true."

"It is. We were just walking around in the woods and climbing trees." I knew it was useless and looked at my feet. She was standing much to close to me.

"Look at me," she commanded."

I looked, straining my neck because she was standing so close, and

I do not know how I knew what I knew. Her face was dark. The whole atmosphere was dark, and I knew she expected a confession, but I really did not know what to confess to—yet I understood clearly that this was the same atmosphere I had come to associate with sexual bondage and the horrible origin of babies.

"What were you doing in the woods with Joachim?" she asked again through clenched teeth.

"Nothing," I said again and without hope, which she interpreted as guilt. I knew she was never going to let up.

"I hear guilt in your voice, I will get to the bottom of this, and I will call in your mother for a conference."

This was going to be the ultimate horror and I knew it. I had to say something to prevent that. "We didn't do anything, *Frau Merz*."

"Tell me the truth," she roared, "I know you were not just walking around. WHAT WERE YOU DOING?"

"Everything," I whispered, "that is bad and evil."

"I knew it," she said, satisfied, and left me standing there. She went into her home, which was also the school office.

I remained standing in the middle of the place, which was in the middle of the whole school, and hated her with all my heart for making something ugly out of my friendship with Joachim. And the whole world, every detail in it, looked totally evil. Then it came to me that I had better clue in Joachim so he knew what was up in case she questioned him too.

I raced to the metal workshop as fast as I could. He was hammering away at a piece of copper. "I told her we did everything that was bad and evil," I whispered.

"Why?? We didn't do anything wrong!"

"I know, but she wouldn't let up. She was gonna call my mom for a conference. I had to give her something."

"Well, I'm not going to tell her anything just 'cause she wants to hear it. Meet me after school at the *Frauenkopf*."

I had not even got started bending my wires, when the horrible apprentice from the bookbindery showed up and told Joachim with evil glee in his face and ugly satisfaction in his voice, "You're wanted in the office."

After school and bouncing furiously on the junipers, Joachim said,

"I don't understand why you told her anything. We didn't do anything wrong. I told her you said what you said because she was torturing you. Of course, she denied torturing you. But I really want to know why you said anything that dumb—besides 'bad and evil' doesn't mean anything."

I could not explain. I could only feel we were being accused of the most dark and evil thing in the world, but I did not understand it, and I confessed to it as best I could to get *Frau Merz* off my back so she would not tell my mother because she, I was sure, would never forgive me.

So how could I risk my mother and *Frau Merz* weaving their dark and hateful atmosphere and accusing me of sexual bondage to Joachim? And how could I explain any of this to him? Boys and men never seemed to have sexual bondage on their minds like women did.

He did not speak to me for a few days, but then the whole thing blew over, and he said during recess, "We have to be careful about being absent from school on the same day, but I guess we could do it every once in a while." And anyway, by that time it was almost summer vacation, so we were careful it until then.

The summer was glorious—filled with huge amounts of doing nothing with Joachim, and nothing much happening in the fields and in town. Of course, I also spent a lot of time out in the fields with Johannes learning to read plants. And of course, Joachim and I made obscene amounts of money collecting cigarette butts and other useable stuff. Once we even found a radio in a American garbage can. It just needed a little bit of repair that Vimsie took care of and then it was fine, and we had lunch in town twice that week.

Just about the time we started to miss school, it was September, and we happily went back to our classroom and our workshops. Fall was a long and gentle season in southern Germany. My grandmother got to know Joachim's grandmother, and we all enjoyed collecting mushrooms after school and the little three-cornered beechnuts that my grandma used to make oil. You needed a ton of them to make a drop of oil.

And then, when I woke up one fine morning and saw the whole world blanketed in snow, I jumped out of my bed on the upper shelf in the closet, knowing Joachim and I would have a day to remember. We had agreed that with the first really big snowfall, we would miss school, meet at the *Frauenkopf,* and hatch the perfect plan.

We decided not to miss the morning session, but the afternoon session was to be in the leather workshop, and neither one of us liked working with the stuff.

"It feels like somebody's skin," I told him.

"It *is* somebody's skin, Silly," he answered.

Very surreptitiously, we wrapped up our school lunch, which was called "Hoover food." It is probable that President Hoover (who saved 800 million lives from death by starvation world-wide) had something much more delicious and nutritious in mind, but by the time the food actually got to us, there had been so many people on the take involved in the process that what we got was not often edible by the standard of living Joachim and I had achieved through our American garbage can raids. Yet there were plenty of postwar children grateful for something to swallow.

We successfully got off the campus together without being seen, and we fed our lunches to two splendid woolly dogs, one red and one black and both with really blue blue tongues. They were on the other side of a wall with a wrought iron gate, and they were always on hand to bark at anyone walking past. We were determined to make them our friends, and, someday, climb the wall or the gate to play with them when no one was home. When they smelled us coming, they stopped barking and started wagging their tails.

"Soon," said Joachim.

"Soon," I agreed and continued chanting, "Soon, soon, soon," converting the ominous tones from the Magic Flute into joyous hope.

"Let's go get lunch in town first and then we can plan what to do."

When we got on the streetcar, the driver smiled at us and said,

"*Es scheint die Schule geht heute wohl hinter sich.*
Bei so 'nem schönem Schneefall—da wunderts mich nicht.
Trotzdem, warum fährt ihr denn in die schmutzige Stadt,
Wenn der Silberwald heute mehr Reize hat?"

(It seems that school is going to the dogs today.
But with such lovely snow, am I surprised? No way.
But why are you going to the dirty city
And miss Silver Wood's charm today—what a pity!)

I thought a minute and then answered:

"*Wir gehen essen und machen dann einen Plan.
Auf dem Rückweg nehemen wir deine Strassenbahn.*

(We're going to eat our lunch in a sandwich bar
And then we'll show back up and we'll catch your streetcar).

It was not perfect, but it rhymed and scanned more or less. The thing about talking in rhymes was that it just took a little practice. You have to think backwards in a way. Normally you think a little ahead when talking or writing, but if you want it to rhyme, you start with the sound and then find the meaning, rather than the other way around, although I would have to admit that it is far easier to find rhymes in German or French or Russian than it is in English.

Joachim, who was also getting good at hexameters said,

"*Der Silberwald iss 'ne verdammt gute Idee.
Den ganzen Nachmittag spielen wir dann im Schnee.*"

(Now the Silver Woods is a damned good idea—so
All afternoon we'll play, run, and slide in the snow).

And the driver said:

"*Ich wünsche euch beiden einen herrlichen Tag,
Was immer das Schicksal euch heute bringen mag.*"

(I wish you both a truly magnificent day
Whatever it is that fate is sending your way)

We got pushed towards the back of the car soon since streetcars in those days were really crowded.

A street vendor's cart happened to sit right across from the stop near Hermes the messenger of the gods. And he had some really great hotdogs with excellent mustard—the vendor, of course, not Hermes, who was running through the sky on an errand of his own. We ate and then caught the next streetcar back to Silver Woods—the next driver, as it happened, had talent in a very different poetic genre: he enjoyed producing colorful, prodigious curses and invective so potent as to prompt some citizens to write in protest to the local papers about decorum and the effect on "our children."

We loved the man, of course, and sought to emulate him, as we emulated the street vendors of various gadgets and other wares, and the wonderful driver of the iambic hexameters. It always amazed us how many words could be said about a kitchen gadget. But we often took turns producing or wishing on others fart-born ass-fruit, diaper-slurping pig hounds, ass-slime sucking bear toads and the like.

The whole wood was carpeted in soft white. The wind had come from the east during the night, and so the huge soft flakes had clothed the east side of all the trees, leaving their silver bark exposed to the pale afternoon sun. Some of the gold bronze leaves still clung to branches, making it that much easier for the snow to collect there in huge, soft mounds and the grey and complicated designs of twigs and branches against the snow looked like mysterious writing. Soon we could nothing of the world, except the silver trees, and the white snow.

It snowed off and on, but no wind this time: just silent softly falling huge flakes to catch on our tongues and to veil the woods and then again to reveal them. Beech trees have many eyes on their trunks, eyes lined with kohl, equally black pupils, and dark grey irises.

First we had a glorious snowball fight. Then we made snow angels on the ground, which were peach colored and powder blue in the slant light of the setting sun. Then we built a snow woman with enormous breasts. Then we made more snow angels. Then we had a race, which we tied, and, tired and out of breath, we just walked. Sometimes big snow flakes were falling, sometimes the pale gold afternoon sun threw purple shadows and made even the silver tree trunks look soft and lavender. The alternating snowfall and the pale gold light made the falling snow seem like shifting veils until they, too, seemed to have eyes.

And then, somehow, in the darkening blue light after sunset, we ended up at the black entrance of the bunker—more black and more visible because of the white snow and in spite of the branches and sticks my grandfather and Nikolai had piled in front of it.

"This place is really dangerous, Joachim. I'm not allowed to be here by myself."

"You're not by yourself."

"I'm sure that's not what my grandpa meant. We have to get out of here."

"First tell me why the place is so dangerous."

"My grandpa got dynamite here, and I've been inside, there are bombs and guns and stuff."

"Really? Help me pull these branches away."

"No Achim. This place is too dangerous."

"Well, I'm not leaving 'til I have a look. You can help or not."

"Promise you'll just look."

"Sure."

So I helped him pull the branches away, and we crawled into the bunker.

"There's not much to see. We have to come back with a flashlight," he said, crawling back out, "Can you imagine how much money we can make on the black market with this stuff? And look at this thing I found."

"Throw it away, and let's get out of here!!" I was truly frightened. I had seen hand grenades and what they could do.

German does not have "scaredy-cats"; it has "scaredy-rabbits," and that is what he called me: *Du bist so 'n richtiger Angsthase.*

But I was seriously frightened now. He made a quick motion, and I ran and screamed, "THROW IT AWAY!!"

The explosion was literally deafening; I screamed, "Achim!! ACHIM!!" and could not hear myself. One of the trees, hundreds of years old with a massive trunk, had saved me.

I sat leaning against the age-old tree, stunned—I do not know how long. Then I screamed his name repeatedly until I could hear my own voice again. There was nothing but silence in the alternating snowy veils and the pale gold light.

Slowly I got up and slowly walked to the center of the explosion, which was clear and easy to see. Joachim was not there. Small fires burned here and there, but would not for long. Everything was very wet, and an old beech forest does not have much undergrowth to act as kindling.

I looked around and saw Joachim lying on his back as if getting ready to make another snow angel. He must have thrown the grenade;

or there would have been nothing but shreds left of him.

He was bleeding. His blood, like a living being, was spreading in the snow. It had a strange and minutely angular movement to it—as if each drop of blood asked each crystalline snowflake for admission and then occupied it suddenly, completely.

Was he dead? "Achim!" I yelled. And again, "Achim!" It seemed wrong to leave him there, but I had to go to get help. Still, I waited until the soft snow had thrown a thin veil over him and then I saw him stir a little. "Achim?" He opened his eyes, but it did not look like he saw anything. "Achim, can you hear me?"

I saw recognition come back into his eyes. "I can't move," he whispered.

"Stay there," I told him, which seemed redundant, but I saw him understand what I really meant. "I'll go get help," I started to leave, but then turned and said, "I saw them tie things around people's arms or legs when they were bleeding at the Elbe River, so I'm going to tie your scarf around your leg. It might hurt."

"Go ahead," he whispered.

I didn't think to go to the streetcar stop, and just walked in the direction of home in a strange kind of trance. I had often chosen to walk home instead of taking the streetcar—the trip was only around five kilometers (just over three miles). Just walking and not thinking, I did not even notice that the sun had set, the sky had cleared, and the full moon and the stars came out to light my way.

Then the sound of a motor pulled me out of my trance. A car in the middle of the woods? Should I hide? "Don't be such a scaredy-rabbit" I heard Joachim's voice say in my mind, and so I stood and waited for the car to approach. The headlights blinded me, and I did not see until the car stopped right next to me that my mother was in the passenger seat, and an American soldier was driving. It was the kind of vehicle that can go over any kind of ground.

"We've been worried sick about you. Where in the world have you been? We heard an explosion," said my mother.

"Joachim's hurt."

"Joachim's hurt?"

"He's bleeding."

"Were you near that explosion? Why are you wandering around by yourself in the middle of the woods in the middle of the night? We've been driving all through this forest for hours looking for you."

"Ali," said the American soldier who spoke almost perfect German, "I think she's in shock." Then he said to me, "Who is Joachim?"

"My best friend and, he's hurt."

"How did it happen?" asked the soldier.

"There was a big explosion…and…it…." I did not want to say what it had done to him.

"Can you take us to him?"

"Yes."

My mother said, "If she's in shock, she needs a doctor."

"We have to get the boy," said the soldier. As we were driving, he asked what had caused the explosion. I described what Joachim had found and detonated; it was, of course, a hand grenade—the German kind that looks a little like a potato masher, not the American kind that looks like a pineapple.

The snow had almost covered Joachim, but in the headlights of the vehicle, you could see his blood shining through the snow. And of course, they saw the bunker. They carefully put Joachim in the back of the jeep, and I sat on my mother's lap. But before we drove away, the soldier got on his walkie-talkie and spoke English, so I could only understand a word here and there. He did say "bunker" several times —the German and the English word are spelled the same way, just pronounced a little differently.

After he drove out of the woods and onto the road, he started going really fast, and before long, an ambulance came toward us, braying like a donkey. They stopped, and we did also just about opposite one another, and two soldiers from the ambulance came running with a stretcher to transfer Joachim. Then the ambulance turned around, and we followed them to the Karl-Olga Hospital. A doctor there said I was good to go home, but they kept Joachim. I showed my mother and the soldier where Joachim lived in Degerloch so they could tell his grandmother where he was and that he was going to be OK.

When I finally got home, my grandmother gave me linden flowers and hot milk, and I told the story of what had happened to Joachim.

"Oh, Lord, forgive me," said my grandfather, "I blame myself. It's a miracle," he said, "That the whole bunker didn't blow up and take a good piece of the forest with it, including you two. And it's another miracle Joachim didn't get killed—count it a very great blessing."

"I don't understand, Grandpa. How can it be a blessing that Joachim got hurt?"

"Well, because he could easily have been killed. Too many children are killed in left over mine fields and by abandoned explosives."

"But Grandpa, you always say that when people die, they go home to God in heaven."

"Well, Rabbit, I see your point, but don't you think it is a blessing that you won't have to miss your friend?"

I crawled up into my grandpa's lap, hugged him around the neck and whispered in his ear, "I told no one that this was the same bunker where you got the dynamite and I never will."

"We'll talk about it tomorrow, my Rabbit. Now get some sleep."

Even so, it was a couple of decades before I felt normal when anyone opened a can of pop, and I could not do it myself. That hand movement is too similar to pulling the pin on a hand grenade.

CHAPTER TWENTY-FOUR
Prisoner of War Train to Arrive from the East

It happened one night as I was listening to the evening news with my grandfather that there was an announcement: a prisoner of war train was due to arrive in downtown Stuttgart. I asked if we would go to meet that train—maybe my father would be on that train. The answer was "no" because his name was not on the list.

I told Joachim about the train next day at school and he said he had heard about it too and was wondering if maybe his dad was on that train, but his grandmother had also said that his father's name was not on the list. His father was missing in action, as mine was, and his mother had gotten killed in Dresden when the whole city was utterly destroyed by American bombs. Joachim had managed somehow to stay alive through the raging firestorms after the bombing. So now he lived with his grandmother in Stuttgart-Degerloch.

"I think we should go anyway," I told him, "Maybe the list doesn't know everything."

"I was thinking that too. I heard about this prisoner of war that came back using his best friend's name because his friend died in the prison camp and he didn't want to use his own name for some reason, I forget what."

"Well, then we have to go for sure."

"It'll be day after tomorrow—where do you want to meet?"

"Let's meet by Hermes, 'cause the terminal will be too crowded, and we might miss each others."

"Hermes? What's Hermes?"

"I told you before, the really tall column with a ball on top and a naked man running through the sky with one toe touching the ball and wings on his feet and his head."

"That's Mercury."

"Well, my aunt Lilo said 'Mercury' is the Latin name and 'Hermes' is the Greek name." I preferred the Greek name because in German I never heard the name "Hermes" without also hearing "*der Götterbote*," or "Hermes the messenger of the gods." Nobody ever said that about Mercury.

So we met under the golden statue of Hermes and then went to the downtown train terminal together. The place really was more crowded than any place I had ever seen including the field by the Elbe River. Joachim and I had to hold hands to make sure we did not get separated in the crowd. There were flowers and banners everywhere, and they had built a platform with a microphone on it. A band was already there tuning up.

Why do they need a band?" said Joachim.

"It was probably the mayor's idea," I told him. "My grandpa said the mayor is really stupid, and that he'd probably be here with a lot of band music."

"Really? Maybe he has a son coming home?"

"My grandpa said he would be the most superfluous person here, but he'd be here anyway because he'd use any excuse to make a speech….. Joachim, do you see those people everywhere carrying posters? Do you know what they are for?"

"Read what they say. 'Have you seen him?' 'Do you know him?' Those are pictures of soldiers missing in action. My grandma used to meet every prisoner of war train with a picture of my dad on a poster like that. She was hoping that maybe some prisoner coming home would remember him and what happened to him, but she says she can't do it anymore because it makes her cry too much. And she won't let me do it either. She tore up the poster and threw it out." He was silent for a moment and then he asked, "Hasn't your mom ever looked for your dad with a poster? You must have some photographs—they can make big posters out of them, you know."

"I don't know," I said. "They said the Pope looked for my dad because the Pope or somebody like that was a friend of my Aunt Editta, and nobody could find my dad. But I'm sure he's not dead."

"Why don't you ask her to bring a poster like this to the station next time?"

"You can't ask my mom anything important. She loves questions, but they can't be about anything important. I can maybe ask my dad's mom, but she's too old to come downtown. Why won't your grandma let you carry a poster of your dad?"

"I don't know. She won't talk about important stuff either."

"Maybe it's 'cause you're a boy—'cause look, no men. Women are carrying them."

"I'd do it if my grandma would let me. I'd do it anyway, but I don't know how to get a poster."

"Achim, let's get out of here. I don't like it here. And anyway I don't think I'd know my dad. I don't remember his face."

"It's too late…listen…the train is coming." And it did come, like a giant sausage made of steel and spitting steam; I felt pinned down and wanted to run, but could not.

And then they came. With dark grey faces and hollow eyes, and their ears were too big, and their clothes too, with sleeves or trouser legs that dangled empty.

How could anybody know them, I thought. To Joachim I said, "They don't look normal. They don't look anything like the people on the posters."

"That's just cause they're wearing new uniforms in the posters and they were younger and not so thin. I'd know my dad. I'm sure."

"Look," I said, "Do you see the man leaning against that pillar over there just in front of the bandstand? I think that could be my dad."

"You just got done saying you wouldn't recognize him, and if you're looking at the same guy I'm looking at, he's got his back to us."

"Well, that's the one I mean."

"He's got his back to us."

"That's why he looks familiar. My dad had his arm in a cast, and I used to help him put on his jacket. I'd climb on a chair to do it, and I really got to know the back of his neck and shoulders."

"Well, let's get closer."

The band had begun to play—not military music, and not the national anthem either, because that was against the law. In fact, people used to say that if you ever needed the police to help you at night, yelling "HELP" would not be as effective as singing, "*Deutschland über Alles*" at the top of your lungs. Instead, the band played a song every ex-soldier street organ grinder played everywhere all over town

Kein schöner Land in dieser Zeit
Als hier das unsere weit und breit
Wo wir uns finden
Wohl unter Linden
Zur Abendzeit....

(No lovelier land here in this time
Than this our land both far and wide
Meeting our dearest friends
Under the lindens
At eventide....)

Joachim and I fought our way through the crowd. The band stopped playing and the mayor was making a really enthusiastic speech about "*Wideraufbau*," or the rebuilding of Germany, in which the returning prisoners of war would play an important role. And the man who could maybe be my dad was walking away from us towards the exit.

We fought harder to get through the crowd so as not to lose him. He stood in front of a large poster for a minute, reading it, but then he continued toward the exit. We reached the poster, and it told prisoners where they should go to look through photographs of war orphans in the hopes of helping to identify them.

We were frantic. We pushed our way past men and women hugging each other or just standing and looking into each other's eyes. Some people scolded us for being rude. We heard all kinds of strange snippets of conversation between the returning prisoners of war and their relatives. Everyone was laughing and crying and hugging each other or just standing and staring as we pushed past: "She was killed in an air raid." Said an old lady to a man without arms, and I could see he wanted to hide his face with his hands as he was crying, but he could not, and so I started to cry too. "Just come on," said Joachim.

"Yes, I knew him, he died in the salt mines of Tashkent," said a prisoner to a lady with a poster of a handsome smiling young man in a clean uniform just like the one my dad used to wear.

"I know where that is," I told Joachim. I know where those salt mines are." But he just pulled me after him past a little boy who was stamping his foot and yelling over and over again, "I don't want a daddy without legs…I don't want a daddy without legs…"

And then we caught up with the man just at the exit to the terminal.

I touched him, and he turned:

Holes where his nose had been.

I almost screamed and covered my mouth with my hands as if my soul were escaping. Red streaks and blue scar tissue like cruel brush strokes entered my dreams: This is your father's face: an empty eye socket, a wound oozing green, his teeth exposed on one side, long and yellow like a dog's teeth.

I hid my face against Joachim's shoulder, and he put his arm around me. The man said with a calm and really beautiful and gentle voice: "You don't have to be afraid. These are just battle wounds like any others—they just happen to be on my face."

I looked at him again and saw that even such a face can smile with just one eye like an island in a monstrous sea.

"Are you my daddy, maybe?" I finally asked.

"I have no children of my own, Honey," he said. "Why don't you two walk with me for a bit, unless you're with someone?"

"We're by ourselves. If you want, you could have lunch with us at a restaurant," said Joachim.

"You have money? Because I don't."

"Man, what kind of question is that? We are rich," Joachim told him with authority.

"Isn't anyone waiting for you at the train station?" I asked.

"No," he said, "I have no family left; I came to Stuttgart because there is a doctor here who might be able to do something with my face—without my face, I can't really do my job. I used to be an opera singer. But say, if you kids really do have enough money, I'd love to have lunch with you today."

"We have tons of money," I told him, "But it's a little early for lunch."

"We could wait in the rose garden behind the old castle," said Joachim.

And so we did. No one was there, probably because of the prisoner-of-war train.

"If you're an opera singer, do you know The Magic Flute?" I asked.

"Yes, I do. Would you like to hear a song from it? Singing is still a little painful, but I'd love to sing you a song, fair lady—stand on the bench here and pretend you're a painting of Pamina."

And then he sang a song about a picture of enchanting beauty.

The waiter seated us at the back of the restaurant and had our new friend sitting with his back to the whole place. Of course, we questioned him over lunch if he had ever met my dad or Joachim's dad in any of the places he had been in Russia. He had not.

"I just don't think he's dead," I said. "They're going to declare him dead though. I don't see how they can do that—just declare someone dead."

"It helps those who are waiting to get on with their lives," he said and added, "Declaring someone dead doesn't kill him."

"Well, it feels like it."

"Don't let an official government paper influence how you feel. It's just a piece of paper. It should mean nothing to you if you don't want it to mean anything. Now, tell me why you are so rich that you can buy lunch for a returning prisoner of war in an elegant restaurant."

So we told him about our cigarette butt and coffee grounds business, and he congratulated us on our perspicacious entrepreneurship—big words in English, but, again, German words are more transparent than English ones: "*Scharfsinnige Unternehmungslust*" may look like big words, but any German child can understand them.

We parted company after lunch and promised to visit him at the Karl and Olga Hospital. Joachim and I spent the rest of the day at the Willhelma, a marvelous complex of gardens and greenhouses. We looked at birds and plants and lizards.

"Is everything OK?" asked my grandmother when I got home. "You look a little strange."

"I'm fine."

And my grandfather asked, "How was school today?"

"Fine."

"Hmmm," he said, "You sure?"

"Yeah," I said.

"Learn anything?"

"Sure, lots of stuff."

CHAPTER TWENTY-FIVE
The Village School and the Music of the Spheres

One day, my mother came home from an extended absence in the late winter of 1951 and informed my sister and me that, come late March, we would leave the Merz Schule and attend the village school instead. Probably I asked why. But I do not remember the answer, if, in fact, there was one. I could not imagine life without the Merz Schule.

The public school was just a couple of blocks north of our streetcar stop; however, fifth grade was taught in the "Old Village," which really was a village and it was old—the first records date back to 1264. New Sillenbuch, where we lived, was some indescribable mixture of things like villas and apartment buildings—and I remember only one farmhouse, the one next to our place, although there must have been a couple more. The Old Village was just what its name said it was with old farmhouses and their barns and manure piles with roosters standing on top of them and telling the whole world about their amazingly high status in it.

To get there was quite a walk down a steep hill. The best thing about the hill was that, come winter, you could get to school in no time by sled. You would not use the road, of course, since that was for cars, but next to the road there were small fields and gardens covered with snow in winter. When you got to the bottom of the hill, there was a wire fence, and you had to lie down flat on your sled at the right moment to slide under it, otherwise you might be decapitated.

The single classroom and the living quarters for the teacher above it was in a small building on the west side of the village square, a space where the fairs were held. I do not remember the teacher's name, but we will call him *"Herr Drescher,"* may he rest in peace.

As I think back, *Herr Drescher*'s living quarters must have been quite cramped. So was his mind. And he was cruel. If he taught anything, I do not remember it, but it was an education to see him use a cane, take children over his knee, and beat them viciously.

I also learned to be really good with a slingshot. There was a pillar in the middle of the classroom, and if you banked shots off that, *Herr Drescher* could not really tell where they had come from. Of course, we wanted to hit him square in the face with wadded up paper bullets, but it was plenty good enough to see them fly in his vicinity to enrage him. He had no mercy for us, and we had none for him. When the fair came to the village, a bunch of us got together, collected garbage and, somehow, we managed to dump it in his apartment above the classroom.

Of course, he knew we had done it. But he could not pinpoint any one of us, so all we accomplished was to make him angrier and more cruel. We tore up blotting paper and stuffed it into his inkwell, so that when he dipped his pen, he'd pick up a blob and drop it on whatever he was writing. The poor man really had to watch his back with us.

Then one day, it was my turn to get switched. I forgot why, but I do remember that he said something about how I would bring shame to my mother. The fact that I was a girl meant that some red streaks were visible on the backs of my thighs just below the hem of my skirt.

"What happened to you?" asked my grandfather.

"Nothing, Grandpa."

"Those red streaks on your legs, my dear Rabbit, they didn't just get there."

"*Herr Drescher*..."

"He hit you?"

"Grandpa, please don't tell Mom."

"What did you do to make him angry?"

In a very small voice, I answered, "He said I would bring shame to her. Please, Grandpa, don't tell her."

"He quoted the Bible?"

"I don't know. Is it in the Bible?"

"Yes, Rabbit. There are three places in Proverbs that talk about hitting children. Come, I'll show you. I know exactly which ones they are."

He opened his big print Bible, and it did not take him long to find Proverbs 13:24:

"He that spareth his rod hateth his son: but he that loveth him chastneth him betimes";

And then, Proverbs 22:15: "Folly is bound up in the heart of a child. But the rod of discipline drives it far from him"; and after that, Proverbs 29:15: "The rod and reproof give wisdom, but a child left to himself brings shame to his mother."

In Luther's German, it is even clearer than it is in King James, that the verses are talking about sons, not daughters; moreover, the verses implicated fathers in these thrashings, but not teachers, and I pointed out both these Biblical facts with some hope for my future. My grandfather smiled his barely perceptible and fleeting smile and said, "Well, it also doesn't say anything about Rabbits." I breathed a sigh of relief. "We've talked before," he continued, "about how, sometimes, the Bible says things I no longer believe, and these verses…" he sighed, "these verses used to give me comfort a long time ago, but now I no longer believe them. I will talk to your mother about this."

"But Grandpa, you promised not to tell Mom."

"I did?"

"Yes, Grandpa, you promised," I said with profound seriousness.

"My memory is getting really bad. But you don't have to worry. The reason I'm going to talk to your mother is that she will make sure *Herr Drescher* never touches you again."

A little while later, I came to school one day, and *Herr Drescher* re-assigned my seat to a bench in the back of the room, and from that day on, I might as well have been invisible. Even when I played hooky occasionally to meet with Joachim, or Hannes, *Herr Drescher* never asked me for the usual written excuse signed by somebody official.

***

Though we no longer attended the same school, Joachim and I continued to be friends, and one of our favorite places to meet was the Wilhelma. This was a complex of amazing gardens and greenhouses that had belonged to some king named Wilhelm. There were tropical plants and even a few strange birds with feathers so fantastic their owners seemed to have flown in from another planet. They also had lizards that could change color and lizards whose feet allowed them to walk on walls and even ceilings and lizards who could blow up colorful balloons under their chins. They even had blue frogs! They had plants whose leaves ate flies or that floated on water, huge leaves with fluted rims like torte pans. And one time when we came while the place was mostly empty on a weekday, one of the attendants let us sit on these.

"Are you skipping school?" he asked, "Because if you are, I won't let you sit on the leaves. I'm not aware of any school holiday today."

"We go to the Merz Schule," I lied and wished it were true.

"Well," he said, "I've got a scale here. Let me weigh you. You both look like you're less than 30 kilos, but I have to make sure."

We passed. And then Joachim, sitting on his leaf-island said to me, as I was sitting on mine, "Want to meet at the *Frauenkopf* tomorrow?"

"Sure."

But I could not meet Joachim on the following morning. That night, after the bedtime story, I crawled out on the garage roof to throw rocks and to do with the words of the day what Mary did. And I fell asleep. The roof, as I remember it, was covered with the usual German clay roof tiles the color of flowerpots and deeply grooved to channel rainwater. I've wondered since how anyone could sleep on a surface like that, but then, in India and in China, I saw people sleep in spaces far more difficult than my garage roof.

I woke to many voices far and near calling my name, and as I listened, I heard concern. I crawled to the edge of the roof and yelled, "I'm here, I'm here!"

"Oh my God!" shouted my mother, "What are you doing on the roof?!" But she didn't wait for an answer and commanded, "Stay there, don't move. Just don't move. We'll get a ladder."

A policeman came running, and everyone in the neighborhood seemed to be out and milling about. "We found her," hollered the policeman, "Somebody get a ladder."

I wanted to say that I did not need a ladder, I could just crawl through the window and back into my closet, but the entire atmosphere was frightening: "Was I going to be arrested?" Maybe I had skipped school too often.

Somebody brought a ladder, and the policeman climbed up, grabbed me, and slung me over his shoulder like a rag doll. When he set me on the ground, my mother was right there with questions.

"What were you doing on the roof? And I don't want to hear any of your 'I don't knows' or your 'nothings' because you had the whole neighborhood worried and out looking for you. Why were you on the garage roof? I want the truth out of you." I did not know what to say. I knew she would not understand throwing rocks or doing with words what Mary did, so I told her the only other thing that was true of my times on the garage roof: "I was listening to the stars singing."

Stunned silence. Then somebody said, "She must have been hearing somebody's radio." And everyone was chattering again. I saw my grandfather not far away and went to find shelter under his arm. Then it occurred to my mother that she really did not want to know what I was doing on the roof, but instead how I had got there. I told her, and she, speaking casually to my grandfather over my head, said one of the hardest things I had heard in my entire life: "Papa, get some slats from your junk collection, would you, and nail them over the window so Angela can't go sleepwalking on roof." Then she turned to me and said, "Stars don't sing. You must have been dreaming or you heard the Krauses' radio."

I think I understand how an innocent man must feel when he stands in a courtroom and hears that he is sentenced to life-imprisonment. I wanted to yell, "No, please, no!" but I knew that this would only make things worse. I also wanted to say that I could definitely tell the difference between stars singing and a radio that somehow takes away the space the music lived in, flattens out all overtones, and adds scratchy noises of its own. Instead of fighting for my freedom and my knowledge, I studied my feet in silence.

That night, my grandfather apologized for the slats. "I'm sorry, Rabbit, but your mother means well. She's really worried about you."

"Grandpa, can the stars sing?"

"Rabbit, I can't hear them, but the Bible—it says they can."

"Can you show me, Grandpa?" He opened his Bible to the *Book of Job*, and it wasn't long before his stubby finger ran under the words "... When the morning stars sang together...."

I have never heard the stars sing since that time, but I would recognize the indescribable sound I heard, a sound half like an organ, half like wind, yet not wind, and not in any scale I could name.

***

And then one day, when I came home from the Wilhelma (instead of school), my mother was home, and she had box after box of brand new household and kitchen goods that she was repacking into other boxes as my grandmother helped with tears in her eyes. I remember especially a set of silverware that was not silver, but made of something called *Cromargan* from the *Würtembergische Metallwaren Fabrik*. I still have a soup ladle and a gravy ladle, and I still love the clean utilitarian design free of all ornamentation and yet not without grace.

"Why are we getting all new stuff?" I asked. As tears rolled down my grandmother's face, my mother said, "You and Ina and I—we're going to America."

And so the time came for me to sneak through the garden of my uncle Walter, the famous asshole of Sillenbuch, to say good-bye to him and to my excellent aunt Editta, and, of course, to Grandmamma. After my curtsey, her request for a recited poem, and then her invitation for me to sit down, she smiled, laid aside her needlework and said, "*Pensa dei biancospini.*"

She had told me often, "When sorrow comes, think of the whitethorns." I had never asked her why, but this time I did ask, "Grandmamma, what does the whitethorn have to do with anything, why should I think of it?"

"I won't see you again," she said, "I'm old; America is far away." She gave me a ring, rose gold and shaped like a snake with a diamond on its head. "It's almost two hundred years old, "she said, "Give it to your daughter or grand daughter when the time comes. Meanwhile, let your mother keep it 'til your hand is big enough. But most important, Child, remember the hawthorn." As it happened, I did see her again for a last and memorable time, but that's for later.

***

I went to find Hannes in the fields to say good-bye to him also. He did not seem sad about my going, and we talked of throwing rocks and all that this had come to mean. And then he said, "Remember the larks playing with swan's down?"

"Yes; you told me not to forget them."

"Well, I'm telling you again."

"Why do I have to remember them?"

"Maybe we'll see each other again, maybe not. If we do meet again, I'll tell you then. If we don't, you'll figure it out by yourself eventually."

***

I have not said much about Mr. Bauer, the painter who lived in the old village down the hill. That is not because he was unimportant, quite the contrary. Instead, it is because it is difficult to say much about a man whose relationship to me was almost entirely silent. If the mood hit me to spend some time painting, I would show up at his door (no telephone at our house), and he would either welcome me, or he would say something like, "Tomorrow afternoon would be a better time."

If I was allowed in, then he would either say, "Join me in the studio" or he would say, "Go play with the kids." He had twelve of them. How an artist supported twelve children is something I wish I had quizzed him about. I learned much later from my mother that he only had six biological children, but, every time his wife had a baby, the couple adopted a war orphan to be that baby's companion. The amazing thing was that all twelve children had musical talent, as did their mother. So the family was also a little symphony orchestra.

Mr. Bauer liked to paint to the cacophony of twelve instruments being practiced at various levels of proficiency. But, somehow, absolute silence pervaded his studio in spite of the noise. If I was allowed in, he'd give me some equipment for watercolors, pencils, or pastels, and that was it—that was all there was of conversation or instruction. And we painted in silence. Once, though, when I'd painted a black cat and a crow not looking at each other, but keenly aware of one another's presence against the background of bare trees and the snowy village, Mr. Bauer had said, "You have talent."

When I came to say "Good-bye," he reminded me: "Don't forget you have talent. Talent is a responsibility, come hell or high water."

And that was it. I never said good-bye to my grandparents. Maybe it was too hard. Maybe it was that it never really sunk in that it would be a long time before I saw them again.

CHAPTER TWENTY-SIX

A Lousy Story

"Just what have you been doing all morning?" asked my mother, clearly not pleased.

"Nothing," I said. "There's nothing to do around here."

"I asked you to make the beds, why didn't you do at least that? It really wasn't too much to ask, was it? Answer me."

"No."

"So why didn't you do it?"

"I don't know."

"That's just not good enough—why do I even bother talking to you, I might as well be talking to the walls. I'm tired of your 'I-don't-knows.' Why didn't you do what I asked you to do? I want an answer out of you."

"I guess I forgot."

"You forgot. You are twelve years old, and I'm going to have to count on you. I asked you to make the beds, and all you've done is sit around all morning. When we get to America, I'm going to have to work, and we won't have Grandma to take care of things. You'll just have to do your share. When I was your age, I had to work in the fields with Grandpa and Grandma—I put in a good day's work after school. Sometimes we brought in the harvest by lantern light, and I'm not asking you to do that much. Right now you're not even going to school and you're too old for the day care center. You can't just sit around and do nothing. Come on—help me make the beds. Of course, we'll be late getting to the cafeteria, and you know what that means."

There was always something awkward about my mother's long speeches when she could not make her children do what she wanted done. Usually she would say the same thing over and over several times (and I will spare you that part). And so my sister and I always understood the gist of it about 1/4 through the harangue, after which we tuned out. My daughters tell me I had the same tendency. Of course, I totally deny it.

I knew the fact that I had not made the beds meant more than one thing. Among these was that the cafeteria line was going to be even longer than usual. I hated the cafeteria. It was interesting for one day, but one day only, because I had never seen a restaurant before where there were no waiters. But then the concept of a restaurant without waiters felt weird and uncivilized. And the food was horrible in its own right. Moreover, I was nauseated almost all the time anyway for reasons soon to be made clear. And the lines were always long, stifling, and you had to wait at least an hour before it was your turn to have some hash slung on your tray.

My mother, my sister and I had been living in this camp for three weeks, along with thousands of other refugees waiting to get their final medical, political, legal, and moral clearances (yes, moral clearance) to board a troop transport ship bound for the United States of America. We had packed all our belongings and had said good-bye to everyone, and now, at this camp in Bremerhafen, we were waiting week after week to get clearances from various bureaucratic departments.

"What happens if we don't get clearance?" I asked.

"Well," said my mother, "I guess we'd just have to go back to Stuttgart, but I hope that doesn't happen. Deciding to go was hard, and now I've given up everything."

I could not decide whether to wish for going to America or wish for going back home. At first I had been excited and curious about the United States of America, but I had not fully realized until the time came to get on the train for Bremerhafen at the terminal in downtown Stuttgart, that going to America meant leaving my grandmother and grandfather and Hannes and Joachim and Grandmamma and Aunt Editta and Kellermanns and Nikolai and Mohrle and Uncle Walter, the asshole of Sillenbuch, behind. Klaus Bach and Michael Ende had already gone off to university. Klara had married a good man.

And all that saying good-bye was long before I knew that leaving your mother tongue behind was going to be even more difficult than leaving all the people I loved. Of course, I thought of Mohrle as a person. And then, there was another, a secret worry I could not talk about: what if my father came back from some prisoner-of-war camp in Russia, how would he ever find us in America? And now, at this immigration camp, I had lots of misgivings, although my mother had reassured me many times that America was not going to be like this camp, even though the Americans were running it—and anyway, this camp was not a concentration camp. The country, she said, would be run differently. We would have our own apartment in America and we would not have to sleep in barracks with hundreds of other people in the same room. We would do our own cooking. There would be a whole new country to explore. Life would be great. Just as it was in the book about America she had brought home for us to read. That book planted a desire for a big lawn, a big house, and a yellow Cadillac convertible. But then, when I really did see my first lawn, I just did not get it. What was so great about a piece of ground with nothing on it but grass? Short grass, too, with no wildflowers amongst it. And I missed the small, fenced-in flower and vegetable gardens of Sillenbuch and the pastures and all their abundance.

After we had gotten a glob of something allegedly edible plopped onto our trays, and I do mean trays, not plates, and had found a space at a crowded table, I said, "You know the bowls of water that you put the legs of our beds in?"

"What about them?"

"You can forget about them."

"What do you mean?" she said, "Didn't you see all the drowned bed bugs I fished out this morning?"

"Well, they won't be drowning any more. I watched them this morning. They're in our beds now."

"That's impossible. There is no way they could get to our beds without drowning."

"Yes there is. I saw it."

"OK, tell me."

"They crawled up the walls, and then they crawled upside down across the ceiling. It took them almost all morning to do it. And when they got over the beds, they just let themselves drop. I could almost hear them yell, 'Geronimo!'" I said.

My mother looked at me in horror-struck disbelief. "So that's what you've been doing all morning?! You really are hopeless. And if you saw them, why didn't you kill them?"

"Well, I didn't know what they were going to do, and I wanted to find out, and then, after they worked so hard to get up the wall—it must be like a really big desert for them—anyway, I felt sorry for them. Besides, it was too late. I couldn't reach them. And after they dropped, they just disappeared." The truth was that it had never occurred to me to kill them.

"If the beds had been made, you could have just brushed them off. You won't be feeling sorry for them when they bite you bloody tonight."

"I was thinking about how small they were compared to the room, and how can they know enough about geography to figure out they could get to our beds by dropping from the ceiling? That must have taken a lot of planning. After their friends and relatives drowned, they knew they couldn't do it by swimming. And how can they walk upside down on the ceiling? One minute they were walking on the ceiling and the next second they just dropped."

My mother looked a tad encouraging, so I continued, "They were walking single file—how do they decide who goes first and second? And when they got to the corner where the wall ends and the ceiling starts, they crawled around in circles for while before they organized again to walk across the ceiling. And when they got over the middle of the beds, they crawled around in circles again, just as if they were talking to each other and thinking about what to do."

"Animals do things by instinct, they don't think and plan, and they don't talk to each other—you know that."

"What's instinct?"

"You've asked that question about a thousand times—animals inherit an inner biological sense from their parents, and they're born knowing what to do. They do it automatically because they can't think and plan. And so because of their instinct, they don't have to. That's why mice always act like mice and birds always act like birds. That's how storks know to fly to Egypt in the fall, that's how they know their way. Each animal always acts the same way, generation after generation."

"Don't humans always act like humans?"

"No, they don't. Humans are different. They can learn and think and plan and remember. And they can do things differently from their parents. Humans are free to choose—animals aren't.

"Well, Mohrle can choose. There is some food he definitely doesn't like." And I realized with a sick feeling in my stomach that I would never see my kitty again. America just was not worth leaving everything for, and I began to hope we would never get there.

"Food is different," she said.

"What?"

"Food is different. Have you been listening?"

"I miss Mohrle," I said, very miserable and close to tears.

I thought about these things for a very long time since there was absolutely nothing for me to do at this camp, and I was dying of boredom. "Only stupid people get bored," said my mother. And I thought, if my grandfather were here, he would find lots of stuff to do. Maybe I really was stupid. I felt very stupid sitting around all day.

Meanwhile, the bed bugs foiled our next attempt to thwart them. Using beanpoles, we draped a sheet over each bed to make a tent, making sure that no part of the sheet touched the floor or the walls or the bed itself. But the bed bugs just let themselves drop from the ceiling onto the top of the canopy, then they crawled down the sheet to the bottom edge, and then they crawled up on the inside of the canopy and let themselves drop into the beds. If they inherited these ways of solving problems from their parents by instinct, then instinct was a lot better than thinking, remembering, planning, and learning, so far as I could tell. I wished that I, too, had been born knowing how to do all the right things automatically, and said so.

"You are very good at doing things without thinking," said my mother, "That's just the trouble with you."

***

The bedbugs were not the only vermin we could not get rid of in that immigration camp. We also could not get rid of head lice—which, by the way, do not just stay on your head. The American army personnel sprayed us once a week with DDT. We had to stand in line, men and women separately. When we got inside the building, we had to take all our clothes off and go through a special room where we were sprayed by people who looked really scary. "Those are just gas masks," said my mother. But even knowing the word "gas mask" did not help me deal with the way they looked. The procedure was truly awful, and it was all for nothing. The lice just kept coming back. The Americans intensified the DDT treatments, but nothing helped. People were starting to get sick, especially old people and babies, and I was feeling nauseous almost all the time.

Finally, my mother decided to speak to the camp's commander about this situation. And since I was too old for the day care center, I got to come along to observe the whole thing. Even now, I still look back with pleasure to this small episode of my life. The lousy situation lifted my spirits and saved me from death by boredom.

Of course, my mother spoke English to the camp commander, but she translated everything for me after each meeting, and so I can reconstruct all the wonderful conversations about lice, which took place that spring of 1952 at the immigration camp at Bremerhaven.

We went to the commander's office, and my mother told his secretary that she wanted to speak to Captain Rogers about the lice.

"About the lice?"

"Yes, I wish to speak to Captain Rogers concerning lice."

"Would you mind telling me what this is all about? Captain Rogers is a very busy man."

"This is about lice."

"I understood that part. If you know how to get rid of the lice, Mrs. Mailänder, why don't you just tell me, and then Captain Rogers can decide on the feasibility of your suggestion."

"I'm afraid I must speak to him personally. This is an extremely complicated intercultural situation. If the Captain does not wish to allow lice to immigrate to the United States, he will have to solve the cultural problem in which these lice are embedded—so to speak."

"Lice are not a cultural problem. They're a health hazard."

"I really must insist on seeing the Captain personally. The older people in the camp and some of the infants are starting to get sick from overexposure to DDT, and I'm sure the Captain would not want to deal with infant mortality due to the overuse of DDT. He might be able to deal with old people dying, but if too many babies die, there would be an investigation."

We had an appointment with Captain Rogers that afternoon. He was frowning and shuffling papers as we were ushered into his office. Finally, he looked up and said, "Well, Mrs. Mailänder, how can I help you." It didn't really sound like a question.

"I do not need help, Sir—you do, if you want to get rid of the lice in this camp."

"Don't tell me DDT is ineffective on European lice—some of my people have already suggested that."

"DDT works very well, Sir, but some of our Russian refugees do all they can to save the lives of their lice."

"What??"

"Sir, they even put lice in their mouths…"

"That's just nuts!! God, that's disgusting! Are you putting me on? If you're putting me on, Mrs. Mailänder, I assure you, you are never getting to America through my camp."

"Hear me out, Sir. Some of the Russian refugees will do anything to save the lice. They put them in their mouths, and then they rush to the barracks to shower to get rid of the poison, and then they put the lice back on their heads. Some of them are starting to think they shall become ill from all the showers they must take."

"Well, if that's the truth, we'll just issue an order to stop this crazy practice."

"Sir, I'm afraid it is not going to be that simple. It is a matter of life and death for these people. They'll find another way to save the lice."

"What? What do you mean it's a matter of life and death…this is not making sense. Lice are not a matter of life and death."

"Sir, they believe they will die without their lice."

"That is the craziest superstition I have ever heard of—we'll just have to re-educate these people. Now, if you'll excuse me, I have a lot of work to do."

An assembly was called for all the Russians in the camp. The camp's chief doctor, wearing a freshly starched and ironed white lab coat and a stethoscope around his neck, gave a speech, which my mother translated into Russian because the camp's translator had died of a heart attack on the day we had arrived, and his replacement had not yet shown up. The doctor spoke at length about the importance of hygiene and the fact that in America people lived long healthy lives without lice. Getting rid of lice, he said several times, was not going to kill anyone, that, on the contrary, lice carried many diseases, and that people's chances of living long and healthy lives were much better without lice. Everyone listened politely, and when it was over, the audience applauded enthusiastically.

However, nothing changed. Captain Rogers sent a couple of MP's to find my mother to tell her that he wanted to talk to her again.

"What part of the speech didn't they understand?" asked the Captain, "Did you translate everything the doctor said correctly?"

"Yes, Sir, but it is not a matter of understanding. It is a matter of believing. Sir, it does not matter what you tell them; their experience for generations back is that when you see the lice leave a person, that person is going to die."

"Is that a fact? The lice leave a person when he is going to die? Why is that?"

"Lice are parasites, Sir, they need a living host."

"And they actually know when a person is going to die and then they just leave? That's preposterous—lice can't see the future or make that kind of diagnosis."

"It's instinct, Sir. My mother was an herbalist in Russia, and when you see the lice leaving…"

"You can actually see them leave? Lice are pretty small."

"They all leave at the same time, Sir—you see crowds of them leave, like a reddish dark brown spot moving across the pillow in a regular Biblical Exodus. Everyone starts to grieve right then because that is a sure sign that the end is near—within a very few days. Sometimes the lice leave even before it is clear to the family or the doctor that death is near."

"Well, but the lice leaving is not the cause of death—that is so obvious."

"It is a 100% correlation, Sir. We are not dealing with educated people here. How are you going to explain the difference between a cause and a 100% correlation to them?"

"Are there any educated people among the Russian refugees who don't think they need to have lice for survival?"

"Yes, Sir, of course; Russia is a civilized country. Many people are highly educated."

"Well, I wouldn't know about *that*; they *are* Communists."

"Except the Communists, of course."

"Do you personally know any of these educated people who are not

Communists in this camp?"

"Yes, Sir."

"Who?"

"Well, there is *Prince Fyodor Anatoly Sviatoslavich, vnuk Vsevolod, pravnuk Olgov, pravnuk Sviatoslavl', prapravnuk Iaroslavl*, just for example," said my mother with a completely straight face.

"Jesus Christ! I didn't ask for the whole damn Russian army."

"That is the full name of the Prince, Sir."

"Do the Russian people respect this fellow?"

"Yes, Sir, very much. He is a kind and compassionate man, a truly cultured man."

"Well, get this prince in here right now, I want to talk to him—what's his name again?"

"*Prince Fyodor Anatoly Sviatoslavich, vnuk Vsevolod, pravnuk Olgov, pravnuk Sviatoslavl', prapravnuk Iaroslavl*, Sir,"

"Ffuh...uh, excuse me," said the Captain, "Prince Vvv—hell, what does this fellow go by?"

"Excuse me, Sir, I am not familiar with that expression."

"What do his friends call him?"

"'Anatoly Sviatoslavich' is one possibility, but, Sir, you cannot possibly call him that."

"Well, he's going to have a tough time adjusting to America—what do you suggest I call him? And I can tell you right now, I'm not going to call him 'Your Highness' and I'm for sure not spitting out that whole crazy alphabet soup his folks saw fit to baptize him with."

"I think you could just call him Prince, Sir."

"I'm not calling him Prince Sir."

"I mean just Prince."

"OK, go find this guy and bring him back here today. I want the louse problem solved now."

My mother and I went to find the Prince, who was a very dignified and white-haired gentleman and who walked with a cane that had a gold lion's head on the top of it. As we were walking back to the Captain's office, she explained the situation to him. He listened attentively, and when she was finished, he said, "I am not a teacher, Alexandra Maximovna—how could we explain the difference between a cause and a 100% correlation to peasants? It is, in fact, not always possible to tell the difference.

It depends on the state of the art in each science—one could even argue that scientific progress consists precisely of discovering that what was thought to be a cause turns out to be merely a correlation. Or the other way around. And, sometimes, the difference between a cause and an effect is by no means clear."

"I am not a teacher either, Anatoly Sviatoslavich. Maybe we could think of several examples of correlations that really are not causes, and everyone knows it."

"Like what, Alexandra Maximovna? I can't think of a single example just off hand."

"Brides wear white at weddings, but the dress is not the cause of the marriage?"

"That sounds pretty good, Alexandra Maximovna. How about the bride and the groom always kiss each other, but this is not the cause of pregnancy?"

"Yes, that is excellent, Anatoly Sviatoslavich. How about widows always wear black, but the black dress is not the cause of widowhood?"

"Yes, yes, Alexandra Maximovna. How about snow always melts in the spring, but the melting snow is not the cause of spring? Or dogs always bark at thieves, but dogs are not the cause of theft."

By the time we got to the Captain's office, they were feeling confident they had the problem solved, and I was feeling confused. The Captain said, "Hello there, Prince, how you doin'? I'm very glad you could make it, and I really hope you can help us out here."

My mother translated into Russian: "How do you do, Prince Anatoly Sviatoslavich, welcome to my office. I am most honored that you made time for me and I hope you can help us in the very difficult situation that we face here."

"Damn," said the Captain, "Did I say all that?"

"Russian words are much longer than English words, Sir," said my mother. The Prince smiled ever so slightly and told my mother that, of course, he understood English, but that he was not entirely comfortable with speaking the language.

My mother said to the Captain, "The Prince says, 'Sir, I am delighted to make your acquaintance, and I am entirely at your disposal with whatever small service I might offer.'"

"Right," said the Captain, "Tell the Prince that I'm going to call an assembly for all Russian refugees tomorrow morning, and this time, he is going to explain to them what the difference is between a cause and a correlation. And I want him to be sure to mention that lice are very dangerous. Lice cause typhus. I do not want a typhus epidemic in this camp. Is that clear?"

"Yes, indeed, Sir," said the Prince after my mother had translated the import of the Captain's words.

The Prince continued with my mother as translator, "May I make a suggestion, Sir?"

"I need all the ideas I can get," said the Captain.

"We might end the lecture with a discussion. We might give the people a chance to ask questions and to tell us what they have understood and what they have not understood."

"That's a great idea," said Captain Rogers, "Very democratic. I'll make sure some of the medical personnel are on hand if any medical questions come up."

The speech went very well. The Russians all listened attentively, but when Anatoly Sviatoslavich asked if there was any discussion or any question, the hall went dead silent for a long minute. Then, as if on command, everyone started talking all at once. Prince Anatoly Sviatoslavich let them talk for a few minutes and then called them to order and asked for a show of hands. The upshot was that there were two objections from the people about the speech. The first one was that no one understood what all the analogies in the speech were about. What did a widow wearing a black dress have to do with lice? What did a bride wearing white dress have to do with lice? What in the world did a bridegroom kissing a bride have to do with lice?

And the second objection was that nobody believed that lice caused typhus. It was exactly the other way around. Everyone knows, they said, that eating lice is the only known cure for typhus. What if they ever got typhus? How could they cure it if they did not have any lice? Lice were the only hope if typhoid fever struck.

After my mother had translated these two objections for Captain Rogers, he said, "Damn—they eat lice?? I've never heard of anything so disgusting and so nuts. And they really think it cures typhus?? Are they all crazy?"

"Sir," said the camp's head doctor, "In the absence of modern medicine, eating lice does make some kind of sense. They'd have to be eaten live, I imagine..."

"Yes, Sir, that's right," said my mother, "They enclose the lice in dough capsules and swallow them."

"Well, I'll be damned!" said the Captain. "That is the most unbelievable thing I've ever heard."

"Sir," said the camp doctor, "Eating lice would have a similar effect to inoculation. The dosage would have to be exactly right, but it would work, since lice are known carriers of typhus—in both cases, by inoculation and by eating small amounts of the pathogen, a weakened form of it is introduced into the system which can then begin to produce antibodies."

"Well, halleluiah," said Captain Rogers, "Tell the people that we have much better and much more effective medicines against typhus in America—no more need to eat lice. They should be very glad to hear it."

My mother translated this message for the Prince, and the Prince told the people. Again, the hall broke out into excited and loud chatter. Again, the Prince asked for a show of hands. And this time, the people objected on the grounds that Americans were very different from Russians in many ways, and they did not want to experiment to find out if they were the same or different with respect to lice, since this was a matter of life and death. The Prince told the people that he would be more than willing to trust the Americans on this point. But the people objected again, saying that the Prince was as different from ordinary Russian people as they were from Americans. My mother translated for the Captain, and he was visibly discouraged by the message. "Well, what are we going to do? I can't ship louse-infected people to the States—Washington is breathing down my neck about that."

"If I may make a suggestion, Sir," said the Prince.

"I'll try anything."

"You might offer a large reward to any Russian of the peasant classes who would offer his person to radical, absolute and permanent delousing. In the case of potato eating, the example of Frederick the Great, eating potatoes on his balcony at Potsdam had convinced the peasantry that potatoes were indeed wholesome food after they had mistakenly eaten the berries that the plants produce, which are, of course, very poisonous."

The offer was made, and the Russians again went into a noisy discussion. This time, the upshot was that even if a person could be found who was desperate enough to risk his life so his family could inherit the reward and even if, by some miracle, he survived, this would prove nothing, since one swallow did not make a summer. In any case, one might have to wait years to learn if that person would survive typhus in case he became ill.

"I believe this is a hopeless situation," said the Prince to my mother in French.

"Unfortunately, I believe you are right," answered my mother.

The Americans, hoist on their own democratic and scientific petard, changed their tactics. MP's began patrolling the lines to the spraying rooms. It did not help; it was too difficult to watch every Russian every minute. Then they hit on the idea that they could make Russians rinse out their mouths after spraying. That did not help either. The Russians simply went back to the beginning of the line and borrowed some lice still waiting to be sprayed. Some put lice in small vials or wrappers and protected them in other bodily orifices. Others paid Lithuanians, Estonians, and Poles to secrete lice for them. My mother told me that many of these refugees were not as poor as they looked and were smuggling diamonds and other precious stones to the States. Lice, too, became a precious commodity.

***

I do not know if Captain Rogers ever solved the problem. He had not by the time we finally got our clearances and boarded a big, grey troop-transport ship, the General Hersey, along with thousands of other refugees, including Russians determined to carry their lice live into the New World.

I went on board excited because I had never been on a ship before. I was also a little worried because I knew stories about shipwrecks. I wondered, too, why some bed bugs drowned in bowls of water while others were born understanding the geography of a room. And how could lice know a person was going to die?

"Hurry, hurry, time is money," said the sergeant on the gangplank—my first English words spoken on American soil, as a ship is considered just that, even though it is made of metal. Time is money? How could one thing be another? These words seemed as mysterious and as strange to me as my grandfather's favorite phrase, "God is love."

I do not remember much about my first ocean voyage. A troop transport ship is not a slave ship, but it is not a passenger ship either; we were crammed in with no room to spare, nor was there much air below decks, and the smell of thousands of sea-sick women and children alone would have made anyone deathly ill, and that is not even counting the diaper pails. The bunks were so close on top of each other from floor to ceiling, so that even I, short as I was, could not sit up in bed. And in the cafeteria, there were no chairs—you stood while eating from your tray. And the tables, designed for American men, were so high that I stood under one of them like a dog begging for scraps. But I did not have to endure any of it for long. The English Channel is always choppy, and by the time we saw the White Cliffs of Dover (which were very dirty that day), the combination of overexposure to DDT and the rolling ship and its accommodations were too much for me. I got so sea-sick that I was strapped down in the ship's hospital where I spent all eleven days of that voyage, mostly unconscious and in convulsions even under heavy sedation. I lost eleven pounds, and had been skin and bones to start with. No one, my mother told me later, had expected me to live.

But as soon as we sailed into the harbor on the 12th of June in 1952 in the New World, I came on deck in time to paint a watercolor of the dark New York skyline with the most violently colored sunset I had ever seen behind it and reflected in the water, so that the black, backlit city looked as if it swam in a sea of blood.

APPENDIX 1

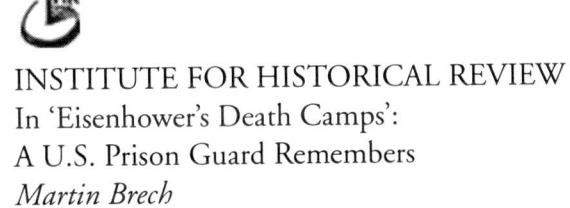

INSTITUTE FOR HISTORICAL REVIEW
In 'Eisenhower's Death Camps':
A U.S. Prison Guard Remembers
Martin Brech

In October 1944, at age eighteen, I was drafted into the U.S. army. Largely because of the "Battle of the Bulge," my training was cut short, my furlough was halved, and I was sent overseas immediately. Upon arrival in Le Havre, France, we were quickly loaded into box cars and shipped to the front. When we got there, I was suffering increasingly severe symptoms of mononucleosis, and was sent to a hospital in Belgium. Since mononucleosis was then known as the "kissing disease," I mailed a letter of thanks to my girlfriend.

By the time I left the hospital, the outfit I had trained with in Spartanburg, South Carolina, was deep inside Germany, so, despite my protests, I was placed in a "repo depot" (replacement depot). I lost interest in the units to which I was assigned, and don't recall all of them: non-combat units were ridiculed at that time. My separation qualification record states I was mostly with Company C, 14th Infantry Regiment, during my seventeen-month stay in Germany, but I remember being transferred to other outfits also.

In late March or early April 1945, I was sent to guard a POW camp near Andernach along the Rhine. I had four years of high school German, so I was able to talk to the prisoners, although this was forbidden. Gradually, however, I was used as an interpreter and asked to ferret out members of the S.S. (I found none.)

In Andernach about 50,000 prisoners of all ages were held in an open field surrounded by barbed wire. The women were kept in a separate enclosure that I did not see until later. The men I guarded had no shelter and no blankets. Many had no coats. They slept in the mud, wet and cold, with inadequate slit trenches for excrement. It was a cold, wet spring, and their misery from exposure alone was evident.

Even more shocking was to see the prisoners throwing grass and weeds into a tin can containing a thin soup. They told me they did this to help ease their hunger pains. Quickly they grew emaciated. Dysentery raged, and soon they were sleeping in their own excrement, too weak and crowded to reach the slit trenches. Many were begging for food, sickening and dying before our eyes. We had ample food and supplies, but did nothing to help them, including no medical assistance.

Outraged, I protested to my officers and was met with hostility or bland indifference. When pressed, they explained they were under strict orders from "higher up." No officer would dare do this to 50,000 men if he felt that it was "out of line," leaving him open to charges. Realizing my protests were useless, I asked a friend working in the kitchen if he could slip me some extra food for the prisoners. He too said they were under strict orders to severely ration the prisoners' food, and that these orders came from "higher up." But he said they had more food than they knew what to do with, and would sneak me some.

When I threw this food over the barbed wire to the prisoners, I was caught and threatened with imprisonment. I repeated the "offense," and one officer angrily threatened to shoot me. I assumed this was a bluff until I encountered a captain on a hill above the Rhine shooting down at a group of German civilian women with his .45 caliber pistol. When I asked, "Why?," he mumbled, "Target practice," and fired until his pistol was empty. I saw the women running for cover, but, at that distance, couldn't tell if any had been hit.

This is when I realized I was dealing with cold-blooded killers filled with moralistic hatred. They considered the Germans subhuman and worthy of extermination; another expression of the downward spiral of racism. Articles in the G.I. newspaper, *Stars and Stripes*, played up the German concentration camps, complete with photos of emaciated bodies. This amplified our self-righteous cruelty, and made it easier to imitate behavior we were supposed to oppose. Also, I think, soldiers not exposed to combat were trying to prove how tough they were by taking it out on the prisoners and civilians.

These prisoners, I found out, were mostly farmers and workingmen, as simple and ignorant as many of our own troops. As time went on, more of them lapsed into a zombie-like state of listlessness, while others tried to escape in a demented or suicidal fashion, running through open fields in broad daylight towards the Rhine to quench their thirst. They were mowed down.

Some prisoners were as eager for cigarettes as for food, saying they took the edge off their hunger. Accordingly, enterprising G.I. "Yankee traders" were acquiring hordes of watches and rings in exchange for handfuls of cigarettes or less. When I began throwing cartons of cigarettes to the prisoners to ruin this trade, I was threatened by rank-and-file G.I.s too.

The only bright spot in this gloomy picture came one night when. I was put on the "graveyard shift," from two to four a.m. Actually, there was a graveyard on the uphill side of this enclosure, not many yards away. My superiors had forgotten to give me a flashlight and I hadn't bothered to ask for one, disgusted as I was with the whole situation by that time. It was a fairly bright night and I soon became aware of a prisoner crawling under the wires towards the graveyard. We were supposed to shoot escapees on sight, so I started to get up from the ground to warn him to get back. Suddenly I noticed another prisoner crawling from the graveyard back to the enclosure. They were risking their lives to get to the graveyard for something. I had to investigate.

When I entered the gloom of this shrubby, tree-shaded cemetery, I felt completely vulnerable, but somehow curiosity kept me moving. Despite my caution, I tripped over the legs of someone in a prone position. Whipping my rifle around while stumbling and trying to regain composure of mind and body, I soon was relieved I hadn't reflexively fired. The figure sat up. Gradually, I could see the beautiful but terror-stricken face of a woman with a picnic basket nearby. German civilians were not allowed to feed, nor even come near the prisoners, so I quickly assured her I approved of what she was doing, not to be afraid, and that I would leave the graveyard to get out of the way.

I did so immediately and sat down, leaning against a tree at the edge of the cemetery to be inconspicuous and not frighten the prisoners. I imagined then, and still do now, what it would be like to meet a beautiful woman with a picnic basket under those conditions as a prisoner. I have never forgotten her face.

Eventually, more prisoners crawled back to the enclosure. I saw they were dragging food to their comrades, and could only admire their courage and devotion.

On May 8, V.E. Day [1945], I decided to celebrate with some prisoners I was guarding who were baking bread the other prisoners occasionally received. This group had all the bread they could eat, and shared the jovial mood generated by the end of the war. We all thought we were going home soon, a pathetic hope on their part. We were in what was to become the French zone [of occupation], where I soon would witness the brutality of the French soldiers when we transferred our prisoners to them for their slave labor camps.

On this day, however, we were happy.

As a gesture of friendliness, I emptied my rifle and stood it in the corner, even allowing them to play with it at their request. This thoroughly "broke the ice," and soon we were singing songs we taught each other, or that I had learned in high school German class ("Du, du, liegst mir im Herzen"). Out of gratitude, they baked me a special small loaf of sweet bread, the only possible present they had left to offer. I stuffed it in my "Eisenhower jacket," and snuck it back to my barracks, eating it when I had privacy. I have never tasted more delicious bread, nor felt a deeper sense of communion while eating it. I believe a cosmic sense of Christ (the Oneness of all Being) revealed its normally hidden presence to me on that occasion, influencing my later decision to major in philosophy and religion.

Shortly afterwards, some of our weak and sickly prisoners were marched off by French soldiers to their camp. We were riding on a truck behind this column. Temporarily, it slowed down and dropped back, perhaps because the driver was as shocked as I was. Whenever a German prisoner staggered or dropped back, he was hit on the head with a club and killed. The bodies were rolled to the side of the road to be picked up by another truck. For many, this quick death might have been preferable to slow starvation in our "killing fields."

When I finally saw the German women held in a separate enclosure, I asked why we were holding them prisoner. I was told they were "camp followers," selected as breeding stock for the S.S. to create a super-race. I spoke to some, and must say I never met a more spirited or attractive group of women. I certainly didn't think they deserved imprisonment.

More and more I was used as an interpreter, and was able to prevent some particularly unfortunate arrests. One somewhat amusing incident involved an old farmer who was being dragged away by several M.P.s. I was told he had a "fancy Nazi medal," which they showed me. Fortunately, I had a chart identifying such medals. He'd been awarded it for having five children! Perhaps his wife was somewhat relieved to get him "off her back," but I didn't think one of our death camps was a fair punishment for his contribution to Germany. The M.P.s agreed and released him to continue his "dirty work."

Famine began to spread among the German civilians also. It was a common sight to see German women up to their elbows in our garbage cans looking for something edible—that is, if they weren't chased away.

When I interviewed mayors of small towns and villages, I was told that their supply of food had been taken away by "displaced persons" (foreigners who had worked in Germany), who packed the food on trucks and drove away. When I reported this, the response was a shrug. I never saw any Red Cross at the camp or helping civilians, although their coffee and doughnut stands were available everywhere else for us. In the meantime, the Germans had to rely on the sharing of hidden stores until the next harvest.

Hunger made German women more "available," but despite this, rape was prevalent and often accompanied by additional violence. In particular I remember an eighteen-year old woman who had the side of her faced smashed with a rifle butt, and was then raped by two G.I.s. Even the French complained that the rapes, looting and drunken destructiveness on the part of our troops was excessive. In Le Havre, we'd been given booklets warning us that the German soldiers had maintained a high standard of behavior with French civilians who were peaceful, and that we should do the same. In this we failed miserably.

"So what?" some would say. "The enemy's atrocities were worse than ours." It is true that I experienced only the end of the war, when we were already the victors. The German opportunity for atrocities had faded, while ours was at hand. But two wrongs don't make a right. Rather than copying our enemy's crimes, we should aim once and for all to break the cycle of hatred and vengeance that has plagued and distorted human history. This is why I am speaking out now, 45 years after the crime. We can never prevent individual war crimes, but we can, if enough of us speak out, influence government policy. We can reject government propaganda that depicts our enemies as subhuman and encourages the kind of outrages I witnessed. We can protest the bombing of civilian targets, which still goes on today. And we can refuse ever to condone our government's murder of unarmed and defeated prisoners of war.

I realize it's difficult for the average citizen to admit witnessing a crime of this magnitude, especially if implicated himself. Even G.I.s sympathetic to the victims were afraid to complain and get into trouble, they told me. And the danger has not ceased. Since I spoke out a few weeks ago, I have received threatening calls and had my mailbox smashed. But its been worth it. Writing about these atrocities has been a catharsis of feelings suppressed too long, a liberation, that perhaps will remind other witnesses that "the truth will make us free, have no fear." We may even learn a supreme lesson from all this: only love can conquer all.

About the author

Martin Brech lives in Mahopac, New York. When he wrote this memoir essay in 1990, he was an Adjunct Professor of Philosophy and Religion at Mercy College in Dobbs Ferry, New York. Brech holds a master's degree in theology from Columbia University, and is a Unitarian-Universalist minister.

This essay was published in *The Journal of Historical Review,* Summer 1990 (Vol. 10, No. 2), pp. 161-166. (Revised, updated: Nov. 2008)

For Further Reading

James Bacque, *Crimes and Mercies: The Fate of German Civilians Under Allied Occupation, 1944-1950* (Toronto: Little, Brown and Co., 1997)

James Bacque, *Other Losses: An investigation into the mass deaths of German prisoners at the hands of the French and Americans after World War II* (Toronto: Stoddart, 1989)

Alfred-Maurice de Zayas, *Nemesis at Postsdam* (Lincoln, Neb.: 1990)

Alfred-Maurice de Zayas, *A Terrible Revenge: The Ethnic Cleansing of the Eastern European Germans, 1944-1950* (New York: St. Martin's Press, 1994)

John Dietrich, *The Morgenthau Plan: Soviet Influence on American Postwar Policy* (New York: Algora, 2002)

Ralph Franklin Keeling, *Gruesome Harvest: The Allies' Postwar War Against the German People* (IHR, 1992). Originally published in Chicago in 1947.

Giles MacDonogh, *After the Reich: The Brutal History of the Allied Occupation* (New York: Basic Books, 2007)

John Sack, *An Eye for an Eye: The Story of Jews Who Sought Revenge for the Holocaust* (2000)

Mark Weber, "New Book Details Mass Killings and Brutal Mistreatment of Germans at the End of World War Two" (Summer 2007) (http://www.ihr.org/other/afterthereich072007.html)

Appendix II

As my grandparents' story is part of me, you have heard snippets of it here and there throughout mine. Here I will tell all I know about two of the people this book is dedicated to, the woman and the man who were mother and father to me.

Maria Abramovna and Maxim Pavlovich

My grandfather, Maxim Pavlovitch (a.k.a. Maximillian Zeitner) told me the Dnepr River in Ukraine was clear as glass, so clean that you could see the snow-white sand on the river bottom tinted in shades of aqua in the undulating light. And every detail of every fish and waterweed was distinct and luminous. Wealthy passengers on river boats, like those on the Mississippi at that same time, the 1880s, and just as full of luxury and light, would throw rubles overboard to watch their slow and silvery spin to the bottom, enticing the wild village boys to dive for them. Among his friends, my grandfather was counted as wealthy, for he was a diver without equal. As an old man, he could still hold his breath for four minutes and he claimed that when he was young, he could go without breathing for longer than five.

I have never seen a river like that. I thought maybe my grandfather had made it up, just as my students in China thought I'd made up blue skies, dragon-shaped clouds, and millions of stars. But then one day, when I had asked some students to tell me a little about themselves, one young man with the light of truth in his face said, "I come from village ver, ver small-ah." He cupped his hands to show how small, and my heart flowed at the gesture. "We cannot afford school-ah," he continued, "But-ah we have river ver, ver clear like-ah glass-ah. "We see fish in deep-ah water. We see beautiful life of them." And because I know my grandfather, and because I saw truth in this young man's face, I have an idea of what sort of a fine education such a river might be for a man.

When I was six, I imagined my grandfather swimming under water, as clear as prairie air, for hours at a time, meeting mermaids and talking to Russian water creatures unheard of in Germany.

His parents were of German origin, Baptists, who, along with Mennonite and Amish people, had fled to Russia because Russia, like America long ago, had promised asylum, freedom of religion, and freedom from military service, forever or a hundred years—the Russian language does not make a most important distinction between those two concepts: forever and a hundred years. My grandfather's family came somewhat later than the well-known waves of people who left Germany for Russia. When my mother, my sister, and I arrived as new immigrants in New York City on the 12th of June in 1952, she said, "Amazing. It is a hundred years to the day that your great grandfather arrived in Russia as an immigrant from Germany."

Maxim Pavlovich, born in Russia[1] in about 1880, yet retaining German citizenship, was short, stocky, and powerfully built with a barrel chest and short arms. And so when he was fourteen, he was apprenticed to a master craftsman in a foundry because, like a mountain-woodland gnome, he had the build for metalwork. At the foundry he learned to make church bells. Famous Russian church bells. One of his brothers made some of the wrought iron grillwork for which Petersburg is famous.

My grandmother said that as a teenager Max had also found a way to make rubles, using the fine white river sand to make molds, and he almost landed in Siberia for it. In the end, the judge let him go because Maxim Pavlovich was young and appeared not to have known that you can't just fabricate money (unless you call it "quantitative easing" and your name is something like Warburg or Yellen). "It wasn't fake money," he had insisted in court, "I made them all of real silver." And he would never have been caught—his workmanship was that good—had he not been too innocent to appreciate the need to keep the whole thing under wraps.

When he became a man, Maxim Pavlovich traveled to Krasnodar[2]

---
[1] Both my grandparents thought of Ukraine as part of Russia.
[2] It was then called Yekaterinodar, which means "Katharine's Gift," but then in about 1922 the Communists renamed it "Krasnodar," which means "Red Gift" or "Beautiful Gift," as if we could just change our minds as to whose gift it really was.

in the Caucasus Mountains, a city famous for the most beautiful Mennonite girls in the world. He lived near Chernobyl; the distance from there to Krasnodar by air is almost 700 miles—so that tells you just how far the fame of their beauty had traveled. He got one of them to go with him as his bride, though they'd had to deal with objections from Mennonites and Baptists both. Then she and her third child had died in labor, and Maxim Pavlovich was left alone with twin boys. So he went back to Krasnodar to find a second wife, Maria Abramovna, my grandmother.

***

My grandmother's people had come to Russia about a hundred years earlier than my grandfather's family. They had come under Catherine the Great who had herself come from Germany, from a hog farm, in fact, and she hoped that the Amish and the Mennonites would modernize Russian farming methods.

Maria Abrahmovna, my grandmother, was a beauty with a waist the hands of a man could encompass entirely. An expert seamstress and a somewhat moody and rebellious girl, she had learned the healing arts, acupuncture and herb lore, from her mother, Sarah, from her grandmother, and, briefly, even her great-grandmother, who had learned from a Chinese traveler who had come through Mongolia. It meant that my grandmother thought of the human body as a system of river-like energies that must be kept balanced and flowing freely. And plants, to her, were living spirits who helped to make this happen.

Her father, Abraham, was a schoolteacher who had refused to allow his daughters to learn to read and write on the grounds that these were "sacred arts," though he had taught his sons. My grandmother had resented it bitterly and, no more than four or five years old, she had learned secretly, bribing one of her brothers with saved up sweets to instruct her in the forbidden art.

One morning her father went off to work and didn't come back that night. Then, after twenty years had gone by as years go, he showed up suddenly out of the blue and he was chock full of the strangest ideas. He had walked into Persia and had kept walking into Tibet and India. No one understood him except his wife, Sarah, who loved him, and Maria, his youngest daughter. Both listened patiently and nursed him when he became ill soon after returning home. It was a long and difficult illness, which kept my great-grandmother housebound until his death.

When Sarah returned to church after the funeral, the elders took her to task in front of the whole congregation for her long absence. She explained that her husband had been too ill to be left alone, as was well known in the village, but the elders would not relent. She was a tall, slender woman, dressed in black and also wearing a black veil of mourning to cover her face. She stood, faced the congregation, tore her veil, cursed them, walked out...

...and never again attended church. Until her marriage to my grandfather, neither did Maria. There had subsequently been some effort to try my great-grandmother as a witch, especially as it seemed she had become infected with the strange ideas her husband had brought back from his travels, but the village thought better of it in the end since, for miles and miles around, there was no one else who understood the healing arts for humans and other animals.

All the other children were already married, except for my grandmother, though she was engaged. But now that mother and daughter no longer attended church and there were rumors of witchcraft, the young man broke off the engagement under pressure from his family, and my grandmother would have remained single had Maxim Pavlovich not come calling. As his two little boys needed a mother, there was no time for courtship—my grandmother simply trusted her life to him. And so he brought to Sengeyevka on the Dnieper River a girl skilled in the healing arts, a girl who could read, and one schooled in the "strange" ideas of the East. Maria Abrahmovna's mother soon joined the young couple.

***

My grandfather, Max, worked in the foundry along with two of his eleven brothers, Alexander and Otto. At this time, Russia began to import farm machinery from England. No such machines were made in Russia back then, and when the English machines broke down, parts from England took a long time to arrive. So my grandfather, who had made rubles, suggested to the master craftsman that making machine parts would not be a big deal. And my grandmother—she kept telling him, "Max, why are you making parts when you could make the whole machine?" And he kept answering, "You talk like any fool of a woman would talk about things you don't understand."

But one Sunday after church, his brothers Alexander and Otto heard her talking and said, "Listen Max, she might have something there." And the three of them wrote letters to Krupp and to Thyssen, two of Germany's industrial barons. They got money (and, maybe, Max even made some—again out of real silver). In any case, he went on several business trips to Germany. Then the brothers began traveling to look for land. They found it in Urbach, a German village on the Volga River further east. And, with help from the Krupp steel mills, it wasn't long before Maxim Pavlovich was the "John Deere" of the whole Volga region.

My grandfather did right as Bessie Smith says a man should do, "You gotta get it, you gotta bring it home, and you gotta put it right here." So my grandmother began to manage her husband's wealth and made it grow. Fabulous wealth it must have been, too, wealth unheard of in the early 1900s for anyone not of the aristocracy. There was china from Dresden, crystal from Bohemia and silver from France; there were stable boys and servants; there were tutors and nannies who spoke French and English, and my grandmother kept two big St. Bernard dogs with English names, Lord and Lady, who, when commanded to speak, would blow out all the candles on the dinner table to the delight of the children. Besides Max's twins, there were two girls, Rebecca and Maria, and a boy, Franz.

There was even enough money for my Great Uncle Alexander (Sasha, for short) to start his own factory making oil from sunflower seeds shipped from Ukraine, while my Great Uncle Otto also started a factory making machines. He made machines so new and so outrageously strange and mind-bending that no one in those parts had ever seen them before: he made automobiles.

Life seemed perfect and without a care for the whole family. But then, World War I began in September of 1914. In that same month, my grandfather was arrested as an enemy alien and taken from his home. No one knew, including him, where he was to be taken, or when, if ever, he would come back, or even if he would be allowed to live. My grandmother, four months pregnant with my mother, fainted—mercifully, since she did not have to witness the rape of her eight-year-old daughter Rebecca.

Soldiers took the horses, put barbed wire around the home, and my grandmother and the children were prisoners. Food was scarce. Rebecca died: weak from the loss of blood and then starvation, she could not fight the infection, which soon spread through the whole abdomen.

The lack of food became desperate. Most of the servants managed to escape. Lord and Lady were slaughtered. Nevertheless, two of the children died of starvation.

As soon as my grandmother gathered her wits about her after all these horrors, she began to teach Franz the skills of a midwife. He was the age of boys I've taught. If you've raised them right, such boys can do anything. People forget, teachers especially, that Alexander the Great was only sixteen years old when he led men into battle, conquering the whole world. Boys that age simply do not comprehend danger, and death is not a viable concept for them.

Franz was thirteen when he learned how to deliver a baby. Together he and my grandmother went over all possible scenarios including Cesarean section. She drew diagrams. She had instruments, showed him how to use them and how, in case a Caesarean section was necessary, to give a primitive anesthetic with wood smoke and with great care so as not to asphyxiate the patient. "It should be a normal delivery," she told him, "And after so many babies, I should be able to remain conscious to give you instructions. But women in labor often become irrational, so be prepared for that."

"I can't do this, Mama," he would say countless times.

"You can," she would say quietly, "Of course you can. You can because you have to. There is no one else, and this baby will come—that much is certain if we all live till the end of December or early January."

"Mama, women can die in childbirth."

"If it comes to a choice between my life and the baby's, choose mine."

"Mother, I can't do that."

"If you don't, the baby and I could both die. Son, don't be afraid. Death is a great mercy; so if it comes to a choice between me and the baby, free the baby's spirit, and don't look back. I have to live if I am to help us all get through this difficult time."

And so even before she was born, terror and grief came to my mother through her mother's blood. And then, when my mother was three weeks old, the same soldiers that had arrested my grandfather loaded my grandmother, Maria, and Franz onto a train. The train was crowded with soldiers and other prisoners. It was moving east—that was all they knew, and so my mother drank fear and grief with her mother's milk.

It was an endless train ride into deepening snow over vast plains and into dark, trackless forests, then mountains, and beyond them more snow and wind-swept plains. She longed for her husband. Never mind that there had been an Annie in Tarau, a far away city in Germany, who had broken her heart. Now, on that train, a black worm crawling through a white plain, leaving no visible sign of its path and soon forgotten, she wanted to tell him all is forgiven. "There is nothing more important in life," she would say to me growing up, "Than learning to forgive. Without forgiveness, nothing could even move, nothing could live."

I don't know how long they traveled on that train. I don't know what she did about washing diapers. When I heard these stories, I was too young to think of asking about that. I do know that, often, the train was stopped because snow was always drifting across the tracks, burying them so deeply that soldiers and prisoners might shovel for days before the train could move on.

They arrived at the end of the line: Chelyabinsk. They were told to wait in the train station, where they ate and slept on the station platform, thousands of prisoners, guarded by hundreds of soldiers. Ever after, when my grandmother saw a mess, she'd say, "Would you clean up your mess, please? This place looks like the train station at Chelyabinsk." Chelyabinsk was a fine, big city, and maybe that was hope and maybe not. Maybe they would be allowed stay here and wait for the end of the war. They waited.

And Franz explored the length of the train. When he came back from his exploration, he said, "I talked to some men shoveling coal into the engines. They were prisoners, Germans, like us. They said another big group of German prisoners has come through since they got here, and that group went further on by caravan and, well, Mama, I just know Papa is with them."

My grandmother had expected the caravan to be either horse-drawn sleighs or camels; how else could you travel in the trackless wilderness of a Siberian winter? I was surprised when I heard about camels in that part of the world, but apparently they are as good on snow as they are on sand. And they wear camelhair coats, naturally, with camelhair blankets on top of that. Both my grandparents had traveled in caravans like that, but I can't piece together all the details. I do know, however, that on this particular occasion my grandmother and her children traveled in a manner completely unexpected.

***

In the eastern mines of Siberia, iron ore was dug from the mountains in the brief summer. In winter, it was loaded into wicker baskets—baskets almost as big as a small hut with low walls. These were set on ski-like boards and pulled by small, but powerful, white horses in caravans to the railroad center at Chelyabinsk, and from there the ore was shipped to Russia's dark, Satanic mills. For the return trip, the baskets would be loaded with fresh supplies and fresh prisoners to work the mines, where life expectancy was about two brutal years—less for women, children, and old people. It was in one of these baskets that my grandmother, Franz, Maria, and the newborn baby traveled through the frozen Siberian wasteland in a caravan of perhaps fifty such contraptions. Maria asked and asked, "Where are we going, Mama?" With the newborn at her breast, my grandmother's answer was a mindless gaze into the distance. I, too, have seen that look in her eyes when I was five and asked questions with death all around us: as if she were seeing beyond a white prairie that went as far as the eye could see and then blended, seamless, into the white winter sky.

Franz, who had soothed his mother's heart with that story of his father traveling this way, tried to keep his little sister quiet. "Stop asking her dumb questions, will you?" he whispered in her ear. "Look at her, can't you see she doesn't know? But I know: we're going to find Papa, so you just be good and let her feed the baby."

During the long winter nights they camped under the dancing stars to the music of wolves and jackals—strangely beautiful music, my grandmother told me, almost like human singing in a minor key. And as terrible as that journey must have been for her, she longed to hear that music again. "It touched your heart," she said, "They would have torn us limb from limb, but they sang as if they, too, loved God."

The small white-haired horses were freed for the night, and the mares would form a great circle around the foals and the prisoners. All night, they'd ward off the wolves with their back hooves, wolves whose eyes burned in the dark and whose shadowy shapes were barely visible as they circled round the encampment just out of reach of the horses' hooves. The stallions ran around the perimeter of the circle all night to help the mares fend off the wolves. Every night the weakest were sacrificed. Every day the weakest traveled at the end of the caravan. If they made it through the day, would they last the night?

To make sure there would be enough horses to get to the mines, as many horses ran free with the caravan as were pulling sleds— to replace those that had fallen prey to the wolves or the jackals, and to relieve those too tired to pull.

There were three Bashkir drivers who carried guns, not to guard the prisoners—nature did that—but to defend against wolves during the short days of travel and to help the stallions guard the mares, the foals and the prisoners during the long nights.

The caravan was so long, you could travel half a day without seeing any of those drivers. The straw-lined wicker baskets were designed for the heavy iron ore, not for human cargo. Going across the Ural Mountain passes they would sometimes topple, and prisoners, especially their children, were lost in the snow. The wolves would find them soon enough. Often sleighs were separated, and you'd travel long distances praying no wolves found you and trusting the horses to choose life and return to the line. If a basket fell off its scaffolding, you could sometimes scramble into the next one or the one after that, and so there were days when my grandmother didn't know till the next stop if the wolves had killed Franz or Maria. And, of course, no one wanted to travel at the end of the line, yet if you'd fallen out of a basket, you might not be able to scramble into any but the very last. My grandmother always ended her stories of that time by saying, "If it hadn't been for Franz, none of us would have made it. He jumped out into the snow to retrieve Maria and other children. He fought for rations and made sure we got our fair share and then made sure I ate enough to nurse your mother."

Sometimes they stopped in Bashkir villages. The people were Muslims, remnants of indigenous tribes conquered by Genghis Khan in the thirteenth century, who still lived as they had then. Weavers of magic carpets and semi-nomadic, they followed herds of half-wild horses and cattle across the plains in summer. In winter they lived in villages of crude structures, long houses, divided in the middle by a hallway, and the men lived on one side, the women and their children on the other.

Stops in those villages were respite from the cruel journey, and after about six weeks of travel, they arrived in Tazhbulatova, which was larger than the other villages they had seen and more permanent. It was a regular stop for the caravans to rest for several days and to pick up fresh horses and feed for the last part of the journey to the mines. When they arrived in town, my grandmother's sleigh stopped right in front of a man washing clothes in a wooden tub. "Mama, Mama," Franz shouted her out of her desolation, "It's Uncle Sasha!"

She must have wept and struggled to ask a question.

And finally she did ask, "Is Max here?"

"Well," said my Great Uncle Alexander, "He was here, but...Maria, he'll be back." He saw only the newborn, Franz, and six-year old Maria. There was no need to ask about her other children, and he once again put his arms around her. "There's no time to explain, Maria. He stationed me here to make sure I'd find you if you came through—somehow he knew you might, but right now I've got to go look over the rest of the caravan—I'll explain later. Don't worry," he shouted over his shoulder as he got on a horse and rode off.

***

And so Franz had been right after all, my grandfather and his brothers, Alexander and Otto, had traveled the same route. But for the Zeitner boys it had been a very different trip than it had been for my grandmother and her three surviving children. First off, the Zeitners refused to ride in those baskets, waiting to be toppled into the snow and eaten by wolves. Instead, each of them caught one of the free horses and rode it bareback. They wasted no time worrying about what the future held, not about wolves and jackals, nor starvation, nor freezing to death, nor anything else. Instead, they assessed the situation and befriended the caravan drivers, learning as much Bashkiri[3] from them as possible, showing an interest in them, in their work, their love lives, and their religion. Some Arabic was used also: Allahu Akbar (God is great) and Inchallah (God willing) as well as Assalaam-o-Alekum (peace be with you), and Allah Hafiz (God keep you in his care) became part of the Zeitners' vocabulary right away. And learning a new language was not so difficult for them; they were already bilingual, having grown up speaking German and Russian equally well. Once you know two languages, the third is not so difficult. The fourth is easier yet.

So each of the three Zeitner brothers learned as much of the Bashkir language and customs as possible from each of the three drivers every day. In the evening, the brothers would come together and share what they had learned, formulating questions for the next day, testing hypotheses, and brainstorming about what in the things they had learned could spell life for them.

The first thing they learned was that the drivers were paid for each adult prisoner they delivered to the mines and how much each live body was worth, men were worth more than women and boys—old people were practically worthless: they'd eat, produce nothing for it, and were likely to drop dead just looking at a mine. Anyone over twelve counted as an adult. The Zeitner boys also learned that the drivers were not held responsible for any specific number of prisoners—how could they have been, considering the hazardous journey, the wolves, the jackals, the deep snowdrifts, the severe rations, and the cold. And most importantly, the three brothers learned that a man named Adjahn was the leader of the tribe that the drivers belonged to and that he had the respect of his people, though he was getting on in years. His youngest wife had not become pregnant, one of the drivers said with a knowing look that told the Zeitner boys much.

So by the time Max, Otto, and Sasha got to Tazhbulatova, they knew how to communicate with these thirteenth-century nomads who thought like Merlin or like King Uther in times of war. Max had made farm machinery; Alexander had run a factory making oil and related products, while Otto had made cars. And wouldn't they have been able to show these thirteenth-century nomads some pretty stunning magical tricks? They asked to be taken to Adjahn, who lived not far

---

[3] Bashkir is a Turkic language, which uses Arabic terms as they relate to Sunni Islam.

from Tazhbulatova. And when they got there, they told him, "We are weapons smiths; we are masters of fire; we understand the magic of toothwheels." And Max said, "My wife is a great healer. I will go through the Ural Mountains and bring her back. But she might be coming through as a prisoner the way I did, so while I go to Urbach, have one of my brothers here watch for her in Tazhbulatova."

"You will go through the mountains alone in winter?" said Adjahn, giving my grandfather a look through narrowed eyes.

"Inchallah" said my grandfather, "Allahu Akbar. If I never come back, and if my wife never comes through Tazhbulatova, my brothers Alexander and Otto will make it all worth your while anyway."

Basically, the Zeitner boys sold an idea: "Buy us from the drivers for a little more than they'd get for us at the mines, and we will bring you wealth, wisdom, and health." Then, the brothers went yet another step further: "Let us look over the caravans of prisoners that come through Tazhbulatova, let us buy anyone who looks useful for you, and you can sell them at a profit to your friends."

And so of all the infinite and bizarre possibilities that a life can hold, it came to pass that my grandfather was a slave trader for a time, and his brother, Alexander, with the help of Adjahn's son, bought my grandmother and her children from the drivers at a bargain basement price along with a couple of German engineers. Uncle Sasha bragged about it afterwards, about how Adjahn's son had haggled for her, how he had run her down to get a good price. And the driver had not understood why anyone would want a woman who already had three kids, so he sold her cheap.

Buying and selling slaves was a form of triage and a way to improve the lives of these herdsmen, who also were occasional horse thieves and were therefore warring with each other from time to time. They could use better weapons, better wolf traps, and so on. And, at the same time, my grandfather and his brothers could keep a few Germans and other prisoners from going to certain death in the mines. Russian high muck-a-mucks, had they known about this interesting arrangement, would probably not have minded. Siberia is full of treasures, and Russia wanted her tamed, colonized, exploited; and the Germans, as enemy aliens, were conveniently at hand. They would either die or, surviving, they would help to claim and tame the territory.

So as it turned out, my grandfather, with his brothers Alexander and Otto (and Otto's family as well) had been living in a nameless village not far from Tazhbulatova. But my grandmother's anxiety was not to end just yet. As Uncle Sasha had explained, Max had set off on a hair-raising journey back to Urbach to find her. Sasha was sure he'd be back.

But my grandmother was not so sure. She knew first hand that in a bear's *Weltanschauung*, humans are excellent food. And she had seen wolves very recently fight one another over human body parts. There were also avalanches and rockslides to consider. And if sure-footed donkeys can fall off mountains in the middle of summer, and they can, as I learned while riding one of those lovely little beasts in the northern mountains of Greece, well, a man can slip and fall to his death easily enough. In fact, there is no end to the horrible ways a man can meet his doom while walking alone through the Ural Mountains in winter.

Yet Sasha kept saying Max would be back as if it were a fait accompli. Well, if anyone could do it then that would be Max. If Max wanted to do something, he never thought about whether it was possible or not—he just did it, and he did the most improbable things. That's what she had loved about him in the first place. So Sasha was probably right. Max would be back.

On the other hand, did Sasha know about Annie of Tarau?

But in the end, my grandmother gave up thinking about Max. There were three children to keep alive.

The crude houses of the village had no furniture. There was a ledge, high off the ground and about five feet wide all around the walls. In the middle, on the earthen floor, laid among stones piled high and supporting a large kettle, was a lively fire to inspire stories. The only chimney was a hole in the roof. The men sat along the rim of the ledge, mending harnesses, waiting for dinner, telling stories. The houses were crude, but not so their stories or their dances. Rudolf Nureyev, one of the greatest ballet dancers of all time, took his first dance steps as a child in a Bashkir village. Their carpets, too, that they unrolled come bedtime, were as magnificently woven as their stories.

The women's quarters across the hall were identical. But no one knows if their stories were the same as those the men told since my grandmother lived in my grandfather's hut after her arrival. For all I know, they had a secret language that the men didn't understand. This is not as far-fetched as it may seem. Not many such languages survive, but I know of one, Nushu, spoken and written in China today, and it is a language understood only by women, as it was traditionally taught only to girls by their female relatives. And in cultures in which women are bought and sold like breeding stock, how could the existence of such languages be surprising?

Adjahn, as the chief of the tribe, had his own house. And one day, long before my grandmother arrived at the village with her three surviving children, my grandfather was on his way home to his hut after visiting his brother Otto, who was also living in such a hut. Somehow his wife, Lena, and their brood of kids were here as well; but how the gods pulled that one off is beyond me—all I know is that Lena did what the Russian women usually did when their men were sent to Siberia: they followed and tried to find them—there was no other hope for life. So Lena drove one of my Great-Uncle Otto's cars out of Urbach with the intention of finding her husband, and, somehow, she managed. She had abandoned the car somewhere in a snowdrift, and how she traveled after that is a mystery. My grandfather said, "They became animals, as I became an animal, going through the Ural Mountains."

So that day my grandfather was on his way home when a sudden storm came up; tiny shimmering ice crystals lit up by the moon were flying so thick in a luminous cloud that the visibility was near zero; it was blowing hard, dangerously hard, and it was probably somewhere around 60 degrees below zero, not counting the wind-chill factor. "Buran" is the name my grandparents gave to these storms that could arrive as suddenly as a pistol shot out of the blue. It was so cold that his breath formed a solid cloud around his mouth, a cloud that stung your lips like needles and it crackled loud enough to hear. He was bent double against the fierce wind; in fact, he was almost crawling on all fours. And, suddenly, he saw Ahdjan, sitting with his knees drawn up, huddled in furs, and leaning against the wall of his house.

My grandfather, out of breath, sat down beside him and gasped, "What, in hell's name, are you doing out here? Have you noticed there's a Buran?"

"You think this is bad? You should see what's going on inside the house with my wives."

"Seven, is it?"

"Yes, my brother, seven—Allahu Akbar."

"You have my most sincere admiration. How do you do it?"

"Each one must believe she is the queen of your heart. When you are with her, you must be with her. They are like animals: they know what you're thinking, and so you can only think of the one you're with. You get the hang of it after much time passes. Maybe you are lucky, you have only one, and, maybe not so lucky."

"I don't know, Brother; it's hard no matter how you slice it. Sometimes I've wished I could have two, but right at the moment, I don't even have one. When I was taken from my home, my wife was pregnant, and I don't know what happened to her and the children. I must go back and try to find them."

"Yes, you have told me often, and I keep telling you, you could buy a new wife, even two, right here—you should abandon that crazy plan of walking through the mountains."

"No, I think what I need to do is to leave, and soon; I've made the decision, and you won't regret it—I've told you often what she can do for a man's health. But how can I travel in Russia—that's what I've been thinking about ever since I got here."

"And I keep telling you that is not so hard—if you get through the mountains."

"Not hard?"

"Nothing is impossible, Inchallah."

"Do you know a way?"

"Maybe. Tell me, who can travel in Russia without being questioned?"

The two men sat in the snow, wrapped in their wolf furs lined with bear fur. Or, maybe, it was bear fur lined with wolf fur. Sitting under the table in my grandparent's apartment in Sillenbuch, village just outside Stuttgart, Germany, years later, I heard many arguments among my grandparents' Russian friends about whether bear lined with wolf or wolf lined with bear has better insulating properties. Whichever way the two men wore their wolf and bear furs, they leaned against the wall of the house in silence while my grandfather considered the problem of who could travel in Russia without being questioned by uniformed thugs. Inside, the women were still shrieking at each other, which could be heard clearly when the wind stopped howling for a moment. I think the two men understood each other perfectly. Finally my grandfather said, "A priest."

"Then you shall become a priest."

My grandfather went home that night, knowing that nothing else needed to be discussed. I don't know how long it took that improbable Bashkir nomad to arrange things, nor do I know what gods he bribed, nor yet the cost, but not long after that night in the snow and the storm, he showed up at my grandfather's hut with a package. It contained the long black cassock that Russian orthodox priests wore with a million little cloth-covered buttons and loops down the front. No question about it, this was the genuine article. In fact, I've seen Russian priests dressed exactly like this in San Francisco in 1965. Did some hapless priest give his life for those items? Everything my grandfather needed was there: the tall, cylindrical black hat with a wedge around the top and the ornate silver crucifix on a heavy silver chain. The cassock was a little long, but Lena fixed that. There were also the black boots, a rosary, and papers identifying my grandfather as Ahtyets Andreyi Ivanovitch Ilyantsov or "Father Andrew" from Petersburg. There were other accouterments, everything he needed to celebrate mass, a little money for the road, and a gun with plenty of ammunition, just in case.

But all that priestly stuff was for when my grandfather got to the other side of the mountains. Getting through the mountains was his first problem, and Adjahn had realized well enough that my grandfather had had no clue what he was talking about when he said he'd walk through the Ural Mountains alone in winter. It could be done, said Adjahn, but not by an inexperienced person like my grandfather. Did he know how to navigate by the stars? Did he know how to keep from freezing to death? Did he know how to avoid freezing his toes or fingers, and then, if he couldn't, how to avoid gangrene? Did he know what winterberries were good to eat? How to dig under the snow for fiddle-neck ferns for food? How to find wild beehives and make use of them without being stung? Did he know how to avoid avalanches of snow or rocks? Did he know how to defend against wolves, jackals, and bears? A gun might kill a bear, but you can't shoot enough wolves or jackals with a gun to make a difference; they'd just keep coming, jumping over their fallen comrades, knowing they'd keep for eating later. And finally, did he know how to deal with the strange states of mind that inevitably come to a person alone in a frozen wilderness?

"You will not know," said Adjahn, "If you are dead or alive and you will not remember who you are. We send our boys into the mountains in winter. They come back as men, or they don't come back at all."

"If your boys can do it, I sure will try," said my grandfather.

"Then you must allow us to prepare you," said Adjahn. "Have you been sleeping with your head pointing east like I told you?"

"I have, but you have not told me why," said my grandfather.

"Because if you do it all the time, you will always feel where east is—your body will learn it. Otherwise you'll wander around in circles in cloudy weather when you can see neither the sun nor the stars and there are no shadows."

"Well, then, I could sleep pointing North, so long as I'm consistent."

That is not advisable at all," said Adjahn and wouldn't say why not. But he did add, "You might as well trust our experience. And then, there will be a lot to learn."

***

He walked for weeks with the little donkey, and the wilderness got wilder and the going more difficult. He slept huddled next to her for warmth, and she counted on him for her food. He walked until the world seemed a frozen blur of exhaustion. And still he walked and kept going. He looked up into the early evening sky and it seemed to him he could almost touch the stars. Then the wilderness seemed empty even of him—and yet, who was that black dot that was walking, small and alone, in the expanse of white snow?

He came near death often enough from the cold, from bears, from wolves, from climbing boulders in his path and almost falling to his death. Once he had sat in the snow, sure death held him in a warm embrace and showed him a vision of golden trees. But the little donkey nudged him softly with her nose and looked at him with her dark eyes, and he remembered that he still had far to go.

It seemed to him he was being followed. There was no sound in the mountains except his footsteps and the donkey's—soft in the snow or crunching—or it was the hard sound of metal clicking on ice. And yet, someone was watching him, he was sure of it.

He walked warily, looking around often, but could discover no one. Still, it seemed someone was here, and suddenly he realized it was he who was here. I am the watcher. I am watching this small man walk among these golden trees. Have I become two?

He kept walking, and, suddenly, he first heard and then saw an avalanche of snow coming down from a cliff. He and the donkey ran, but it buried them. Luckily the avalanche had been small, and running had brought him closer to the edge of the mound of snow. He could lift his arms and feel his hands were free, so he was able to dig himself and the donkey out of the snow. But it had taken all his strength, and he rested for a day. That was not so bad, but he had also eaten more than he should have and, while eating restored his strength, he had not covered any distance for it. Rations were not plentiful in the first place, and so he was always hungry.

Then he began to notice beauty. Never had he seen it before. The snow he realized with surprise was not white at all, it was a pale peach color and the shadows were deepening shades of blue. He looked at the little donkey and he loved her. He saw the sun set between two rounded mountains and the world seemed to him alive and intelligent. How could you loose your way in a world like that? When he reached the cleft between the mountains, he'd been out of food for three days, and he knew it was time to kill the donkey, but he could not do it. After three days of fasting, hunger disappears and beauty becomes more intense. He waited, and the little donkey asked for food, but he had none to give her. "I wept for her life," he said, when he told me the story for the last time when I was almost a woman, eighteen years old in 1958 and he was dying. "I named her Khadija and I killed her."

"Did you eat her?"

"I did, and she gave me life," he said, and then, after a long pause, he added "It doesn't matter whether you see a burning bush or the sun set between two mountains. You find honey in the wilderness either way."

The going downhill was relatively easy. He no longer cared whether he lived or died. "They seemed the same," he said. "I fell asleep and watched the moment my body and mind moved from waking to sleeping. There was hardly any difference. If waking and sleeping are almost the same, how can life and death be so different from each other?" He lost a toe to frostbite, but the wound healed clean, thanks to a charcoal burner's knowledge about the value of cauterization. The charcoal burner was the first human being he had encountered after his journey alone through the mountains. "The strangeness," he said, "Of another human being when I had seen no one and had been no one for so long was huge. Breath-taking. Like meeting God." He stayed with the charcoal burner until he could walk again.

He put on the priest's vestments and became the priest, Ahtyetz Andreyi or Father Andrew, who bought a ticket on a riverboat going down the Volga towards the Black Sea. On that boat he met three Russian priests who welcomed him as their brother because they needed a fourth player for their card games. And so, one way or another, my grandfather was a man of God who, for the moment, was playing poker with three allegedly real priests, while also exchanging theological banter, talk of politics, news of the war, as well as racial slurs against Germans.

"No culture," he said, using the Russian word for "culture," which is not about computers, cars, and refrigerators as American culture is, or about Goethe and Mozart, as German culture was. Instead, the Russian word "culture," "cooltoorah" is all about the values of the heart. "No culture," he told those Russian priests playing cards on a riverboat, "Germans have no heart. But they fight like machines."

"That's why our boys will win," said the priest from Moscow.

"It won't do any good if the Bolsheviks have their way," allowed the priest going home to Odessa. "We will not be safe then, my Brothers," he said, and added prophetically while shuffling the deck for the next round, "They will kill us in cold blood and burn our churches."

"Yes," said my grandfather, raking in silver and gold, "I heard of a priest back in Petersburg, who robbed his church of all her treasures. They say he escaped to the West."

"Do you know his name?" asked the third priest who had not revealed where he was from or where he was going.

"No," said my grandfather, "Was it you?" Everyone laughed, and he ordered another bottle of vodka since he was winning. This was a bottle of vodka that had been kept on ice after having cured for three months, stuffed full of the hottest peppers in the known universe.

So he was cruising down the Volga River in style with all possibilities before him. Where was his heart; what was he thinking? How to say mass convincingly. A wife in trouble somewhere, or, possibly, dead already. A lover in Germany. Freedom in America, the land of all possibilities. Or Tibet and the life of a monk giving up identity. Was he free going down that river flowing south? Who, in the end, defined him?

I asked him that question when he was dying, and, apparently, he made a decision based on literary appreciation: "What is the story I want told about me in the end; what is the story I want you to remember, my Rabbit?" And so, as he threw down the last trump in a theological argument supporting polygamy, prostitution, and slavery with divine sanction, my grandfather said, "Nice playing with you fellows, but I get off at Urbach."

***

When my grandmother and her children had suddenly met Uncle Sasha in Tazhbulatova after weeks and weeks of traveling through snow drifts on those rickety sleds, she allowed hope to spring in her heart, but then, when he left her standing in the snow, hurriedly saying he'd explain later as he got on a horse and rode off, she was immediately plunged into terror again.

Adjahn had sent his eldest son Abdul together with Uncle Sasha to watch for caravans in Tazhbulatova because Abdul, among all his sons, was the shrewdest trader.

You could always calculate, give or take a couple weeks, when the next load of prisoners—slaves for the mines—would be coming through. So Adjahn's eldest wife's sister had a lot of household help whenever a caravan was due because Uncle Sasha was doing whatever it took to be in front of her house, look naturally busy, and be on the lookout for my grandmother and her children.

Adjahn didn't want the news of his slave business to spread too soon—he understood a fundamental principle of marketing: The early bird gets the worm, but the second mouse gets the cheese—unless the early bird understands the value of controlling a large market share before the second mouse realizes there is something to grab. So Adjahn wanted his prisoners bought away from the caravan going to the mines as quickly and as furtively as possible. The minute Abdul saw Sasha leave my grandmother standing there and going to look over the rest of the caravan, he approached the head driver and said, "That one won't bring you much at the mines. Look at her. Looks like she hasn't worked a day in her life. Bet you couldn't even use her as a breeder—I'll take her and her kids off your hands for more than you'd get for her at the mines."

"Something tells me you find her attractive enough, Abdul—how's it going?

"I'm doing great, Humayun, Allahu Akbar. Your youngest boy doing better?

"Yeah, he's out of danger. But lets talk business. You actually want to buy this infidel woman and her kids? She's worthless, but her boy looks useful," said Humayun, the caravan driver, though it was six-year old Maria's cheek he pinched while saying it. My grandmother didn't speak Bashkiri, but the tone and look of the men was universal enough. She pulled Maria towards her and, to her supreme horror, watched herself and her children being sold to a Bashkir tribesman. For what dark purpose? Where was Sasha?

He came riding back with a couple of German men, whom Adjahn's son also haggled for. Uncle Sasha said to Franz, "Come with me—you're to ride with us at the front." They went to the back of the house and brought out saddled horses.

So now my grandmother was riding a horse with the baby in her arms and Maria clinging to her back. The two men, whom she knew slightly from the brief noon day stops of the caravan, were on either side of her, also on horseback, but from their conversation all she could gather was that they, too, did not know where they were going and why. They, too, had come to the incredible conclusion that they had been bought away from that caravan. Why? And, all around them, Bashkir riders with guns seemed to be guarding them or, maybe, protecting them from wolves.

She told the Germans, "The man riding with the Bashkir up front with my son is my brother-in-law. He didn't have time to tell me anything."

"If he's your brother-in-law," said one of the Germans, "I suspect we'll be alright."

But the other German said, "Well, that would depend on whether he has any say in things."

Before they could discuss it much further, Franz came riding back from the front of the troop, where he had been riding between his Uncle Sasha and Adjahn's eldest son Abdul.

"Mama," he said, "Papa is brilliant."

"Where is he?"

"He went to Urbach to find us, and when he doesn't, he'll come back here—and Mama, you won't believe this, he went dressed like a priest and he stationed Uncle Sasha here so he could find us in case we came this way. Papa bought us so we wouldn't end up in the mines where all the other Germans are going."

"You mean Papa bought us, not the Bashkir?"

"Yup—well, kind of."

"And us?" asked one of the Germans, "We were bought too, that was easy to see, but why?"

"Uncle Sasha thought you looked useful," said the boy with innocent simplicity, "He says he's sorry he couldn't buy everybody, but saving some people from the mines is better than saving nobody."

The purchase of slaves, it seems, was a form of triage.

They came at last to several of the Bashkir long houses, huts, really, that stood empty. Uncle Sasha explained that the Bashkirs had no way of protecting their homes from mice, rats, bugs, and other vermin. So when a house got too overpopulated with undesirables to suit the Bashkirs, they just built a new house. It was into one of these abandoned huts that my grandmother and her children moved and soon called home. But it would be wrong to think that they moved in with all kinds of horrid little creatures—horrid only from a merely human point of view, of course. Once the humans go, most of the critters go too. Most, but not all. Centipedes, spiders, and sow bugs will happily claim squatter's rights, but a determined householder can deal with them. Fleas, lice, and bedbugs are not entirely easy to deal with, especially in winter when you can find no plants to help you, but these leave in caravans of their own in search for warm-blooded creatures elsewhere as soon as the humans go.

Things were not as great for my grandmother as they had been when the two St. Bernards, Lord and Lady, blew out the candles when told to speak, but, on the other hand, things were not as bad as they might have been. She dealt with the bugs and she prayed every night Max would come back through those mountains.

Fortunately, my grandmother had work to do to keep her mind occupied. She'd had the sense to bring her acupuncture needles, obstetrical instruments, as well as some other tools of her trade. The Bashkirs rarely had difficulty in delivering babies; but, occasionally, her services as a midwife were welcome not only by the women, but by the mares as well. Mostly, however, it was acupuncture. Adjahn's knees got better, his digestion improved, and he slept better. When my aunt Maria was dying in the late seventies and I was nursing her, she told me that my grandmother even knew what herbs combined with acupuncture would help the man get it up again. Was it Solomon's seal? Or did some more potent herbs grow in that region? My grandmother didn't know the German names of most of the plants she used, and I've forgotten their Russian names. In any case, Adjahn's youngest wife got pregnant, and the tribe, especially Adjahn himself, revered my grandmother—Adjahn, in fact, practically worshipped her. But that was later. Now it was still winter, and acupuncture was pretty much all my grandmother had available to help the sick.

Acupuncture and stories. She knew that a good story can heal your heart as well as foxgloves can. For my grandmother, reading and writing were sacred and forbidden arts, and when she mastered them, she knew how stories and lives are made together. She didn't know till very much later what a placebo was, but when she learned the word, she laughed and said, "It's just a good story in pill form."

Siberian spring comes suddenly and it's sweet enough to reverberate throughout the universe because nature has to give it all she's got to orchestrate something like that. She directs all her strength and beauty through one small channel—a controlled explosion of sweetness. The first signs are the trees, of course, as everywhere in regions with deciduous trees. Suddenly, they no longer look stark and lonely against the winter sky, but somehow soft and mysterious, as if veiled. And then the snow tulips thaw out their small and luminous spaces under the snow so you can see a red or yellow tint shine through the ice roof of the little greenhouses they've made for themselves.

Did foxglove grow there for the heart? Hepatica for the liver? Or milkweed, one of the most useful plants in all creation: you can eat the young shoots; you can eat the young flower buds when they're still green; you can eat the young seedpods when they're still firm, and you can use the silky fluff that helps the seeds fly to make pillows or warm, quilted clothing. Something my grandmother called "puchki" grew there. She said it's a plant with edible stems better than asparagus—and not only better tasting, according to her, but it also had better diuretic properties than asparagus.

When I was growing up, I heard more stories about Siberia than I did about the time of wealth in Urbach, and it is my experience as well: among the sweet uses of adversity is the fact that it is a great source of all kinds of fabulous stories. My grandparents were useful among the Bashkirs. Strangely, these people ate only meat and some grains, but no vegetables even though the Siberian spring and summer are rich in herbs and edible wild plants. And the people did suffer from vitamin deficiencies, especially vitamin C, as a result of not eating enough fruits and vegetables. You'd think nature would orchestrate an animal's diet a little better than that, but I guess once an elaborated language enters the picture, the pictures get too strange to fathom. Maybe their diet had been programmed during an ice age, and they were doing things the way their ancestors had always done things.

Of course, my grandmother didn't know anything about vitamin C, but she knew as well as any self-respecting sheep that long before a set of gums starts to bleed, you go find a lot of sheep's sorrel to eat as soon as the snow thaws. And, as a human, you go a step further and make sure you dry or salt enough to last through the following winter. She taught the women how to dry, pickle, or preserve in honey the berries, wild fruits, and herbs that grew there for winter use; how to dig a root cellar, how to make oil from nuts and seeds.

The Bashkir people felt that a body needs washing on only three occasions: after birth, before marriage, and after death. I heard from some of my students in China that there are people in the western and northwestern parts of the country even today who don't know the pleasures and benefits of frequent and regular bathing and washing your hair—so my grandmother's efforts had been small and very local.

The Bashkirs also did not wash their clothes. When my grandmother had found Uncle Sasha washing clothes in a wooden tub, it had been his own. The Bashkirs wore their clothes till they just dropped off. My grandmother taught the women how to make soap and showed them that clothes not only smell better, but also last longer if they are washed regularly.

Otto, Alexander, and the two German engineers, meanwhile, made simple machines to grind seeds and grain, plows to till the soil, and other implements to make life easier. Better wolf traps. And the people were truly grateful for the new knowledge. My grandparents always spoke of their time with the Bashkirs with love and appreciation because they had been loved and appreciated.

For my Uncle Franz, the time the family spent with the Bashkir tribesmen and their half-wild horses was nothing short of magic. He was thirteen going on fourteen and free to ride with the young men of the tribe. He joined their games and their dances. He learned to ride so well that he could go at a full gallop, bareback, bend to the ground and pick up his girl's silk handkerchief with his teeth. That's according to my grandmother, and she believed that truthfulness is good for one's soul. My grandfather might well embroider a story, or pretend to be someone he clearly was not, but not my grandmother.

So Franz and one of Adjahn's daughters, a dark and slant-eyed beauty (mysterious, but not to be mistaken for all that) were hanging out together. And, what could be more natural, my grandmother sends them to collect bird eggs. She'd boil them and pickle them in brine and spices for winter use. There are wild geese and ducks as well as cranes, swans and quail. There are small, wild chickens with speckled feathers and speckled eggs; there are wild chickens with purplish black skin under their iridescent feathers, and pheasants with golden throats. There are pale green eggs, deep turquoise eggs, pale blue eggs, eggs of ivory, copper, and gold. "Take eggs only if there are more than two in a nest" she tells them, "And always leave two. Leave crane and heron eggs alone though, since they'll taste too fishy. But duck eggs are better than chicken eggs."

Now, I realize that many American parents reading about a mother who sends a teenage boy and girl out egg hunting together in spring with only the company of wild flowers will wonder if my grandma had her head screwed on right. Chinese parents, on the other hand, wouldn't think a thing of it. My first year teaching in China in 2002, it took me two months to figure out that the river of hormones, which had been animating my students in America since seventh grade or earlier, was only a mountain spring with just a trickle having broken ground and murmuring now and then in my Chinese college freshmen (and women).

***

My grandfather, meanwhile, had gotten off the luxurious Russian riverboat in Urbach as a fairly rich man, for the moment, anyway. It was still early evening, and too light to be seen in the village in spite of his priestly outfit. He'd grown a nice beard that he'd started when the decision had been made to become a priest. That beard helped to disguise him, but he was afraid to take chances, and so he decided to kill some time by having dinner at the riverside inn rather than the cheaper and better one in town. He ordered a lavish dinner fit for a priest.

As soon as the crepuscular hour made evening light deceptive, he made for Boris Borisevitch Bilokhatnuk's house, an old Ukranian friend of his, a man whom he was sure he could trust. When Boris Borisevitch answered the knock at his door, he didn't recognize my grandfather right away and was not really pleased to see a clergyman standing there.

"It's me, Boris, Maxim—let me in before anyone recognizes me," said my grandfather.

"No one would in that get-up; have you eaten?" said Boris and pulled him inside. "What are you doing here dressed like that?" asked Boris.

"Yes, I've eaten, thanks. I've come for my wife and children."

"Ah, Maxim, I am so sorry; they were taken away. I don't know where they went. They were prisoners in your home—we tried to get food to them, but we could not."

"Do you know where they were taken?"

"No, Maxim, but the same soldiers that arrested you, took them."

"Good," said my grandfather.

"Good!? Why good?"

"It means I think I know where they went if they made it alive. I've suspected it anyway."

"Still there is very bad news."

"Tell me."

"Three of your children died, Rebecca and the twins."

My grandfather put his elbows on the table and hid his face with his hands. Then he asked, "But my wife was alright?"

"She was, and so was the newborn baby and Maria and Franz. She named the baby Alexandra."

"Yes, that's what we had agreed if it was a girl. Tell me, Boris, how long can you hide me—I only need a few days—I'll make it worth your while."

"No need to talk of making things worthwhile—of course you can stay. I'll say my cousin is visiting from the Ukraine. We can go walking together in the evening—I'll have to put up with some talk for having a priest for a cousin, but I'll deal with it. I'm sure no one could possibly recognize you with that beard and those clothes. People are scared to look at priests too close anyway. Besides, it seems to me you've lost a lot of weight and you've got a little limp? That will also help."

"Lost a toe coming through the mountains. But it's healing clean. I guess you could be right about my not being recognized. I'll need a good horse, Boris; I'll give you the money to get it. You've always been good at finding the best horses at the best price. And then I'll go back across the mountains to Siberia."

"You are crazy Maxim Pavlovitch—dressed like that you could go anywhere; why don't you try to escape to Germany?"

"I made a promise, and I left Otto and Alexander in Siberia. I'm almost sure Maria and the children were sent to the same place."

"Well, if you're crazy enough to go back to Siberia, why don't you go by train as far as Chelyabinsk? It would be a much shorter and more comfortable trip. You could stay with me till snowfall and then you could get a horse in Chelyabinsk. You could ride with the caravans to the mines. It'll be a lot safer than going through those mountains on your own."

"I came through those mountains in winter, Boris, and I want to see them again now that it's spring—the going should be easy this time."

"Well, I guess you've always had a crazy streak in you Maxim Pavlovitch."

And so my grandfather left his friend and the town of his wealth and the man he had been forever. When he got to the last city before he had to travel into the wilderness, he got himself outfitted properly for a mountain journey. He got a fresh horse and a pack mule. He packed up his priestly vestments, and he traveled into the mountains in style with the rich glory of the Siberian spring all around him.

"I felt like a real Kazakh in those mountains," he told me—I was eighteen and sitting by his bedside at St. Luke's Hospital on 116th Street in Cleveland, Ohio, and he, who had been my best friend when I was a child, was dying.

"Which one do you mean, Grandpa, a free man, or a vagabond, or an adventurer?" The word, "Kazakh," (formerly "Cossack") can mean all three.

"All of them, my Rabbit, but mostly free. I have never felt so free as I did alone in those mountains. Free and simple—so simple, I even forgot to have thoughts. And then, when I put on the clothes of that priest—I was that priest. And when I took them off, I was nobody. I was tempted to just stay in the mountains. I found the charcoal burner again—almost decided to build me a hut and become his neighbor. "

But then, I guess, he thought of his family, and so one day in high summer he came walking into town on his horse to see Franz competing successfully in some riding competition with the rest of the village boys. Maybe my grandmother hardly expected him since her father had taken extraordinary leave from his family for twenty years.

Franz delivered the next baby, born nine months after my grandfather had casually walked into town on his bay mare, a boy who did not survive the Siberian winter that followed.

Adjahn had maintained that this was because they didn't do with the newborn what always had to be done. When my grandmother and Franz had attended Ahdjan's youngest wife with the birth of twin boys, both in breach position, my grandmother gave the babies, still red and wet with blood, into Adjan's hands. He put them next to his skin under several layers of fur clothing, and then he rode a hard day out and a cold night back. That's how they always dealt with newborns; Allahu Akbar, if they lived and Allahu Akbar if they didn't. And if they did live, you could be pretty sure they weren't weak.

For the rest of that summer and that winter the responsibilities of a man trying to keep a family together in Siberia must have become a bit much for my grandfather. I've done some reading about Siberia, and all the books mention a kind of typically Siberian freak-out syndrome. Of course, freak-outs have to assume a local name and habitation, just as inspirations do. Maybe it was just ordinary culture shock. Maybe it was the Buran that made you as crazy as the hot wind that comes from the Sahara and manages to travel through the Alps without losing all of its fury and heat. Every police department in the world knows about winds like that, as well as the effects of the full moon.

And so, for a time, Siberia brought out the worst in my grandfather. He became sort of like a were-wolf. He became the cruel tyrant that my Aunt Ruth and I have never seen in him, but that my Aunt Maria and my mother remember clearly and swear was real. I don't know exactly what it was he did to my grandmother, but he was abusive—too abusive.

So far, this story is not unusual. Many people experience sides of themselves they wish they didn't have to exactly look at—and lots actually manage not to look, telling themselves stories about their own virtue. I remember, for example, the story of the old man who was brought to be a witness against Adolf Eichmann. Eichmann was the first of the Nazi war criminals to be tried in Jerusalem. Because feelings ran so high against him, he had to be put in a bulletproof glass cage, which sat on a platform. The courtroom was sunken, so you had to go down a few steps after you came in the door. That made the visual dynamics bizarre, to say the least; for it meant that the people who sat in judgment of him had to look up at him—it meant his monstrosity was glorified. But when you first came into the room, you saw him at eye-level. So when the old man was brought in and he saw Eichmann for the first time in years and years, he fainted. Later, when reporters asked him if seeing Eichmann had brought flooding back so much of the horrors he'd seen and had been through at Eichmann's hands that he fainted, he simply said, "No.

"No, I saw there an old man like myself, and I realized that whatever Eichmann was capable of I am capable of. It was this realization that made me faint."

Well, some people never get to that realization, and some spend their lives fainting on the steps to the courtroom.

Anyway, one way or another, my grandfather began to abuse his wife. Not so unusual. But the way Ahdjan's tribe handled my grandfather's case was most unusual, beyond interesting, and far more drastic than taking newborn babies horseback riding in snow or in summer heat. Adjahn came to my grandfather's hut and warned him. He said, "Listen Maxim Pavlovich, you can't do that. That's not how we do things. This is no way to treat a woman. We won't tolerate it." He quoted Qur'an about how a good man treats even his animals. But I do not know what, precisely, those semi-nomadic herdsmen (who bought and sold their women) would have considered "no way to treat a woman."

Max did not listen. Who did these semi-nomadic tribesmen think they were anyways, telling him, a good Christian and the head of a family, how he ought to treat his wife? So Adjahn came again. "Maxim Pavlovich, listen, you can't treat a woman like that. It's not sophisticated. Especially not a woman like your wife. A woman like that comes about as often as a blue fox or a white raven. She is a great healer. You will ruin her healing powers."

Max did not listen. Or, maybe, Max could not help himself, which would mean he was incapable of listening deeply enough. Guys more stubborn than Max hardly exist. Adjahn came again. "Listen Maxim Pavlovich, I am telling you for the third time, you are not to treat a woman as you are treating your wife," he said, "My youngest son has just come back from taking his first son for his first ride. Allahu Akbar, the baby lived." Now, I don't know if Max understood why the baby was an important thing to mention in this context. After living in China, the intention is clear to me: A threat against his life was hiding in that "Allahu Akbar, the baby lived."

Max did not listen. Even if he didn't understand the threat, he should have known that this was a serious wake-up call. Adjahn had warned him three times. There is something profoundly magical about that: Once for the knower, once for the known, and once for the spirit that ties the one to the other. After three warnings, there is no excuse—every teller of tales knows this: three is deep magic.

But, as I said an obligatory number of times, my grandfather did not listen, and, come a beautiful spring sun-set evening, the Bashkirs came and bodily took him from his house and transported him to a pit dug in the ground too deep to escape from. They performed a sacred ceremony involving many songs, dances, wild drum-beats and prayers, and then, as soon as the sun went below the horizon, they took off all his clothes and threw my grandfather into the pit which was crawling with poisonous snakes. Then they went home, unrolled their magic carpets, and went to sleep.

In the morning, exactly at sunrise, the Bashkirs came back and, Allahu Akbar, my grandfather was still alive, but much changed. For one thing, his hair had turned snow white. "What was it like in that snake pit, Grandpa?" I must have asked each one of the hundreds of times I asked him to retell the story as I was growing up. I knew about snake pits from Grimm's Fairy Tales, which my grandmother read to me daily, repeating all *those* stories many times as well. And the fairy tale snake pits were real to me because my grandfather's snake pit was real.

And what was that night like for my grandmother, what was she thinking all night long? I doubt she slept, and I know for a fact that the abuser and the abused fit like hand in glove.

***

For "snake pit," my dictionary says, "mental institution," and gives no history of the term. Could it be that the snake pit as born in a human mind and lives only as metaphor? But, while the human world is full of such snake pits, I found no reference to the existence of literal snake pits anywhere. Yet the whole family affirmed that my grandfather spent time in a real and literal snake pit that turned his hair white overnight. And he said, "That snake pit was a miraculously successful collaboration between God, Man, and Nature to produce a changed man. It was as if I really came to life that night for the first time and I began to understand what Jesus meant when he said, 'Except a man be born again, he cannot see the kingdom of God.' I saw the kingdom of God in that snake pit, and it changed me. But the funny thing is I still felt exactly like me—I'm still puzzling about that." According to my mother, the snakes drove him insane that night and he never recovered.

If he really did spend time in a pit with poisonous snakes, how did he live? They definitely were poisonous; he said he saw their fangs—non-poisonous snakes do not have them. And so how could he have lived?

The story of my grandfather's stint in the snake pit sat around in my mind till 1956 when I was sixteen, and then I took the bus to the far west side of Cleveland, Ohio got off at the zoo, found the curator of reptiles, and asked if he needed any volunteers to help out with the snakes. As it turned out, he was curator of arachnids as well. So I got to know all kinds of snakes and spiders—you can actually make eye contact with some kinds of spiders and you can establish a friendly relationship with them more easily than with snakes. Some big furry spiders even like to be petted, and I swear to God they would purr if they knew how—they do rhythmic little knee bends instead of purring, looking for all the world like four little girls with fuzzy leg warmers doing demi-pliés in third position. And spiders have the most amazing eyes. But whether spiders or snakes, I found them all to be creatures like myself, beautiful as well as terrible and certainly intelligent.

And here is the straight scoop on serpents. They are not too interested in biting folks at night. Snakes are cold-blooded animals and they need the sun. At night they sleep and dream of biting into juicy warm-blooded animals they can eat—why waste the poison on my grandfather, a beast too huge to swallow—even for me on occasion.

Also, the Bashkir tribesmen had probably "milked" these deadly vipers, which must have been collected for the express purpose of re-educating my grandfather via shock therapy to scramble the synapses in his brain. If you grab a snake just behind the head or use a forked stick (longer than striking distance), he is easily controlled—unless he is gigantic, bigger than you. Pin him—I have seen eagles swoop to do it in Iowa—and the snake opens his mouth with a hissing sound known to cause heart attacks. So you give him something to sink his fangs into—an apple, for instance or a rubber bottle if you actually want to collect the poison for some extremely sinister purpose. Then, after you have got him to shoot his wad, he is not really dangerous since it takes time for his body to manufacture enough venom to fill up the little sacks behind his teeth. He could inflict some nasty puncture wounds, but they would not kill you—unless you have a really weak heart.

My grandfather's explanation about how he got through that night was that God had softened the hearts of the snakes. Anything is possible, and I do not think 20th century thought has come anywhere close to solving the problem of causation, and 21st century thought has not figured itself out yet. My guess is that since those snakes were in a pit so deep a man could not climb out, those poor animals were freezing and were probably trying to snuggle up to my grandfather for warmth—and it was this that scared the b-Jesus out of him enough to turn his hair white.

**

After Max had had a chance to re-install the b-Jesus, he explored the countryside as far as he could go on long and frequent camping trips alone with his shadow and in hopes of finding somewhere else to live, someplace where people didn't use snake pits to cure wife-beaters.

He found Werch Kisilsk, on the Kisilsk River, which snakes its way through fertile grasslands lush with water willows, Siberian iris, sweet flag, swamp marigolds, water mint, forget-me-nots, loosestrife, native orchids, ferns and myriads of other flowers and wild vegetables. Werch Kisilsk was a big place by local standards, a town of about eight hundred souls. In the early nineties, I lived in the forest on the Allegheny River near a town of eight hundred souls in Pennsylvania—it had seven churches, one traffic light (which did not work), one policeman, and a cathouse (which worked) right outside of town by the highway exit just a bit south of the truck plaza. The people were mostly lawless rednecks and religious rednecks, though there were a few more unfathomable types also. But that was Emlenton, PA; I can't even begin to imagine what sort of humanity hung out in Werch Kisilsk.

In Werch Kisilsk the people were mostly Kazakhs which sounds more romantic than rednecks, and I suspect the reality was as interesting as the famous intergalactic bar scene in the movie Star Wars. Kazakhs were commissioned by the Tsars of Russia to breed the best horses in the world. Like the Bashkirs, the Kazakhs had lived in symbiotic relationship with horses for eons. They were allegedly more civilized than the Bashkirs. They spoke Russian in addition to Kazakh. They had amazing dancers and riders to rival the Bashkir dancers and riders. And Franz was immediately at home with them. For like Hector, Franz was a tamer of horses—when he wasn't being a midwife.

When most of the Bashkirs had left to follow their half-wild horses across the grasslands, my grandfather packed up his family, a few of the other "slaves" he had accumulated, and what little belongings they had amongst them, and they walked for some weeks, arriving in Werch Kisilsk to the amazement of the locals who quickly got used to the little troop of stunningly weird looking foreigners with hideously open and pale eyes, "double eyelids" (as Western eyelids are known in China), and big noses, because they were short of men on account of the war. And my grandfather and his friends immediately got busy making farm and kitchen tools. My grandmother was soon sewing and dispensing herbal medicines. They moved into an abandoned house next to the river, and it was still early enough in the season to plant some vegetables in the rich, black river bottomland.

Life in Werch Kisilsk definitely seemed a vast improvement over the little nameless village near Tazhbulatova. But my grandparents' new and improved living conditions were extremely temporary. Before the first lettuces could be harvested, one of the nastier entities of the place showed up on my grandparents' doorstep accompanied by three men, and informed them that the whole family had just volunteered to make bricks in a brickyard for the greater glory of Mother Russia. But, though they had volunteered, the three men, armed to the teeth, who stood around telling each other jokes to pass the time, guarded them day and night; so escaping back to the Baskirs was not possible.

They were installed in a one-room cabin next to the brickyard and told that their daily quota was 1,500 bricks. Five brick makers should not have a problem, they were told. That one of the laborers was two years old, one was nine, and a third was once again pregnant just wasn't deemed relevant.

The work was all done by hand—from digging the clay and the sand to chopping the straw and mixing the heavy, sticky mass by stomping through it with bare feet and then, finally, shoveling it into wooden forms open on the bottom and the top. My grandfather and Franz learned to lift the forms and turn them with just the right motion at just the right speed, so the soft mix didn't plop out like cow pies. Eventually, the drying process shrank them away from the wood, and then they had to dry slowly, sometimes under wet cloth, so they would not crack. Turning them was my mother's job, and it was not easy to keep a two-year old focused on it since sow bugs found the dark, wet spaces under the drying bricks a comfortable home, and she remembered running scared of them.

Everybody's fingers bled, and the guards said to my grandfather, "If you can't discipline your workers, we'll shoot 'em for you." My grandparents were not paid for their work—after all, they had volunteered—but they were promised sufficient food. Sufficient food meant that my grandfather and Franz went hunting or fishing after the long and grueling day's work, and Maria and Alexandra were sent into the streets of Werch Kisilsk to beg. Maria went door-to-door, and my mother huddled next to a large rock in the center of town and, her gathered fingers repeatedly touching her lower lip, she said to everyone that passed: "Radi Boga, dah-yetye minye kussock khleba." It means, "A piece of bread, please, in God's name," but nobody needs that translation, the hand-gesture is enough. I have seen girls her age beg for food that way in India, and according to the latest stats I could dig up, 50% of the world's population goes to bed hungry tonight—if in fact they have a bed— while some CEO' fortune increases by five billion, all of which doesn't say much for the milk of human kindness or the state of our evolution. This whole planet is a snake pit, if you ask me.

And then there came the day when Franz went out into the fields early in the morning, even before the music of the morning birds began, with a bucket and a spade to bury the little boy whom he had helped to deliver during the night, choosing his mother's life, freeing the baby's spirit, and not looking back. "I don't think I've had enough food to nurse a baby," my grandmother had said shortly before it was due. "How can I bear watching it starve to death?" After the birth, my grandmother could not work for a few days, and that meant rations were cut.

Fortunately, you cannot make clay bricks in winter, and Siberian summers are short. So when winter came, my grandfather was asked to teach school in Werch Kisilsk because the only teacher in the town, Sergeij Ivanovich, was just getting too old to do it. "They tell you," he croaked, "That you lose your mind when you get older." Then he cackled hoarsely and added, "But they forget to mention that you really don't miss it all that much." He handed over a few books to my grandfather and gave him quick instructions about his new trade: "They have to trust you; that's the main thing. If they don't trust you, they don't learn. When I was child, they told me I could learn from a teacher I hated as well as I could from a teacher I loved. But that's just not so." And my grandfather, he said, "A peaceful life. Had I known how peaceful the life of a teacher is, I'd have chosen that trade to begin with."

But his peaceful life as a schoolteacher was brief. In the middle of the summer of 1918 the war between the Red and the White army reached Werch Kisilsk.

People who have not seen war on their own soil lately seem to believe that war is between countries and their soldiers. War is not against civilian populations or against non-military targets. But I do not see how any thinking person could believe such nonsense. This has never been true. If the civilian population feels safe and has enough food, they are an eternal source of new soldiers and other resources for their fighting men. Terrorizing and destroying the civilian population as cruelly as possible is part of the whole point. War, in the 20th century especially, is organized (i.e. corporate) crime and it is as savage as possible by design: a collective snake pit: shock therapy to make a new social and economic structure possible.

Werch Kisilsk was taken by the Red Army and then taken back by the White Army. And then taken again by the Red Army. By this time, everyone, military as well as civilian, is just about equally savage. There were the usual looting, pillaging, and the more unmentionable atrocities. While Franz and my grandfather went out to gather news and kill, when necessary, for food, my grandmother and her two girls spent most of their time huddled in wolf furs in the "ice house." This was a pit dug into the ground where ice, cut from the river in winter, was stored, insulated by straw so that it would remain unthawed for most of the summer. It was cold there and uncomfortable, especially for my grandmother who was once again pregnant, but it was safer than the wooden house that could have burst into flames at any moment.

Finally, with the whole town in flames, the old schoolteacher gave my grandfather a rickety wooden cart and an equally rickety old mare. "I want to die here in my home," said Sergeij Ivanovitch, "You take the horse and the cart. I don't know how long the horse will last—she has trouble making the trip to the river for water every day, but you can have her and try to get as far from here as you can with your family." Sergeij Ivanovich could not imagine how far you might have to go when the war is a world war.

And in that rickety cart, with the red sunset before them and the red flames of Werch Kisilsk behind them, Franz helped my grandmother deliver yet another baby, a little girl this time, named Gertrude for the hope of reaching Germany somehow. Food was hard to find on that journey, and, after four months, Gertrude stopped crying from hunger and was buried by the side of the road. Somehow, the family kept going. Somehow, the old horse kept going until she was slaughtered for food. My grandmother rode in the rickety cart with her gaze in the distance. Three more babies were born, died of starvation, and were buried in shallow graves during the years my family wandered from place to place looking only for food. Sometimes soldiers would show up and grab one of them for a work detail somewhere. My grandmother, once again pregnant, did time digging ditches. My grandfather and Franz might be grabbed for some unimaginably torturous labor without much food. How they managed to find each other afterwards is unimaginable. Nature arranged it. My grandfather and Franz did stints in the salt mines because salt was more valuable than gold, and you could sometimes buy food with it. Somehow, they also lived in Kyrgystan for long enough to learn another Turkic language. But I cannot write this story; I have tried, but another-day-another-dead-baby just does not make good reading.

Twenty-eight million people starved to death in Russia between 1915, the year my mother was born and the family was sent to Siberia, and 1922 when what was left of them was re-united in Berlin, Germany after several separations and reunions. And the terror of such times is not just what you suffer, but what you would do to others for a crust of bread. They arrived in Berlin just in time for a depression that made the one in the U.S. look lush. And I do mean that. In China, I showed my college students the movie, "Places in the Heart," which takes place in the Depression, and Hollywood does what it can to portray the poverty of the times. It looked like enviable wealth to my students in China.

The bitterest grief for my grandmother during the years they wandered like stray animals were not the babies that starved to death and were buried by the side of the road, it was the loss of Franz. Franz who was a rider without equal and the boy hero of my childhood, looked equally good to the Red Army. He would obviously make a good cavalryman, and so they inducted him. My grandfather tried to stop them, arguing that Franz was a German citizen, but the soldiers made it clear that they would take Franz, the only question was whether they would kill his father first or whether they would let him live. Franz was never heard from again.

Somehow, Maxim Pavlovich and Maria Abrahmovna made it to Germany with their two daughters, my aunt Maria and my mother. When the Great Depression and World War II came, they had much experience in how to survive hard times. And they had learned infinite patience and the kindness to help others in desperate need.

My mother, Alice Zeitner Mailänder, a.k.a. Alexandra Maximovna, who saw her family through WWII, flight from the invading Russian army, and an engineered postwar famine.

My father, Rudolf Mailänder, who probably starved to death in one of General Dwight D. Eisenhower's death camps established *after* WWII had ended.

My father reading to me while he was home on furlough

My maternal grandmother, Maria Zeitner, a.k.a. Maria Abramovna who saw three of her children starve to death, one killed by rape, and one taken by the Red Army. Yet look at that smile.

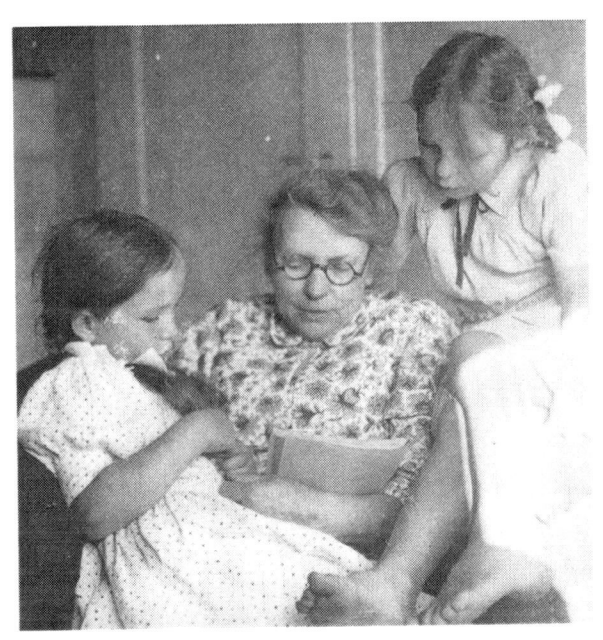

My grandmother reading to my sister and me (on the right).

My maternal grandfather, Max Zeitner, a.k.a. Maxim Pavlovich, who walked through the Ural Mountains alone in winter to save his family.

My grandparents and their oldest two daughters (my mother is on the right) just after escaping from Siberia and coming to Germany, walking most of the way.

My mother's younger sister, my aunt Ruth Zeitner, a.k.a. Princess Irina Maximovna Azarenko-Zarovsky (and more subsequent a.k.a.'s as the prince shifted shape than can be listed here), a.k.a. Felicity Belton. I had almost her talent in choosing the wrong guys.

My mother's older sister, my aunt Maria Zeitner, a.k.a. Maria Maximovna, who was sentenced to life-imprisonment in East Germany by the Russians for Nazi war crimes. She was released after nine years in a prisoner-exchange program.

Maria was allowed to write a 15-line letter once a month from prison. She was allowed to receive one such letter each month.

My grandmother's brother, a forest ranger in Russia.
I'm proud to have such a wild bear in my ancestry.

Albrecht Leo Merz, architect, senator, educational philosopher, artist-teacher, and founder of the Merz Schule, designated as a model school by UNESCO.

Albrecht Leo Merz with my class. The second boy from the left in the second row was my best friend Joachim.

My classroom for four years. The desks were made in the woodshop. Nothing fancy here, but the best school I have seen in 60 years of teaching in five different cultures.

A paperback I bound into a hardcover in 2nd grade, a book that was then assigned for independent reading to all of us. I read it and loved it about a hundred times.

Here you can see my second grade handwriting (it went downhill from there). It says "Christmas 1948".

A page from that book. No pictures, no dumbed-down vocabulary or sentence structure.
A real novel that every second-grader at our school read

One of the hundreds of paper cuts I made between the ages of six and twelve.

A watercolor of my village and my cat, Mohrle (Blackie).

My mother, my sister (left), and I on the train leaving for an immigrant camp in Bremerhaven, from where we would depart for America